EZ SOLUTIONS

TEST PREP SERIES

MATH REVIEW

GEOMETRY

EZ SIMPLIFIED SOLUTIONS – THE BREAKTHROUGH IN TEST PREP!

LEADERS IN TEST PREP SOLUTIONS – WE MAKE IT EZ FOR YOU!

AUTHOR: PUNIT RAJA SURYACHANDRA

WWW.EZMETHODS.COM

EZ SOLUTIONS
USA

EZ SOLUTIONS
P.O. Box 10755
Silver Spring, MD 20914
USA

Conceived, conceptualized, written, and edited by:
Punit Raja SuryaChandra, EZ Solutions

PRINTED AND MANUFACTURED IN THE UNITED STATES OF AMERICA

TABLE OF CONTENTS

PREFACE

▪ABOUT EZ SOLUTIONS

EZ Solutions – *the breakthrough in test-preparation*!

EZ Solutions is an organization formed to provide *simplified solutions* for test-preparation and tutoring. Although EZ Solutions is a fairly new name in the publishing industry, it has quickly become a respected publisher of test-prep books, study guides, study aids, handbooks, and other reference works. EZ publications and educational materials are highly respected, and they continue to receive an unprecedented amount of praise from professionals, instructors, librarians, parents, and students.

OBJECTIVE: Our ultimate objective is to help you *achieve academic and scholastic excellence*. We possess the right blend and matrix of skills and expertise that are required to not only do justice to our programs and publications, but also to handle them most effectively and efficiently. We are confident that our state-of-the-art programs/publications will give you a completely *new dimension* by enhancing your skill set and improving your overall performance.

MISSION: Our mission is to foster continuous knowledge to develop and enhance each student's skills through innovative and methodical programs/publications coupled with our add-on services – leading to a *better career and life* for our students.

OUR PHILOSOPHY: We subscribe to the traditional philosophy that everyone is equally capable of learning and that the natural, though sometimes unfulfilled and unexplored impetus of people is towards growth and development. We know that the human brain is undoubtedly a very powerful and efficient problem-solving tool, and every individual is much more capable than they realize. We strive to implement this philosophy throughout our books by helping our students explore their *potential* so that they can *perform at their optimum level*.

OUR COMMITMENT TOWARDS YOUR SATISFACTION: Reinventing, Redesigning, and Redefining Success: We are committed to providing *total customer satisfaction* that exceeds your expectations! Your satisfaction is extremely important to us, and your approval is one of the most important indicators that we have done our job correctly.

Long-Term Alliance: We, at EZ, look forward to forming a *long-term alliance* with all our readers who buy our book(s), for the days, months, and years to come. Moreover, our commitment to client service is one of our most important and distinguished characteristics. We also encourage our readers to contact us for any further assistance, feedback, suggestions, or inquiries.

EZ Solutions publishing series include books for the following major standardized tests:
- GMAT
- SAT
- PSAT
- ASVAB
- PRAXIS Series
- GRE
- ACT
- CLEP
- TOEFL
- Other (national and state) Standardized Tests

EZ Solutions aims to provide good quality study aides in a wide variety of disciplines to the following:
- Students who have not yet completed high school
- High School students preparing to enter college
- College students preparing to enter graduate or post-graduate school
- Anyone else who is simply looking to improve their skills

Students from every walk of life, of any background, at any level, in any field, with any ambition, can find what they are looking for among EZ Solutions' publications.

FOREIGN STUDENTS: All of our books are designed, keeping in mind the unique needs of students from North and South America, U.K., Europe, Middle East, Far East, and Asia. Foreign students from countries around the world seeking to obtain education in the United States will find the assistance they need in EZ Solutions' publications.

CONTACT US: Feel free to contact us, and one of our friendly specialists will be more than happy to assist you with your queries, or feel free to browse through our website for lots of useful information.
E-Mail: info@EZmethods.com
Phone: (301) 622-9597
Mail: EZ Solutions, P.O. Box 10755, Silver Spring, MD 20914, USA
Website: www.EZmethods.com

FEEDBACK: The staff of EZ Solutions hopes that you find our books helpful and easy to use. If you have any specific suggestions, comments, or feedback, please email us at: feedback@EZmethods.com

BUSINESS DEVELOPMENT: If you are interested in exploring business development opportunities, including forming a partnership alliance with us, kindly email us at: partners@EZmethods.com.

PRODUCT REGISTRATION: In order to get the most up-to-date information about this and our other books, you must register your purchase with EZ solutions by emailing us at: products@EZmethods.com, or by visiting our website www.EZmethods.com.

ERRORS AND INACCURACIES: We are not responsible for any typographical errors or inaccuracies contained in this publication. The information, prices, and discounts given in this book are subject to change without prior notice. To report any kind of errors or inaccuracies in this publication, kindly email us at: errors@EZmethods.com.

▪ABOUT OUR AUTHOR

The name of the man behind EZ publication series is **Punit Raja SuryaChandra**, who is also the founder of our company. He holds a Bachelors in Business and an MBA. It took him many years to write and publish these unique books. He researched every single book available in the market for test-preparation, and actually realized there is not even one book that is truly complete with all the content and concepts. This was the single most important reason that prompted him to write these books, and hence our **EZ prep guidebooks were born**. He has made every effort to make these books as comprehensive and as complete as possible. His expertise and experience are as diverse as the subjects that are represented in our books. He has the breadth and depth of experience required to write books of this magnitude and intensity. Without his unparalleled and unmatched skills and determination, none of this would have been possible.

In developing these books, his primary goal has been to give everyone the same advantages as the students we tutor privately or students who take our classes. Our tutoring and classroom solutions are only available to a limited number of students; however, with these books, any student in any corner of the world can benefit the same level of service at a fraction of the cost. Therefore, you should take this book as your personal EZ tutor or instructor, because that's precisely how it has been designed.

ACKNOWLEDGEMENTS:
Our author would like to extend his vote of appreciation and gratitude to all his family members for their unconditional and continuous support, to all his close friends for their trust and confidence in him, and to all his colleagues for their helpful consultation and generous advice.

Our EZ books have benefited from dedicated efforts and labors of our author and other members of the editorial staff. Here at EZ, we all wish you the best as you get comfortable, and settle down with your EZ tutor to start working on preparing for your test. In pursuing an educational dream, you have a wonderful and an exciting opportunity ahead of you. All of us at EZ Solutions wish you the very best!

.ABOUT EZ BOOKS

THE EZ NAME:
All our books have been written in a very easy to read manner, and in a very easy to understand fashion, so that students of any background, of any aptitude, of any capacity, of any skill-set, of any level, can benefit from them. These books are not specifically written for the **dummies** or for the **geniuses**; instead, they are written for students who fit into any category of intellectual acumen. This is how we acquired the name **"EZ Solutions"** for our publications – and as the name itself suggests, **we make everything EZ for you**!

THE EZ TUTOR:
Like any good tutor, EZ Tutor will work with you **individually and privately**, providing you with all the tools needed to improve your testing skills. It will assist you in recognizing your weaknesses, and enlighten you on how to improve upon them while transforming them into strengths. Of course, it will also point out your strengths as well, so that you can make them even stronger. By employing innovative techniques, EZ tutor will **stimulate, activate, and accelerate your learning process**. Soon after you start working with your EZ tutor, you will see **remarkable and noticeable improvement** in your performance by utilizing your newly acquired learning skills.

Whenever, Wherever, and However: EZ tutor also has the **flexibility** to work with you whenever you like – day or night, wherever you like – indoors or outdoors, and however you like – for as long or as short. While working with your EZ tutor, you can work at your own pace, you can go as fast or as slow as you like, repeat sections as many times as you need, and skip over sections you already know well. Your EZ tutor will also give you explanations, not just correct answers, and it will be **infinitely patient and adaptable**. Hence, our EZ Tutor will make you a more intelligent and smarter test-taker, and will help you maximize your score!

ADD-ON OPTIONS: *Turn your EZ Virtual Tutor into a Real Tutor!*

EZ TUTORING OVER THE PHONE:
Along with buying the entire series of our modules, students can also add on services like email/online support and/or telephone support. In fact, you can get the best preparation for your test by blending our professional 1-on-1 tutoring with our state-of-the-art books. The most important feature of our add-on features is our individualized and personalized approach that works toward building your self-confidence, and enhancing your ability to learn and perform better. This will also invigorate your motivational, organizational, as well as your learning skills. Our phone specialists are highly qualified, experienced, innovative, and well trained. You can do all this in the exclusivity and comfort of your home. Students can get in touch with one of our specialists anytime they need help – we'll be there for you, whenever you need us! We offer several packages with different levels, features, and customizations for tutoring over the phone to suit your individualized needs. Contact us for more details.

EZ 1-ON-1 TEST-TAKING & ADMISSION CONSULTATION:
We understand that standardized tests and school/college admissions can sometimes become very stressful. Our 1-on-1 Test-Taking & Admission Consulting Program can dramatically reduce your stress and anxiety. One of our consultants can personally guide you through the entire process, starting from familiarizing you with a test to getting you successfully admitted into a school/college of your choice. Again, you can do all this in the exclusivity and comfort of your home. We offer several packages with different levels, features, and customizations for test-taking and admission consultation over the phone to suit your individualized needs. Contact us for more details.
The following are some of the features of our EZ 1-on-1 Test-Taking & Admission Consulting Program:
- Familiarize you with a particular test
- Equip you with test-taking skills for each section of your test
- Reduce test-taking anxiety, stress, nervousness, and test-fever with personal counseling
- Draft and edit your essays
- Re-design your resume
- Prepare you for a telephone or personal interview
- Select the right school/college & help with admission application procedures
- Presentation Skills – how to present and market yourself

EZ UNIQUE FEATURES:
Your EZ Tutor offers you the following unique features that will highlight important information, and will let you find them quickly as and when you need to review them.

EZ STRATEGIES: It provides you with many powerful, effective, proven, and time tested strategies for various concepts, and shows you exactly how to use them to attack different question types. Many of these test-taking strategies cannot be found in any other books!

EZ SHORTCUTS: It gives you many time-saving shortcuts you can apply to save yourself some very valuable testing-time while solving a question on your actual test.

EZ TACTICS: It shows you several important tactics to use so that you can solve problems in the smartest way.

EZ DEFINITIONS: It defines all the key definitions in an easy to understand manner so that you get a clear description and concise understanding of all the key terms.

EZ RULES: It presents all the important rules in an orderly manner so that you can learn the basic rules of all the concepts.

EZ STEPS: It walks you through hundreds of concepts, showing you how to tackle every question type in an organized user-friendly step-by-step easy-to-understand methodology that adapts to your understanding and needs so that you get the best procedural knowledge.

EZ MULTIPLE/ALTERNATE METHODS: It gives you a choice of multiple methods of answering the same question so that you can choose the method that seems easiest to you.

EZ SUMMARIES: It lists a complete summary of all the important concepts in an ordered and organized manner so that you will never have to hunt for them.

EZ FACTS: It provides you with numerous key facts about various principles so that you know all the facts-and-figures of the material you are reviewing.

EZ HINTS: It supplies you with innumerable hints and clues so that you can use them to become a smarter and wiser test-taker.

EZ TIPS: It also presents you with many tips and pointers that will prevent you from making any careless mistakes or falling into traps.

EZ NOTES: It reminds you to make notes of some important points that will come handy while answering a question.

EZ WARNINGS/CAUTIONS: It warns you of some obvious mistakes that will prevent you from making them while answering a question.

EZ EXCEPTIONS: It makes you aware of the exceptions and exclusions that apply to any particular rule.

EZ REFERENCES: It gives you references of related materials that you may want to refer to in other parts of the same or different modules, while learning a specific concept.

EZ SPOTS: It lists buzzwords and phrases that will help you easily spot some specific question types.

EZ PROBLEM SET-UP: It converts even some of the most complex problems into an easy to understand mathematical statement so that you understand accurately how to interpret the problems.

EZ PROBLEM EXPLANATIONS: It provides easy to understand explanations within square brackets for each step of the problem so that you know exactly what you need to do in each step.

EZ SOLVED EXAMPLES: It also throws several realistic solved examples with easy to understand detailed explanations for each and every question type explained so that you can understand and learn how to apply the concepts.

EZ PRACTICE EXERCISES: Last but not the least; it also includes intensive realistic practice exercises with easy to understand detailed explanations for each and every question type explained so that you can put to practice what you learned in an actual test question – solved examples will help you understand the concepts & practice will make you perfect!

GUESS WHAT!! No other book offers you so much. Your EZ tutor strives to provide you with the ***best possible training*** for your test, and ***best value for your time and money***; and it is infinitely committed to providing you with ***state-of-the-art*** material.

Advantages: Amazing results in the first few days of the program!

Disadvantages: Only if you don't make use of our programs and publications!

THE EZ ADVANTAGE:

EZ TEST-PREP PROGRAM BROKEN INTO MODULES:
Instead of having a ***big fat ugly scary all-in-one gigantic book***, we have broken our entire test-prep program into ***small easy-to-use modules***.
- **Exclusivity:** Each module is exclusively dedicated to covering one major content area in extensive depth and breadth, allowing you to master each topic by getting an in-depth review.
- **More Content:** You will find many more topics and many more pages per topic than what you can find in all other books combined.
- **Tailored and Customized:** Separated modules offer test-takers of all levels with a more tailored and customized approach towards building specific foundational and advanced skills, and successfully preparing for the test.

EZ TO READ, CARRY, AND MANAGE:
EZ Modules are convenient – they are ***easier to read, carry, and manage***.
- **EZ to Read:** EZ Modules are easier to read with text in spacious pages with a bigger font size than those other books with overcrowded pages with a small print.
- **EZ to Carry:** EZ Modules are easier to carry and hold than those other big fat bulky gigantic books.
- **EZ to Manage:** EZ Modules are overall easier to manage than those other all-in-one books.

BUY ONE MODULE OR THE ENTIRE SERIES:
The individually separated modules give you the flexibility to buy only those modules that cover the areas you think you need to work on; nevertheless, we strongly suggest you buy our entire series of modules. In fact, the most efficient and effective way to get the most out of our publications is to use our entire set of modules in conjunction with each other, and not just a few. Each module can be independently bought and studied; however, the modules are somehow connected with and complement the other modules. Therefore, if you are serious about getting a good score on your test, we sincerely recommend you purchase our entire series of modules. Contact us to order, or go to www.EZmethods.com, or check your local bookstore (look at the EZ Book Store on the last page for more information).

NO NEED TO REFER TO ANY OTHER BOOK:
Almost all other test-prep books contain a small disclaimer in some corner. They themselves spell it out very loud and clear, and admit that their book is only a brief review of some important topics; hence, it should not be considered to be an overall review of all the concepts. Most other test-preparation guides only include information for you to get familiar with the kind of topics that may appear on the test, and they suggest that you refer to additional textbooks, or consult other reference books if you want more detailed information and to get an in-depth knowledge of all the concepts. These books are not designed to be a one-stop book to learn everything you must know; instead, they are more like a

summary of some important points. Moreover, they assume that you already know everything, or at least most of the concepts.

However, if you are using our EZ modules to prepare for your test, it's the opposite case, you don't need to refer or consult any other book or text or any other source for assistance. On the contrary, we, in fact, discourage you from referring to any other book, just because there is absolutely no reason to. Our EZ modules contain everything that you need to know in order to do well on your test. We haven't left anything out, and we don't assume anything. Even if you don't know anything, you will find everything in our modules from topics that are frequently tested to topics that are rarely tested, and everything in between. The only topics that you won't find in our books are the topics that will probably never appear on your test!

Frequently Tested: Included in our review – topics that are repeatedly tested on your test, on a regularly basis
Occasionally Tested: Included in our review – topics that are sometimes tested on your test, every now and then
Rarely Tested: Included in our review – topics that are seldom tested on your test, very infrequently
Never Tested: Not included in our review – since these topics are never tested on your test, we don't even mention them anywhere in our review

The bottom line is, if something can be on your test, you'll find it in our modules; and if something is not going to be on your test, it's not going to be in our modules. Each and every math concept that even has the slightest possibility to be on the test can be found in our modules.

THE OFFICIAL REAL PRACTICE TESTS:
Although we don't suggest you refer to any other book, the only time we recommend using other books is for practicing previously administered tests to exercise your skills. The best resources for actual practice tests are the official guides published by the test makers that have several actual previously administered tests. One can **replicate** these tests as closely as one can, but no one other than the test administrators can **duplicate** them, and have the ability to reproduce or publish them. Therefore, to get the maximum effect of our approach, you must practice the actual tests from the official guide. You can also take a free online practice test by going to their website. EZ's practice tests are also based upon the most recently administered tests, and include every type of question that can be expected on the actual exam.

HOW OUR BOOKS CAN HELP YOU:
Our books are designed to help you identify your strengths and the areas which you need to work on. If you study all our modules, you will be fully equipped with all the tools needed to take your test head-on. Moreover, you'll also have the satisfaction that you did all you possibly could do to prepare yourself for the test, and you didn't leave any stone unturned. The amount of content covered in our books is far more than what you would learn by studying all the other test-prep books that are out there, put together, or by even taking an online or an actual prep course, and of course, spending thousands of dollars in the process. This will give you an idea of how material we have covered in our books.

STRUCTURE OF OUR MODULES:
All our modules are **structured in a highly organized and systematic manner**. The review is divided into different modules. Each module is divided into units. Each unit is further subdivided into chapters. Each chapter covers various topics, and in each specific topic, you are given all that you need to solve questions on that topic in detail – explaining key concepts, rules, and other EZ unique features. Also included in some topics are test-taking strategies specific to the topics discussed. Following each topic are solved sample examples with comprehensive explanations, which are exclusively based on that topic, and utilizing the concepts covered in that topic and section. Finally, there are practice exercises with thorough explanations containing real test-like questions for each topic and section, which are very similar to actual test questions. All units, chapters, and topics are chronologically numbered for easy reference.

Moreover, the modules, units, chapters, and topics are all arranged in sequence so that later modules, units, chapters, and topics assume familiarity with the material covered in earlier modules, units, chapters, and topics. Therefore, the best way to review is to work through from the beginning to the end.

SERIES > MODULES > UNITS > CHAPTERS > TOPICS > SUB-TOPICS > SOLVED EXAMPLES > PRACTICE EXERCISES

THE EZ DIFFERENCE:

DIFFERENCE BETWEEN EZ SOLUTIONS' PUBLICATIONS AND OTHER BOOKS:

Most of the other test-prep books suggest that your exam only tests your ability to take the test, and it does not test any actual content knowledge. In other words, they claim that your test is all about knowing the test-taking strategies, and it has very little to do with the actual knowledge of content; others claim that your test is all about knowing a few most commonly tested topics. While we have great respect for these books and the people who write or publish them, all these books have one thing in common: they all want to give their readers a quick shortcut to success. They actually want their readers to believe that just by learning a few strategies and memorizing some key formulas, they'll be able to ace their test. We are not sure if it's the fault of the people who write these books or the people who use them; but someone is definitely trying to fool someone – either those test-prep books for making the readers believe it, or the readers for actually believing it (no pun intended).

With a test as vast as this, it's simply not possible to cover the entire content in just a few pages. We all wish; however, in life, there really aren't any shortcuts to success, and your test is no exception to this rule. Nothing comes easy in life, and that is also precisely the case with your test. You have to do it the hard way by working your way through. Unfortunately, there is no magic potion, which we can give you to succeed in math! Therefore, if you want to do well on your test – be mentally, physically, and psychologically prepared to do some hard work. In this case, efforts and results are directly proportional, that is, greater the efforts you make, better your results are going to be.

While most test-preparation books present materials that stand very little resemblance to the actual tests, EZ's publication series present tests that accurately depict the official tests in both, degree of difficulty and types of questions.

Our EZ books are like no other books you have ever seen or even heard of. We have a completely different concept, and our books are structured using a totally different model. We have *re-defined the way test-prep books should be*.

STRATEGIES SEPARATED FROM CONTENT:
What we have done in our modules is, *separated the actual content-knowledge from the test-taking strategies*. We truly believe that a test-prep program should be more than just a *cheat-sheet of tricks, tips, and traps*. The test you are preparing for is not a simple game that you can master by learning these quick tactics. What you really need to do well on your test is a program that builds true understanding and knowledge of the content.

PERFECT EQUILIBRIUM BETWEEN STRATEGIES AND CONTENT:
In our modules, we've tried our best to present a *truly unique equilibrium* between two competing and challenging skills: test-taking strategies and comprehensive content-knowledge. We have *blended* the two most important ingredients that are essential for your success on your test. We have *enhanced* the old traditional approach to some of the most advanced forms of test-taking strategies. To top all this, we have *refined* our solved examples with detailed explanations to give you hands-on experience to real test-like questions before you take your actual test.

Other Books: Most of the other test-prep books primarily concentrate on teaching their readers how to *guess* and *use the process of elimination,* and they get so obsessed with the tactics that in the process they completely ignore the actual content. Majority of the content of these books consists of pages of guessing techniques.

EZ Books: With our EZ Content-Knowledge Modules, you'll find *100% pure content* that has a highly organized and structured approach to all the content areas, which actually teaches you the content you need to know to do well on your test. Therefore, if you are looking to learn more than just guessing by process of elimination, and if you are serious about developing your skills and confidence level for your exam, then our highly organized and structured test-prep modules is the solution. By studying our books, you'll learn a systematic approach to any question that you may see on your test, and acquire the tools that will help you get there.

EZ Solutions' publications are packed with important information, sophisticated strategies, useful tips, and extensive practice that the experts know will help you do your best on your test.

You should use whichever concept, fact, or tip from that section that you think is appropriate to answer the question correctly in the least possible time. If you've mastered the material in our review modules and strategy modules, you should be able to answer almost all (99.99%) of the questions.

LEARN BACKWARDS AND MOVE FORWARD: Smart students are the ones who make an honest attempt to learn what they read, and also learn from their mistakes, but at the same time, who moves ahead. Therefore, you should learn backwards, that is, learn from your past experiences, and move forward, that is, keep moving ahead without looking back!

ONE CONCEPT, EZ MULTIPLE METHODS:

Our books often give you a **choice of multiple methods** of answering the same question – you can pick the method that seems easiest to you. Our goal is not to **prescribe** any **hard-and-fast** method for taking the test, but instead, to give you the **flexibility and tools you can use to approach your test with confidence and optimism**.

STRATEGIES OR CONTENT?

In order to do well on your test, it is absolutely essential that you have a pretty good grasp of all the concepts laid out in our review modules. Our review modules contain everything you need to know, or must know to crack your test. They cover everything from basic arithmetic to logical reasoning, and everything in between. Nonetheless, that's not enough. You should be able to use these concepts in ways that may not be so familiar or well known to you. This is where our EZ Strategies kick in.

CONTENT VERSUS STRATEGIES:

There is a **succinct** difference between knowing the math content and knowing the math strategies.

Hypothetically speaking, let's assume there is a student named Alex, who learns only the test-taking strategies; and there is another student named Andria, who learns only the math-content. Now when the test time comes, Andria who learns only the math-content is extremely likely to do a lot better than Alex, who learns only the test-taking strategies.

The truth is that someone who has the knowledge of all the math content, but doesn't know anything about the strategies, will almost always do better on the test than someone who knows all the strategies but doesn't know the content properly.

Now let's assume there is another student named Alexandria, who learns both, the test-taking strategies and the math-content. Yes, now we are talking! This student, Alexandria, who knows both the strategies and the content, is guaranteed to do a lot better than Alex, who only knows the strategies, or Andria who only knows the content.

This brings us to our conclusion on this topic: don't just study the strategies, or just the content; you need to know both simultaneously – the strategies and the content, in order to do well on your test. How quickly and accurately you can answer the math questions will depend on your knowledge of the content and the strategies, and that will have an overall effect on your success on the test.

Hence, the equation to succeed on your test is: **Strategies + Content = Success!**

We are confident that if you study our books on test-taking strategies along with our books on content-knowledge, you'll have everything you possibly need to know in order to do well on your test, in fact, to ace your test, and come out with flying colors!

The good thing is that you made the smart decision to buy this book, or if you are reading this online, or in a bookstore, or in a library, you are going to buy one soon!

CONTENT-KNOWLEDGE REVIEW MODULES:

THOROUGH IN-DEPTH REVIEW:
Most other test-prep books briefly touch upon some of the concepts sporadically. On the other hand, our books start from the basics, but unlike other books, they do not end there – *we go deep inside, beyond just touching up the surface* – all the way from fundamental skills to some of the most advanced content that many other prep books choose to ignore. *Each concept is first explained in detail, and then analyzed for most effective understanding* – each and every concept is covered, and we haven't left any stone unturned. Overall, our program is more challenging – you simply get the *best-of-the-best*, and you get more of everything!

COMPREHENSIVE REVIEW:
Our Content-Knowledge Review Modules provide the *most comprehensive and complete review* of all the concepts, which you need to know to excel in your test. Each module is devoted to one of the main subject areas so that you can focus on the most relevant material. The ideal way to review our modules is to go through each topic thoroughly, understand all the solved examples, and work out all of the practice exercises. You must review each topic, understand every solved example, and work out all of the practice exercises. If you don't have enough time, just glimpse through a section. If you feel comfortable with it, move on to something else that may potentially give you more trouble. If you feel uncomfortable with it, review that topic more thoroughly.

Moreover, if you carefully work through our review, you will probably find some topics that you already know, but you may also find some topics that you need to review more closely. You should have a good sense of areas with which you are most comfortable, and in which areas you feel you have a deficiency. Work on any weaknesses you believe you have in those areas. This should help you organize your review more efficiently. Try to give yourself plenty of time and make sure to review the skills and master the concepts that you are required and expected to know to do well on your test. Of course, the more time you invest preparing for your test and more familiar you are with these fundamental principles, the better you will do on your test.

There is a lot of content reviewed in our modules. Although the amount of material presented in our books may appear to be overwhelming, it's the most complete review to get prepared for your test. To some of you, this may seem like a great deal of information to assimilate; however, when you start reviewing, you'll probably realize that you are already comfortable with many concepts discussed in our review modules. We also suggest that you spread your use of our modules over several weeks, and study different modules at your own pace. Even if you are sure you know the basic concepts, our review will help to warm you up so that you can go into your test with crisp and sharp skills. Hence, we strongly suggest that you at least touch up on each concept. However, depending on your strengths and weaknesses, you may be able to move quickly through some areas, and focus more on the others that seem to be troublesome to you. You should develop a plan of attack for your review of the wide range of content. Work on your weaknesses, and be ready to take advantage of your strengths.

Finally, our main objective in the content review modules is to refresh your knowledge of key concepts on the test and we attempt to keep things as concrete and concise as possible.

PRACTICE MODULES:

BASIC WORKBOOK:
Our math practice basic workbook contains a variety of questions on each and every topic that is covered in our review modules. The best way is to first learn all the concepts from our review modules and then apply your skills to test your knowledge on the actual test-like questions in our basic workbook.

ADVANCED WORKBOOK:
Our math practice advanced workbook also contains a variety of questions on each and every topic that is covered in our review modules. Once you become comfortable with the questions in our basic workbook, you should try your hands on our advanced workbook so that you can gain more experience with some of the most difficult questions. For students who are aiming for a very high score, practicing from our advanced workbook is very important. For students who are aiming for a mediocre score, practicing from our advanced workbook is not so important.

▪ABOUT THIS BOOK

In order to excel on your test, it's important that you master each component of your test. That's why we have broken the entire test into different sections and each book focuses only on only one component. It's important to learn the art of tackling the questions you'll see on the test; nevertheless, it's equally important to get a strong hold of the mathematical fundamentals and principles. Apparently it's not enough to only know the test taking strategies, you also need to have a solid knowledge of the math content, and know how to solve the problems mathematically. This book is exclusively dedicated to the **Geometry** that apply to the math section of your test.

WHAT'S COVERED IN THIS BOOK:

In this book, you will learn everything related to **Geometry** content that can be used on different types of questions throughout the math section. Mastering the content of this book will not only improve your performance on the math section, but will also make you a smarter and wiser test-taker. In this book, you'll learn all the strategies and the content related to geometry, so that you can solve the geometry quickly, correctly, and more efficiently. In fact, being able to solve geometry is one of the most important factors to succeed on the math section.

WHAT'S NOT COVERED IN THIS BOOK:

This book does not cover any content other than Geometry – to learn about other content areas, you must refer to the other books in the series.

PRE-REQUISITES FOR THIS BOOK:

The pre-requisite for this book is your thorough familiarity with arithmetic and algebraic principles and concepts. Hence, when you go through this book, you are already expected to know the content covered in some of the other books in the series.

RELATED MODULES FOR THIS BOOK: You will get the best out of this book if you use it in conjunction with some of the other related books in the series that are listed below.

List of related modules for this book:
▪ EZ Solutions – Test Prep Series – General – Test Taker's Manual
▪ EZ Solutions – Test Prep Series – Math Review – Arithmetic
▪ EZ Solutions – Test Prep Series – Math Review – Algebra
▪ EZ Solutions – Test Prep Series – Math Review – Applications
▪ EZ Solutions – Test Prep Series – Math Review – Geometry
▪ EZ Solutions – Test Prep Series – Math Review – Word Problems
▪ EZ Solutions – Test Prep Series – Math Review – Logic & Stats
▪ EZ Solutions – Test Prep Series – Math Practice – Basic Workbook
▪ EZ Solutions – Test Prep Series – Math Practice – Advanced Workbook
▪ EZ Solutions – Test Prep Series – Math Strategies – Math Test Taking Strategies

Note: Look at the back of the book for a complete list of EZ books

PART 0.0: INTRODUCTION TO GEOMETRY:

Literally speaking, the word geometry comes from two Greek words – *"geo"* which means *"Earth"* and *"metron"* which means *"to measure"*. So *"geometry"* quite literally means *"to measure Earth"*. Geometry was founded in the study of the Earth. However, over the years, the use and study of geometry has become much more vast and diversified. Today, geometry is more the study of shapes (both flat and curved) than the study of Earth. Broadly speaking, geometry is the mathematics of the properties, measurements, and relationships of points, lines, angles, surfaces, and solids.

You must remember that geometry problems cannot be solved in isolation, you would still need to know the concepts you learned in arithmetic and algebra in order to solve most geometry problems. Therefore, you need arithmetic and algebra to solve geometry problems, but you may not necessarily need to know geometry to answer arithmetic or algebra problems. Likewise, since many math questions require knowledge and use of geometry, geometry is an integral part of many math problems, and in order to solve such problems, the basics of geometry should be very clear to you. You should be able to find measure of sides and angles, find area and perimeter of linear figures, find surface area and volume of solid objects, work with the coordinate grid, and use geometric concepts in problem-solving situations.

THIS PAGE HAS BEEN INTENTIONALLY LEFT BLANK

PART 1.0: LINES AND ANGLES:

TABLE OF CONTENTS:

EZ REFERENCE: -To practice easy-to-medium level questions, please refer to our EZ Practice Basic Workbook.
                    -To practice medium-to-difficult level questions, please refer to our EZ Practice Advanced Workbook.

1.1: LINES:

1.1.1: PARTS OF LINES:

(A) POINT:
- A point has no size or dimensions, that is, it has no length, width, or height, and it occupies no space.
- A point is used to identify specific location in space, but it is not an object by itself.

Symbol: A point can be represented on a piece of paper with a small dot (.).

(B) LINE:
- A line is a one-dimensional straight path that has no endpoints.
- A straight line is an infinite set or collection of adjacent or connecting points one next to the other which extends infinitely in both directions since there are no endpoints.
- A minimum of two points are required to make a line, and there is no maximum number of points on a line.
- Lines are infinitely long with no thickness or width, and therefore cannot be measured.
- It is practically impossible to draw a line since any line drawn would have some fixed length and width.
- Given any two distinct points, there can be one and only one line that passes through those two distinct points.

Note: A line can be either curved or straight; however, unless otherwise stated, the term "line" refers to a straight line.

Symbol: The symbol ($\leftrightarrow$) written on top of two letters represents the line $\Rightarrow \overleftrightarrow{AB}$

The arrowheads at each end indicate that the line is infinite in both directions.

The direction of the symbol on top of the letters represents the directions of the line.

Naming Lines: $\Rightarrow$ By a single letter: For example, in the figure below: line "L"

$\Rightarrow$ By two points on the line: Line can be named by selecting one or two points on the line, and labeling them with different letters. For example, in the figure below: line $\overleftrightarrow{AB}$

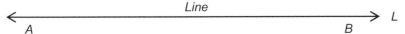

(C) RAY:
- A ray is a part of a line that begins at one labeled fixed endpoint and extends infinitely from that point in the other direction.
- A ray has one endpoint, and consists of an infinite number of points.
- A ray is like a half-line.
- Rays are infinite and therefore cannot be measured.

Symbol: The symbol ($\rightarrow$) written on top of two letters represents the Ray $\Rightarrow \overrightarrow{AB}$

The arrowhead at one end indicates that the ray is infinite in that one direction.

The direction of the symbol on top of the letters represents the direction of the ray.

Naming Rays: A Ray is denoted by selecting two points, one of which should be the endpoint, and labeling them with different letters. For example, in the figure below: Ray AB, consists of point A and all the points on AB that are on the same side of A as B.

(D) LINE SEGMENT:
- Line segment is a segment or part of a line with finite length and two labeled fixed endpoints.
- Line segments are finite and therefore can be measured.

Symbol: The symbol (—) written on top of two letters represents the line segment $\Rightarrow \overline{AB}$

There are no arrowheads that indicate that the line segment is infinite in either direction.

Naming Line Segments: A line segment is denoted by its two endpoints, and by labeling them with different letters. For instance, in the figure below: Line Segment AB, consists of points A and B and all the points that are between them.

A unique line contains any two distinct points; Therefore, line L is the only line that contains both point A and point B.

Congruent Lines: If two line segments have the same length, we say that they are congruent.

For instance, if PQ and RS have the same length, then PQ and RS are congruent $PQ \cong RS$ or $PQ = RS$.

Midpoint of Line Segment: The midpoint of a line segment is the point that divides the line segment into two segments of equal lengths. For instance: The diagram below shows the midpoint M of line segment $\overline{AB}$. If point M on the line segment $\overline{AB}$ is equidistant from both endpoints A and B, then point M is called the midpoint of line segment $\overline{AB}$. In other words, point M, divides or bisects the line segment $\overline{AB}$ into two equal parts, which means, $AM = MB$.

Line Segment

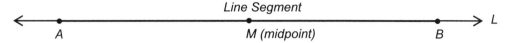

A .... M (midpoint) .... B

1.1.2: ADDING/SUBTRACTING LENGTHS OF LINE SEGMENT:

It's important to understand how to add and subtract the lengths of line segments along the same line when the lengths of different line segments along the same line are given.

For example, in the following diagram: $\Rightarrow EG = EF + FG = 2 + 3 = 5$
$\Rightarrow EF = EG - FG = 5 - 3 = 2$
$\Rightarrow FG = EG - EF = 5 - 2 = 3$

Line Segment

E .... F .... G

FINDING ORDER OF POINTS ALONG A LINE:

It's also important to understand how to find the order of points along the same line when the lengths of different line segments along the same line are given.

Example #1: Points P, Q, and R all lie on line L, with Q to the right of P. If, $PQ = 15$, $QR = 10$, and $PR > QR$. What is the value of PR?

Solution: Let's break the problem and take one step at a time:

Step 1: We can start to solve the problem by drawing the following diagram where P and Q lie on line L, such that, Q is to the right of P, and $PQ = 15$, as given in the problem.

15

P .... Q L

Step 2: Now the question is where to place point R on line L. All we are given is that $QR = 10$, however, we don't know whether R is to the left or to the right of Q. We also have to satisfy the condition that $PR > QR$. So let's evaluate both cases:

Case #1: Where R is to the left of Q by using $QR = 10$, we get the following diagram:

15

P 5 R 10 Q

As you can see in the above diagram, we get $PR = 5$. But we have to satisfy the condition that PR must be greater than QR, and in the diagram, $PR < QR$ (5 < 10). Therefore, R cannot be to the left of Q. This obviously means R must be to the right of Q, but let's evaluate it in case 2.

Case #2: Where R is to the right of Q by using $QR = 10$, we get the following diagram:

2

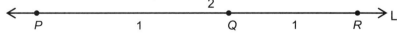

P 1 Q 1 R

As you can see in the above diagram, we get $PR = 25$. We have also satisfied the condition that PR must be greater than QR, and in the diagram, $PR > QR$ (25 > 10), as required. Therefore, this diagram shows the correct order of points P, Q, and R along line L, where R is to the right of Q, and $PR = 25$.

Example #2: If the distance from point X to point Y is 15, and the distance from point X to point Z is 7, what are the possible values of YZ?

Solution: The best way to answer this problem is by drawing a sketch as shown below. We know that the length of XY is 15 and XZ is 7. We don't know if Z is to the left or right of X.

> **Case #1:** Where Z is to the left of X, we get the following diagram:

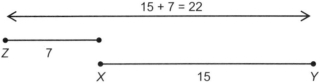

As you can see in the above diagram, YZ = 22.

> **Case #2:** Where Z is to the right of X, we get the following diagram:

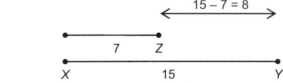

As you can see in the above diagram, YZ = 8.

Therefore, the two possible value of YZ are 8 and 22.

1.1.3: TYPES OF LINES:

(A) PERPENDICULAR LINES:
- Perpendicular lines are two lines that intersect each other to form four angles of equal measure, and each angle has a measure of 90°.
- Perpendicular lines form a right angle at the point of intersection. In other words, if two lines are perpendicular, they are the sides of right angles whose vertex is the point of intersection.

CONVERSELY: When two lines intersect each other to form four angles of equal measure, and each angle has a measure of 90°, the lines are said to be perpendicular.

SYMBOL: The symbol for perpendicular lines is: $\perp$

For Example: In the figure below, m perpendicular to n is written as $m \perp n$.

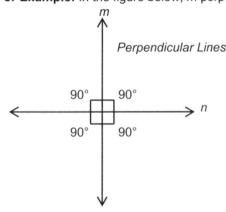

Perpendicular Lines

(B) PARALLEL LINES:
- Parallel lines are lines that remain apart, and maintain an equal and constant distance between each other and never intersect each other if extended infinitely (no matter how far they are extended) in either direction.

- Since parallel lines never intersect each other no matter how far they are extended; therefore, parallel lines do not form any angles.

CONVERSELY: When two lines remain apart, and maintain an equal and constant distance between each other and never intersect each other no matter how far they are extended in either direction, the lines are said to be parallel.

SYMBOL: The symbol for parallel lines is: ‖

For Example: In the figure below, *m* parallel to *n* is written as *m* ‖ *n*.

Distance between parallel Lines: The distance between two parallel lines is the length of the perpendicular segment from any point on one line to the other line.

For example: In the figure below, the distance between parallel lines *m* and *n* is the perpendicular distance *AB*.

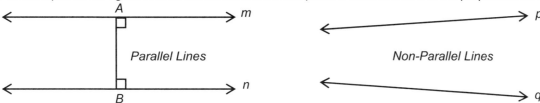

TRANSVERSAL: Transversal is a line that intersects two or more parallel lines.

PROPERTIES OF PARALLEL & PERPENDICULAR LINES:

PROPERTIES #1: If two lines are parallel to the same third line, then they are parallel to each other.
For Example: If *M* ‖ *L* and *N* ‖ *L* ⇒ Then it implies that ⇒ *M* ‖ *N*

PROPERTIES #2: If a line is parallel to one of two parallel lines, then it is also parallel to the other line.
For Example: If *M* ‖ *N* and *L* ‖ *M* ⇒ Then it implies that ⇒ *N* ‖ *L*

PROPERTIES #3: If two (or more) lines in a plane are perpendicular to the same line, then they are parallel to each other.
For Example: If *M* ⊥ *K* and *N* ⊥ *K* ⇒ Then it implies that ⇒ *M* ‖ *N*

PROPERTIES #4: If a line is perpendicular to two or more lines, then those lines are parallel.
For Example: If *K* ⊥ *M* and *K* ⊥ *N* ⇒ Then it implies that ⇒ *M* ‖ *N*

PROPERTIES #5: If a line is perpendicular to one of two parallel lines, then it is perpendicular to the other line as well.
For Example: If *M* ‖ *N* and *K* ⊥ *M* ⇒ Then it implies that ⇒ *K* ⊥ *N*

PROPERTIES #6: If any one of the angles formed when two lines intersect is a right angle, then the lines are perpendicular.
For Example: If ∠*MPK* is a right angle, then *M* ⊥ *K*

PROPERTIES #7: The shortest distance from a point to a line is the line segment drawn from the point to the line such that it is perpendicular to the line.
For Example: If *M* is any point and there is a line *K*, then *MP* is the shortest distance between point *M* and line *K*.

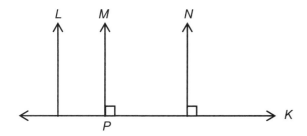

1.2: ANGLES:

1.2.1: PARTS OF ANGLE:

(A) ANGLE:
- An angle is formed by the intersection or union of two lines, line segments, or rays.
- Angles are usually formed by two rays that start from the same endpoint but may go infinitely in different directions.
- Angles are measured in counterclockwise.
- The measure of an angle is always constant between its two sides, no matter how long its sides are; i.e., it doesn't matter how close or far those points are from its vertex.
- Each complete revolution around the vertex creates an angle of 360°.

SYMBOL: $\angle$

(B) SIDES:
- The sides of the angle are two lines, rays, or line segments.

(C) VERTEX:
- The vertex of an angle is the shared endpoint or point-of-intersection at which its two sides meet or intersect.
- The vertex measures the degree of angle.

Note: Vertex – singular; Vertices – plural

(D) DEGREE:
- The degree is a unit of angular measure.
- There are 360° around any given point.
- A degree is 1/360° of complete revolution around the point called the vertex.
- Angles are indicated by a number and the degree symbol (°).

SYMBOL: (°) Symbol for Degree is the small raised circle.

Note: 1° = 60' (minutes) and 1' = 60" (seconds)

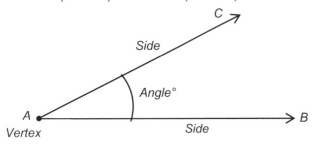

DIFFERENT WAYS OF NAMING AN ANGLE:
- By three capital letters, where the middle letter is the vertex and the other two letters are points on adjacent sides, i.e., $\angle BAC$ or $\angle CAB$, both of which represent the same angle illustrated in the figure above.

When there is no confusion, angles can also be named in the following way:
- By a capital letter which names its vertex, i.e., $\angle A$
- By a lower-case letter or number placed inside the angle, i.e., $\angle x$ or $\angle 1$

Note: $m\angle ABC$ = measure of $\angle ABC$

1.2.2: TYPES OF ANGLES:

Angles are primarily classified according to their degree measure. Any two interesting lines or line segments can form angles of different types and degrees. Following are the different types of angles:

(A) ZERO ANGLE: (Zero Angle = 0°)
- A zero angle is an angle whose degree measure is exactly 0°.
- To visualize forming a zero angle, first think of two lines that form any angle greater than 0° and then envision one of the lines rotating toward the other until they both fall in the same alignment. The angle they create will reduce in size from its original measure to 0°, and hence forming a zero angle.

For Example: In the figure below, ∠ABC is a zero angle.

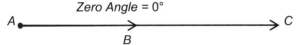

(B) ACUTE ANGLE: (0° < Acute Angle < 90°)
- An acute angle is an angle whose degree measure is greater than 0° but less than 90°.
- An acute angle is less than a right angle.

For Example: In the figure below, ∠ABC is an acute angle.

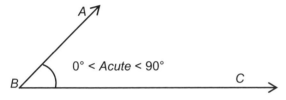

(C) RIGHT ANGLE: (Right Angle = 90°)
- A right angle is an angle whose degree measure is exactly 90°.
- A right angle is half of a straight angle, and quarter of a full revolution.

Symbol: Symbol for right angle is a small square placed on the vertex of the angle: ∟

For Example: In the figure below, ∠ABC is a right angle.

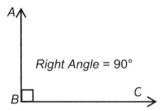

(D) OBTUSE ANGLE: (90° < Obtuse Angle < 180°)
- An obtuse angle is an angle whose degree measure is greater than 90° but less than 180°.
- An obtuse angle is greater than a right angle but less than a straight angle.

For Example: In the figure below, ∠ABC is an obtuse angle.

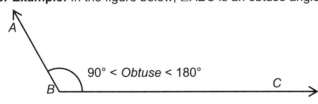

(E) STRAIGHT ANGLE: (Straight Angle = 180°)
- A straight angle is an angle whose degree measure is exactly 180°.
- A straight angle is an angle whose sides lie on a straight side, in other words it forms a straight line.
- A straight angle is twice of a right angle, and half of a full revolution.

For Example: In the figure below, $\angle ABC$ is a straight angle.

Straight Angle = 180°

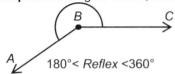

(F) REFLEX ANGLE: (180° < Reflex Angle < 360°)

- A reflex angle is an angle whose degree measure is greater than 180° but less than 360°.
- A reflex angle is greater than a straight angle.

For Example: In the figure below, $\angle ABC$ is a reflex angle.

180° < Reflex < 360°

(G) SUM OF ANGLES AROUND A POINT:

- The sum of all the measures of all the angles around a point is 360°.

360°

EZ NOTE: The above fact is important when the point is the center of a circle, as we shall see later in the section on circles. An angle is formed when two line segments extend from a common point. If you think of that point as the center of a circle, the measure of the angle is the number of degrees enclosed by the lines when they pass through the edge of the circle.

ANGLES IN A CIRCLE & AS FRACTIONS OF A CIRCLE:

- There are 360 degrees in a circle in one revolution. It doesn't matter how large or small a circle is, it still has exactly 360 degrees.
- We can think of angles as part or fractions of circles. All angles less than 360° are angles that are some fraction of 360°.

For instance: If we extended a 45° angle to 90°, we would have a right angle. If we extended it another 90°, we would have a straight angle. Tack on 2 more 90° and we'd have one full revolution, a 360° circle.

$\Rightarrow$ 45° angle represents a one-eighth of a circle, or1/8 of 360°.
$\Rightarrow$ 90° angle represents a one-fourth (quarter) of a circle, or 1/4 of 360°
$\Rightarrow$ 135° angle represents a three-eighth of a circle, or 3/8 of 360°
$\Rightarrow$ 180° angle represents a one-half of a circle, or 1/2 of 360°
$\Rightarrow$ 225° angle represents a five-eighth of a circle, or 5/8 of 360°
$\Rightarrow$ 270° angle represents a three-fourth of a circle, or 3/4 of 360°
$\Rightarrow$ 315° angle represents a seven-eighth of a circle, or 7/8 of 360°
$\Rightarrow$ 360° angle represents one full revolution of a circle, or 360°
$\Rightarrow$ 720° angle represents two full revolutions of a circle, or twice of 360°

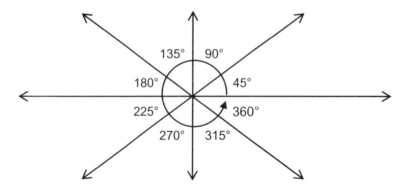

(H) CONGRUENT ANGLE:

- Congruent angles are angles of equal measure.
- If two angles have the same degree measure, they are said to be congruent.

For instance, if ∠ABC and ∠PQR have the same measure, then ∠ABC and ∠PQR are congruent
⇒ ∠ABC ≅ ∠PQR or ABC = PQR

(I) ANGLE BISECTOR:

A line or line segment **"bisects"** an angle as it splits the angle into two smaller and equal angles. The two smaller and equal angles are each half the size of the big angle. So, if an angle is divided into two equal angles by another straight line, then the angle is said to be **"bisected"** and the line that bisects it is called the **"bisector"** of the angle.
For Example: In the figure below, line BD divides ∠ABC into two equal angles. So, line BD is the bisector that bisects ∠ABC into two equal angles ∠ABD and ∠DBC and each one of them is half the size of ∠ABC.

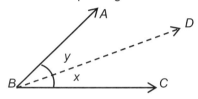

1.2.3: SUM OF ANGLES:

(A) Sum of 90° ⇒ The sum of the measures of the angles in a right angle is 90°.
⇒ If two or more angles form a right angle, the sum of their measures is 90°.
For Example: In the figure below, P + Q + R + S = 90°.

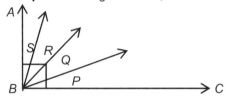

(B) Sum of 180° ⇒ The sum of the measures of the angles on one side of a straight line is 180°.
⇒ If two or more angles form a straight angle, the sum of their measures is 180°.
For Example: In the figure below, P + Q + R + S + T = 180°.

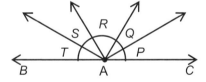

(C) Sum of 360° ⇒ The sum of the measures of the angles around a point is 360°
⇒ If two or more angles form a complete revolution, the sum of their measures is 360°.
For Example: In the figure below, P + Q + R + S + T + U + V + W = 360°.

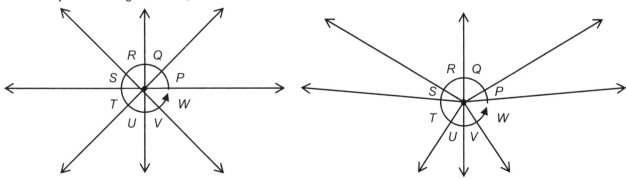

1.2.4: TYPES OF PAIR OF ANGLES:

Following are the different types of pair of angles:

(A) ADJACENT ANGLES:
- Adjacent angles are a pair of two angles that share a common vertex and a common side.

For Example: In the figure below, Pair of Adjacent Angles: ∠BAC and ∠CAD.

EZ CAUTION: In adjacent angles, one angle can't be inside the other.

Note: ∠BAD and ∠CAD are not adjacent angles because one angle is inside the other.

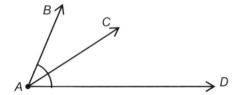

(B) COMPLIMENTARY ANGLE: (Complementary Angle = Pair of angles that sum up to 90°)
- Complementary angles are a pair of two adjacent angles that make up a right angle, i.e., whose degree measurements exactly add up to 90°.

CONVERSELY: When the sum of two adjacent angles is 90°, the angles are complementary.
- Each of the complementary angles is said to be the complement of the other.
- Two adjacent angles that form a right angle are complementary angles.
- If two complementary angles are equal, they must both measure 45° each.
- A line intersecting a right angle cuts it into a pair of complementary angles.

For Example: In the figure below, if x and y is a pair of complementary angles, then: ∠ABD + ∠DBC = 90° or $x + y = 90°$.

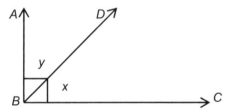

(C) SUPPLEMENTARY ANGLE: (Supplementary Angle = Pair of angle sum up to 180°)
- Supplementary angles are a pair of two adjacent angles that make up a straight angle, i.e., whose degree measurements exactly add up to 180°.

CONVERSELY: When the sum of two adjacent angles is 180°, the angles are supplementary.
- Each of the supplementary angle is said to be the supplement of the other.
- Two adjacent angles that form a straight line are supplementary angles.
- If two supplementary angles are equal, they must both be right angles.
- A line intersecting a straight angle cuts it into a pair of supplementary angles.

For Example: In the figure below, if x and y is a pair of supplementary angles, then: ∠ABD + ∠DBC = 180° or $x + y = 180°$.

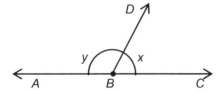

1.3: INTERSECTION OF LINES:

INTERSECTING LINES: Intersecting lines are two lines, rays, or line segments crossing each other at a point.

POINT-OF-INTERSECTION: The point-of-intersection is the point at which two lines, rays, or line segments intersect (cross) each other.

Note: Two different lines cannot have more than one point of intersection, because there is only one line between two points. For instance, in the figure below:

$\Rightarrow$ *P* is said to be the point-of-intersection of *m* and *n*. We can also say that *m* and *n* intersects at *P*.

$\Rightarrow$ *P* is the point-of-intersection of two lines if *P* is a point that is on both of the lines.

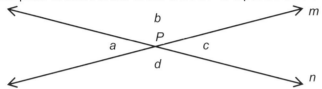

WHEN TWO STRAIGHT LINES INTERSECT, THEN:
- 4 New Angles are formed $\Rightarrow$ *a*, *b*, *c*, *d*.
- 2 Acute/Small Angles are formed that are equal to each other $\Rightarrow$ *a* = *c*
- 2 Obtuse/Big Angles are formed that are equal to each other $\Rightarrow$ *b* = *d*
- Sum of any acute angle and any obtuse angle is 180°
  $\Rightarrow$ Any Acute/Small Angle + Any Obtuse/Big Angle = 180° $\Rightarrow$ (*a* or *c*) + (*b* or *d*) = 180°
- Sum of all four angles is equal to 360° $\Rightarrow$ *a* + *b* + *c* + *d* = 360°

EZ HINT: If the measure of 1 of the 4 angles is known, then the measure of other three angles can be easily figured out.

EZ TIP: If both the lines are perpendicular to each other, then all the 4 angles formed are 90° and are equal in measure.

CLASSIFICATION OF ANGLES FORMED WHEN TWO STRAIGHT LINES INTERSECT EACH OTHER:
When two straight lines intersect each other, four new angles are formed, which can be classified as follows:
(refer to the above figure)

(A) VERTICAL (OPPOSITE) ANGLES:
- Vertical angles are the pair of opposite angles that are formed when two straight lines intersect each other. Two pairs of Vertical angles are formed at the point-of-intersection. The two angles in each pair of opposite angles are known as vertical angles.
- The two angles in a pair of vertical or opposite angles have the same degree measurement, and are therefore equal.
  For Example: Vertical Angle: *a* = *c*; *b* = *d*
- The sum of the measure of all 4 vertical angles equals 360°
  For Example: *a* + *b* + *c* + *d* = 360°

(B) ADJACENT ANGLES ARE SUPPLEMENTARY:
- When two straight lines intersect each other, any two adjacent angles are supplementary angles, that is, they add up to 180°.
- Pair of adjacent angles are supplementary angles, and therefore add up to 180°
  For Example: Adjacent Angles: *a* + *b* = *b* + *c* = *c* + *d* = *d* + *a* = 180°

EZ CAUTION: Vertical angles are equal but are NOT adjacent or supplementary, i.e., they don't add up to 180°:
Note that *a* + *c* ≠ 180° and *b* + *d* ≠ 180° as they do not fit the definition of adjacent angles. (If the vertical angles were all right angles, then any two angles, of course, would sum to 180°.)

1.4: PARALLEL LINES AND TRANSVERSAL:

1.4.1: PARALLEL LINE CUT BY PERPENDICULAR LINE:
When a pair of parallel lines is intersected by a third line (transversal) that is perpendicular to the parallel lines:

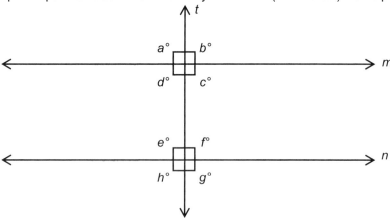

In the figure above m || n and t is perpendicular to m and n

WHEN TWO PARALLEL LINES ARE INTERSECTED BY A PERPENDICULAR TRANSVERSAL, THEN:
- Eight new angles are formed ⇒ a, b, c, d, e, f, g, h
- All eight angles are right angles and are equal to each other ⇒ a = b = c = d = e = f = g = h = 90°

Therefore, when two parallel lines are intersected by a third line in such a way that the third line is perpendicular to the parallel lines, all the angles formed are 90° angles.

EZ TIP: If one of the angles formed by the intersection of two lines is a right angle, then all four angles are right angles.

1.4.2: PARALLEL LINE CUT BY NON-PERPENDICULAR LINE:
When a pair of parallel lines is intersected by a third line (known as transversal) that is not perpendicular to the parallel lines:

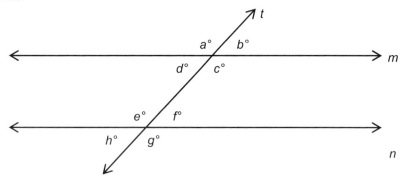

In the figure above m || n and t is the transversal that intersects through m and n

WHEN TWO PARALLEL LINES ARE INTERSECTED BY A NON-PERPENDICULAR TRANSVERSAL, THEN:
- 8 New Angles are formed ⇒ a, b, c, d, e, f, g, h
- 4 Acute (Small) Angles are formed and are equal to each other
  ⇒ Any Acute Angle = Any Acute Angle   ⇒ b = d = f = h
- 4 Obtuse (Big) Angles are formed and are equal to each other.
  ⇒ Any Obtuse Angle = Any Obtuse Angle ⇒ a = c = e = g
- Any pair of acute or small angle and obtuse or big angle forms a linear pair or supplementary angles, i.e., sum of any acute angle and any obtuse angles is 180°
  ⇒ Any Acute (Small) Angle + Any Obtuse (Big) Angle = 180°   ⇒ (b or d or f or h) + (a or c or e or g) = 180°
- Sum of all eight angles is equal to 720°   ⇒ a + b + c + d + e + f + g + h – 720°

EZ TIP: Eyeballing the eight angles usually reveals which angles are acute and which angles are obtuse, and thus which ones are equal in measure and the combinations of angles that add up to 180°.

EZ HINT: If the measure of 1 of the 8 angles is known, then the measure of other seven angles can be easily figured out. Whenever you see a transversal problem, immediately fill in all the known acute and obtuse angles. You will then be able to spot all the angles that are equal, and all the combinations of angles that sum up to 180°. This information alone will usually lead you towards the solution to the problem.

CLASSIFICATION OF ANGLES FORMED WHEN TWO PARALLEL LINES ARE INTERSECTED BY A TRANSVERSAL:

When two parallel lines are intersected by a transversal, then 8 new angles are formed, which can be classified as follows: (refer to the above figure).
Note: The following special terms or definitions are not tested on your test; however, it is important that you know and understand the relationships among these angles.

(A) INTERIOR ANGLES:
- When two parallel lines are intersected by a transversal, then the four angles that are formed inside the two parallel lines are known as interior angles.
  For Example: Interior Angles: c, d, e, f.

(B) EXTERIOR ANGLES:
- When two parallel lines are intersected by a transversal, then the four angles that are formed outside the two parallel lines are known as exterior angles.
  For Example: Exterior Angles: a, b, h, g.

(C) VERTICAL ANGLES: (Vertical Angles are Equal)
- Vertical Angles are the pair of opposite angles that are formed when two straight lines intersect or cross each other. The two angles in each pair of opposite angles are known as vertical angles.
- Vertical Angles have the same degree measurement and are therefore equal.
  For Example: Vertical Angle: $a = c$; $d = b$; $e = g$; $h = f$.

(D) CORRESPONDING ANGLES: (Corresponding Angles are Equal)
- When two parallel lines are intersected by a transversal, then the four pairs of angles that are formed on the same side of the transversal, one of which is exterior angle and the other interior angle, are known as corresponding angles. (Each angle matches another angle in the same position on the transversal.)
- Corresponding angles have the same degree measurement and are therefore equal.
  For Example: Corresponding Angles: $a = e$; $b = f$; $c = g$; $d = h$.

(E) ALTERNATE INTERIOR ANGLES: (Alternate Interior Angles are Equal)
- When two parallel lines are intersected by a transversal, then the two pairs of angles that are formed on alternate (opposite) sides of the transversal and are on the interior sides (inside the parallel lines) are known as alternate interior angles.
- Alternate Interior angles have the same degree measurement and are therefore equal.
  For Example: Alternate Interior Angles: $d = f$; $c = e$.

(F) ALTERNATE EXTERIOR ANGLES: (Alternate Exterior Angles are Equal)
- When two parallel lines are intersected by a transversal, then the two pairs of angles that are formed on alternate (opposite) sides of the transversal and are on the exterior sides (outside the parallel lines) are known as alternate exterior angles.
- Alternate Exterior angles have the same degree measurement and are therefore equal.
  For Example: Alternate Exterior Angles: $a = g$; $b = h$.

(G) SAME-SIDE INTERIOR ANGLES: (Same-Side Interior Angles are Supplementary)
- When two parallel lines are intersected by a transversal, then the two pairs of angles that are formed on the same and interior sides of the transversal are known as same side interior angles.
- Same Side Interior Angles are supplementary angles and therefore their degree measurements add up to 180°
  For Example: Same Side Interior Angles: $c + f = 180°$; $d + e = 180°$.

(H) SAME-SIDE EXTERIOR ANGLES: (Same-Side Exterior Angles are Supplementary)

- When two parallel lines are intersected by a transversal, then the two pairs of angles that are formed on the same and exterior sides of the transversal are known as same side exterior angles.
- Same Side Exterior Angles are supplementary angles and therefore their degree measurements add up to 180°
  For Example: Same Side Exterior Angles: $a + h = 180°$; $b + g = 180°$.

EZ CAUTION: If a pair of lines that are not parallel is cut by a transversal, none of the statements or relationships listed above is true.

CONVERSELY: If a transversal intersects two lines, then those two lines are parallel under the following conditions:
(A) If two lines are cut by a transversal and the resulting corresponding angles are equal in measure, then the two lines are parallel.
(B) If two lines are cut by a transversal and the resulting alternate interior angles are equal, then the two lines are parallel.
(C) If two lines are cut by a transversal and the resulting alternate exterior angles are equal, then the two lines are parallel.
(D) If two lines are cut by a transversal and the resulting same side interior angles are supplementary, then the two lines are parallel.
(E) If two lines are cut by a transversal and the resulting same side exterior angles are supplementary, then the two lines are parallel.
(F) If two lines are cut by a transversal and the resulting four acute angles are equal to each other or the four obtuse angles are equal to each other, then the two lines are parallel.

HIDDEN PARALLEL LINES AND TRANSVERSAL:
(A) Sometimes, you may be presented with a problem in such a way that the parallel lines and the transversal are not easily visible. In such cases, it is a good idea to try to extend the lines so that you can easily see the parallel lines and the transversal more clearly.
(B) Sometimes, the parallel lines and transversals are somewhat mixed in with a few other crossing lines, in such cases, block some of the lines so that you can spot the parallel lines and the transversal.
(C) Sometimes, parallel lines cut by a transversal also appear when a rectangle, a parallelogram, a rhombus, or a trapezoid is cut in half by a diagonal or any other line.
Therefore, always remember to be on the lookout for parallel lines and any line that intersects them; whenever you are able to locate them, start extending or blocking lines and labeling the known acute and obtuse angles.

PRACTICE EXERCISE – QUESTIONS AND ANSWERS WITH EXPLANATIONS: LINES AND ANGLES:

Question #1:   In the figure given below, what is the value of x?

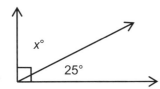

Solution: EZ Problem Set-Up $\Rightarrow$ Sum of the angles formed by perpendicular lines equal 180°
$\Rightarrow 25° + x = 90°$ [Set up the equation]
$\Rightarrow x = 65°$ [Subtract 25° from both sides]

Question #2:   In the figure given below, what is the value of x?

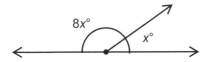

Solution: EZ Problem Set-Up $\Rightarrow$ Sum of the angles of a straight line equal 180°
$\Rightarrow x + 8x = 180°$ [Set up the equation]
$\Rightarrow 9x = 180°$ [Combine like-terms]
$\Rightarrow x = 20°$ [Divide both sides by 9]

Question #3:   In the figure given below, what is the value of x?

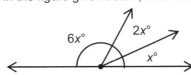

Solution: EZ Problem Set-Up $\Rightarrow$ Sum of the angles of a straight line equal 180°
$\Rightarrow x + 2x + 6x = 180°$ [Set up the equation]
$\Rightarrow 9x = 180°$ [Combine like-terms]
$\Rightarrow x = 20°$ [Divide both sides by 9]

Question #4:   In the figure given below, what is the value of x?

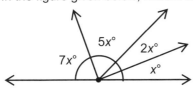

Solution: EZ Problem Set-Up $\Rightarrow$ Sum of the angles of a straight line equal 180°
$\Rightarrow x + 2x + 5x + 7x = 180°$ [Set up the equation]
$\Rightarrow 15x = 180°$ [Combine like-terms]
$\Rightarrow x = 12°$ [Divide both sides by 15]

Question #5:   In the figure given below, what is the value of x?

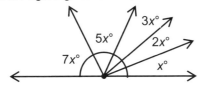

Solution: EZ Problem Set-Up $\Rightarrow$ Sum of the angles of a straight line equal 180°
                                  $\Rightarrow x + 2x + 3x + 5x + 7x = 180°$ [Set up the equation]
                                  $\Rightarrow 18x = 180°$ [Combine like-terms]
                                  $\Rightarrow x = 10°$ [Divide both sides by 18]

Question #6:   In the figure given below, what is the value of x?

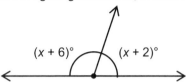

Solution: EZ Problem Set-Up $\Rightarrow$ Sum of the angles of a straight line equal 180°
                                  $\Rightarrow (x + 2) + (x + 6) = 180°$ [Set up the equation]
                                  $\Rightarrow 2x + 8 = 180°$ [Combine like-terms]
                                  $\Rightarrow 2x = 172°$ [Subtract 8 from both sides]
                                  $\Rightarrow x = 86°$ [Divide both sides by 2]

Question #7:   In the figure given below, what is the value of x?

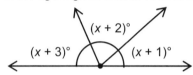

Solution: EZ Problem Set-Up $\Rightarrow$ Sum of the angles of a straight line equal 180°
                                  $\Rightarrow (x + 1) + (x + 2) + (x + 3) = 180°$ [Set up the equation]
                                  $\Rightarrow 3x + 6 = 180°$ [Combine like-terms]
                                  $\Rightarrow 3x = 174°$ [Subtract 6 from both sides]
                                  $\Rightarrow x = 58°$ [Divide both sides by 3]

Question #8:   In the figure given below, what is the value of x?

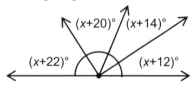

Solution: EZ Problem Set-Up $\Rightarrow$ Sum of the angles of a straight line equal 180°
                                  $\Rightarrow (x + 12) + (x + 14) + (x + 20) + (x + 22) = 180°$ [Set up the equation]
                                  $\Rightarrow 4x + 68 = 180°$ [Combine like-terms]
                                  $\Rightarrow 4x = 112°$ [Subtract 68 from both sides]
                                  $\Rightarrow x = 28°$ [Divide both sides by 4]

Question #9:   In the figure given below, what is the value of x?

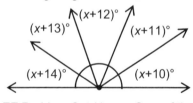

Solution: EZ Problem Set-Up $\Rightarrow$ Sum of the angles of a straight line equal 180°
                                  $\Rightarrow (x + 10) + (x + 11) + (x + 12) + (x + 13) + (x + 14) = 180°$ [Set up the equation]
                                  $\Rightarrow 5x + 60 = 180°$ [Combine like-terms]
                                  $\Rightarrow 5x = 120°$ [Subtract 60 from both sides]
                                  $\Rightarrow x = 24°$ [Divide both sides by 5]

Question #10:   In the figure given below, what is the value of x?

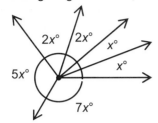

Solution: EZ Problem Set-Up $\Rightarrow$ Sum of the angles around a point equal 180°

                              $\Rightarrow x + x + 2x + 2x + 5x + 7x = 360°$ [Set up the equation]
                              $\Rightarrow 18x = 360°$ [Combine like-terms]
                              $\Rightarrow x = 20°$ [Divide both sides by 18]

Question #11:   In the figure given below, what is the value of x?

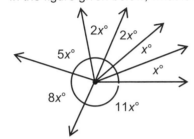

Solution: EZ Problem Set-Up $\Rightarrow$ Sum of the angles around a point equal 180°

                              $\Rightarrow x + x + 2x + 2x + 5x + 8x + 11x = 360°$ [Set up the equation]
                              $\Rightarrow 30x = 360°$ [Combine like-terms]
                              $\Rightarrow x = 12°$ [Divide both sides by 30]

Question #12:.   In the figure given below, what is the value of x and y?

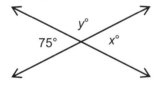

Solution: Measure of $\angle x = 75°$ [Measures of vertical angles are equal to each other]
               Measure of $\angle y = 180 - 75° = 105°$ [Sum of supplementary angles equal 180°]

Question #13:   In the figure given below, what is the value of x?

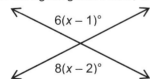

Solution: EZ Problem Set-Up $\Rightarrow$ Measures of vertical angles are equal to each other

                              $\Rightarrow 8(x - 2) = 6(x - 1)$ [Set up the equation]
                              $\Rightarrow 8x - 16 = 6x - 6$ [Apply distributive property]
                              $\Rightarrow 2x - 16 = -6$ [Subtract 6x from both sides]
                              $\Rightarrow 2x = 10$ [Add 16 to both sides]
                              $\Rightarrow x = 5°$ [Divide both sides by 2]

Question #14:   In the figure given below, what is the value of x?

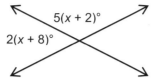

Solution: EZ Problem Set-Up ⇒ Sum of the angles of a straight line equal 180°

⇒ 2(x + 8) + 5(x + 2) = 180	[Set up the equation]
⇒ 2x + 16 + 5x + 10 = 180	[Apply distributive property]
⇒ 7x + 26 = 180	[Combine like-terms]
⇒ 7x = 154	[Subtract 26 from both sides]
⇒ x = 22°	[Divide both sides by 7]

Question #15:   In the figure given below, if $a \parallel b$ and $r = 125°$, what is the value of all the marked angles?

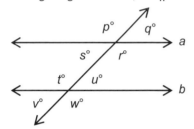

Solution:

Measure of ∠p = 125°	[Measures of vertical angles are equal to each other]
Measure of ∠q = 180° − 125° = 55°	[Sum of supplementary angles equal 180°]
Measure of ∠r = 125°	[Given]
Measure of ∠s = 180° − 125° = 55°	[Sum of supplementary angles equal 180°]
Measure of ∠t = 125°	[Alternate interior angles are equal to each other]
Measure of ∠u = 180° − 125° = 55°	[Sum of same side interior angles equal 180°]
Measure of ∠v = 180° − 125° = 55°	[Sum of interior angle & opposite exterior angle equal 180°]
Measure of ∠w = 125°	[Measures of corresponding angles are equal to each other]

Question #16:   In the figure given below, if $p \parallel q$ and $r \parallel s$, then what is the value of x and y?

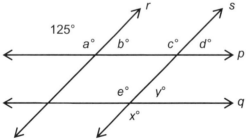

Solution:

Measure of ⇒ ∠a = ∠c = 125°	[Corresponding angles are equal]
Measure of ⇒ ∠c = ∠x = 125°	[Alternate exterior angles are equal]
Measure of ⇒ ∠x + ∠y = 180°	[Supplementary angles]
⇒ 125° + ∠y = 180°	[Substitute ∠x = 125°]
⇒ ∠y = 55°	[Subtract 125° from both sides]

Question #17:   If Q is the midpoint of line segment PS, R is the midpoint of QS, what is the ratio of RS to PQ?
Solution: The best way to solve this problem is to sketch a figure. A good starting point would be to draw PS with a length of 8 units. Then, place Q in the center of PS, which will make PQ & QS each with a length of 4. Next, place R in the center of QS, which will make QR & RS each with a length of 2. Make sure to pick a number for PS, so that it can easily be divided into halves a few times. The figure should look like the following:

Ratio of *RS* to *PQ* = 2:4 = 1:2

Question #18: If *B* is the midpoint of line segment *AE*, *C* is the midpoint of *BE*, and *D* is the midpoint of *CE*, what is the ratio of *DE* to *AE*?

Solution: The best way to solve this problem is to sketch a figure. A good starting point would be to draw *AE* with a length of 8 units. Then, place *B* in the center of *AE*, which will make *AB* & *BE* each with a length of 4. Next, place *C* in the center of *BE*, which will make *BC* & *CE* each with a length of 2. Finally, place *D* in the center of *CE*, which will make *CD* & *DE* each with a length of 1. Make sure to pick a number for *AE*, so that it can easily be divided into halves several times. The figure should look like the following:

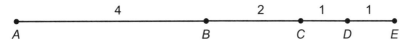

Ratio of *DE* to *AE* ⇒ 1:8

Question #19: In the figure given below, *B* is the midpoint of *AC* and *C* is the midpoint of *AD*. If *AE* = 27 and *BC* = 5, what is the length of *DE*?

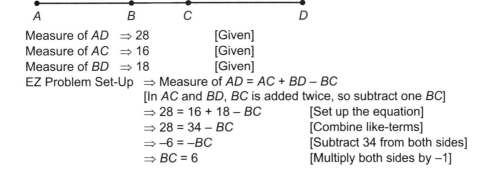

Solution:

Measure of *AE*	⇒ 27	[Given]
Measure of *BC*	⇒ 5	[Given]
Measure of *AB* or *BC*	⇒ 5	[*B* is the midpoint of *AC*]
Measure of *AC*	⇒ *AB* + *BC*	[*AC* is made up of *AB* and *BC*]
	⇒ 5 + 5 = 10	[Substitute *AB* = 5 and *BC* = 5]
Measure of *CD* or *AC*	⇒ 10	[*C* is the midpoint of *AD*]
Measure of *AD*	⇒ *AC* + *CD*	[*AD* is made up of *AC* and *CD*]
	⇒ 10 + 10 = 20	[Substitute *AC* = 10 and *CD* = 10]
Measure of *DE*	⇒ *AE* − *AD*	[To find *DE*, subtract *AD* from *AE*]
	⇒ 27 − 20 = 7	[Substitute *AE* = 27 and *AD* = 20]

Question #20: In the figure given below, points *A*, *B*, *C*, and *D* lie in the same line. The length of *AD* = 28 units, *AC* = 16 units, and *BD* = 18 units. What is the distance of *BC*?

```
    •       •       •               •
    A       B       C               D
```

Solution:

Measure of *AD* ⇒ 28   [Given]
Measure of *AC* ⇒ 16   [Given]
Measure of *BD* ⇒ 18   [Given]
EZ Problem Set-Up ⇒ Measure of *AD* = *AC* + *BD* − *BC*
            [In *AC* and *BD*, *BC* is added twice, so subtract one *BC*]
            ⇒ 28 = 16 + 18 − *BC*   [Set up the equation]
            ⇒ 28 = 34 − *BC*   [Combine like-terms]
            ⇒ −6 = −*BC*   [Subtract 34 from both sides]
            ⇒ *BC* = 6   [Multiply both sides by −1]

THIS PAGE HAS BEEN INTENTIONALLY LEFT BLANK

PART 2.0: POLYGONS:

TABLE OF CONTENTS:

EZ REFERENCE: -To practice easy-to-medium level questions, please refer to our EZ Practice Basic Workbook.
                   -To practice medium-to-difficult level questions, please refer to our EZ Practice Advanced Workbook.

2.1: BASICS ABOUT POLYGONS:

Polygon is formed from the word *"poly,"* which means *"multiple"* or *"many"* and *"gons,"* which means *"sides"*; hence, *"polygon,"* then quite literally means a *"multiple-sided"* figure.

A Polygon is a closed geometric figure in a plane that is composed of and bounded by three or more straight line segments, called the *"sides"* of the polygon. Each side intersects exactly two other sides that are joined together only at their endpoints. The points of intersection of the sides are the *"vertices"* of the polygon. In any polygon, the number of sides is always equal to the number of angles.

For Example: In the diagram below, *ABCD* is a polygon, and *PQRS* is not a polygon since the line segments intersect at points that are not endpoints.

***n*-gon:** A polygon can be referred by the term *"n-gon"*, which refers to a polygon with *"n"* sides.

Convex Polygon: For the purpose of our discussions, the term "polygon" will be used to mean a "convex polygon," that is, a polygon in which the measure of each interior angle is less than 180°.

PARTS OF POLYGONS:

(A) Side of Polygon: The line segments are called sides of the polygon.
  For Example: In the figure below, *AB* is one of the sides of the polygon.

(B) Angle of Polygon: Intersection of two sides results in an angle of the polygon.
  For Example: In the figure below, ∠*ABC* is one of the angles of the polygon.

(C) Vertex of Polygon: The point-of-intersection of line-segments or endpoints of two adjacent sides is called a vertex of the polygon. (Vertex – singular; Vertices – plural)
  For Example: In the figure below, point *A* is one of the vertices of the polygon.

(D) Diagonal of Polygon: Line segment inside the polygon connecting two nonadjacent vertices or whose endpoints are nonadjacent vertices is called diagonal of the polygon.
  For Example: In the diagram below, *AC* is one of the diagonal of the polygon.

(E) Altitude of Polygon: The altitude of a polygon is any line segment that starts from one of its vertices and ends on one of its sides in such a manner that it is perpendicular to that side.
  For Example: In the diagram below, *DE* is the altitude of the polygon.

NAMING POLYGONS: A polygon is usually labeled according to the letters (usually upper case) that mark its vertices given, in order.

For Example: In the diagram below, the polygon can be named as *ABCD*, or *BCDA*, or *CDAB*, or *DABC*.

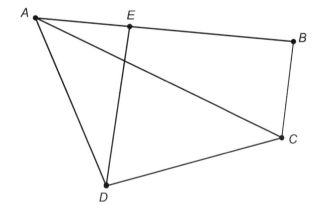 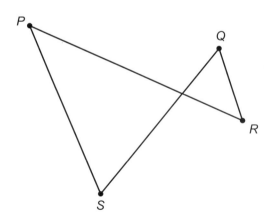

2.2: TYPES OF POLYGONS:

2.2.1: TYPES OF POLYGONS BASED ON EQUALITY:

(A) EQUILATERAL POLYGON: ⇒ **Equal Sides**
Equilateral polygons are polygons whose all sides are of equal measure.

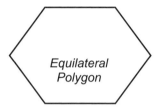

(B) EQUIANGULAR POLYGON: ⇒ **Equal Angles**
Equiangular polygons are polygons whose all angles are of equal measure.

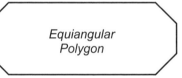

(C) REGULAR POLYGON: ⇒ **Equal Sides & Equal Angles**
Regular polygons are polygons that are both *equilateral* and *equiangular*. In other words, regular polygons are polygons in which all sides are of equal length and in which all interior angles are of equal measure.
Regular Polygon = Equilateral + Equiangular.

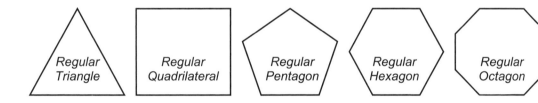

(D) IRREGULAR POLYGONS: ⇒ **Unequal Sides & Unequal Angles**
Irregular polygons are polygons that are neither equilateral nor equiangular. In other words, irregular polygons are polygons in which all or some sides are not of equal length and in which all or some angles are not of equal measure.

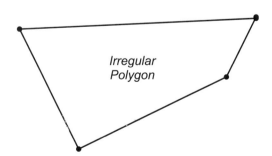

(E) CONGRUENT POLYGONS:

Polygons are congruent with one another if all of their corresponding angles and corresponding sides are equal. Congruent polygons have the same size and the same shape.

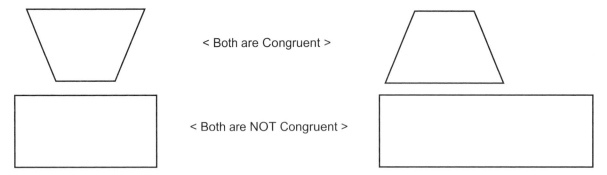

< Both are Congruent >

< Both are NOT Congruent >

Symbol of Congruency: Two or more sides with the same number of small strokes through them indicate that those sides are of equal measure. Similarly, two or more angles with the same number of little arcs around them indicate that those angles are of equal measure.

For Example in the diagram below: $AB = DE$; $BC = EF$; $AC = DF$ and $\angle A = \angle D$; $\angle B = \angle E$; $\angle C = \angle F$

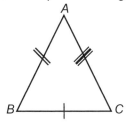 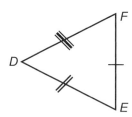

(F) SIMILAR POLYGONS:

Polygons are similar to one another if all of their corresponding angles are equal and the lengths of their corresponding sides are proportional. Similar polygons have the same shape but may not necessarily have the same size.

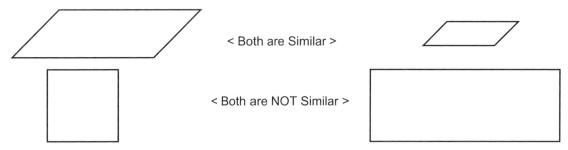

< Both are Similar >

< Both are NOT Similar >

2.2.2: TYPES OF POLYGONS BASED ON NUMBER OF SIDES OR ANGLES:

(A) Triangle   ⇒   Three-Sided Polygon
(B) Quadrilateral   ⇒   Four-Sided Polygon
(C) Pentagon   ⇒   Five-Sided Polygon
(D) Hexagon   ⇒   Six-Sided Polygon
(E) Heptagon   ⇒   Seven-Sided Polygon
(F) Octagon   ⇒   Eight-Sided Polygon
(G) Nonagon   ⇒   Nine-Sided Polygon
(H) Decagon   ⇒   Ten-Sided Polygon
(H) Dodecagon   ⇒   Twelve-Sided Polygon
(H) N-gon   ⇒   N-Sided Polygon

Note: Triangles and Quadrilaterals are the most important types of polygons for the purpose of your test.

2.3: SUM OF ANGLES OF POLYGONS:

2.3.1: SUM OF INTERIOR ANGLES OF POLYGON:
Following are the two methods to find the sum of interior angles of a polygon:

2.3.1.1: BY USING FORMULA:
Sum of the Measures of *"n"* Interior Angles in a Polygon with *"n"* sides $\Rightarrow (n - 2) \times 180°$

Degree Measure of Each Interior Angle of a Regular Polygon with *"n"* sides $\Rightarrow \dfrac{(n - 2) \times 180^0}{n}$

The following table demonstrates the relationship between number of sides of a polygon and sum of its interior angles:

Number of Sides	Sum of Interior Angles
3	180°
4	360°
5	540°
6	720
7	900°
-	-
n	180°(n – 2)

EZ NOTE: The sum of the interior angles of a given polygon is dependant on the number of sides of the polygon. Notice that the sum of the interior angles of a polygon follows a regular pattern that is directly related to *n*, the number of sides of the polygon. Particularly, the sum of the angles of a polygon is always 2 less than *n* (the number of sides) times 180°.

2.3.1.2: BY DIVIDING POLYGON:
The total number of degrees in the interior angles of most polygons can also be found by dividing the polygons into triangles and applying the following steps:

STEP 1: From any vertex, draw diagonals, and divide the polygon into as many non-overlapping adjacent triangles as possible. Only use straight lines as diagonals, and only divide the space inside the polygon into triangles.

STEP 2: Count the number of triangles formed.

STEP 3: Since there is a total of 180° in the angles of each triangle, multiply the number of triangles by 180° $\Rightarrow$ the product will be the sum of the angles in the polygon.

Any Polygon can be Divided into Triangles in Two Different Ways:
(A) By drawing all diagonals emanating from any one given vertex to all other nonadjacent vertices.
(B) By drawing all diagonals connecting all the opposite vertices.
Notice that a four-sided polygon is divided into two triangles, five-sided polygon is divided into three triangles, a six-sided polygon is divided into four triangles, and an eight-sided polygon is divided into six triangles. As a thumb-rule, an *n*-sided polygon is divided into (n – 2) triangles. For instance, the square below is divided into 2 triangles, the pentagon into 3 triangles, the octagon into 6 triangles, and so on.

 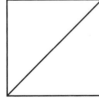   

EZ TIP: To divide polygons into triangles, quadrilaterals would need one diagonal, pentagons would need two diagonals, hexagons would need three diagonals, heptagons would need four diagonals, octagons would need five diagonals, and so on.

For instance: To find the measure of each angle of a regular hexagon (6-sided polygon)
Find the sum of the interior angles and divide by the number of interior angles, which is 6.
Since all angles are equal, each of them is equal to the one-sixth of the sum.

The sum of the interior angles of each triangle is 180°, and since there are 4 triangles in a 6-sided figure, the sum of the interior angles is 4 × 180° = 720° and each of the six interior angles measure 720° ÷ 6 = 120°.

For Example: What is the measure of each angle of a regular pentagon (5-sided polygon)?
Solution:
Sum of the Angles	$\Rightarrow (n - 2) \times 180°$	[Write the appropriate formula]
	$\Rightarrow (5 - 2) \times 180°$	[Substitute the known values]
	$\Rightarrow 3 \times 180°$	[Do the subtraction]
	$\Rightarrow 540°$	[Do the multiplication]
Each Interior Angle	$\Rightarrow$ Sum of Angles ÷ No. of Sides	[Write the appropriate formula]
	$\Rightarrow 540° \div 5$	[Substitute the known values]
	$\Rightarrow 108°$	[Do the division]

2.3.2: SUM OF EXTERIOR ANGLES OF A POLYGON:

In any polygon, the sum of the exterior angles, taking one at each vertex, is always 360°.
Each exterior angle of a regular polygon $\Rightarrow$ **360° ÷ n**

For Example: If each interior angle of a polygon measures 120°, how many sides does the polygon have?
Solution: Since each interior angle = 120°; each exterior angle = 60°
EZ Problem Set-Up $\Rightarrow$ Each exterior angle of a regular polygon = 360° ÷ n

$\Rightarrow \dfrac{60^0}{1} = \dfrac{360^0}{n}$ [Set up the equation]

$\Rightarrow 60°n = 360°$ [Cross-multiply]

$\Rightarrow n = 6°$ [Divide both sides by 60°]

The polygon has 6 sides.

2.3.3: SUM OF INTERIOR AND EXTERIOR ANGLE OF POLYGON:

In any polygon, the sum of an interior angle and an exterior angle is always equal to 180°
$\Rightarrow$ Measure of an exterior angle + Measure of an interior angle in polygon = 180°

For Example: How many sides does a polygon have if the measure of each interior angle is 8 times the measure of each exterior angle?
Solution: Let, the measure of each exterior angle of the polygon $\Rightarrow x$
The, the measure of each interior angle of the polygon $\Rightarrow 8x$
EZ Problem Set-Up $\Rightarrow$ Measure of an exterior angle + Measure of an interior angle in polygon = 180°

$\Rightarrow 1x + 8x = 180°$ [Set up the equation]

$\Rightarrow 9x = 180°$ [Combine like-terms]

$\Rightarrow x = 20°$ [Divide both sides by 9]

Measure of each exterior angle of the polygon $\Rightarrow 20°$
Sum of the measure of all exterior angles of a polygon $\Rightarrow 360°$
Number of angles in the polygon $\Rightarrow 360° \div 20° = 18$
The polygon has 18 angles or 18 sides.

2.4: PERIMETER OF POLYGON:

The perimeter of any figure is nothing but its outer boundary. The perimeter of any polygon (regular or irregular) is equal to the sum of the lengths of all its sides.

PERIMETER OF POLYGON $\Rightarrow$ Sum of lengths of all its sides $\Rightarrow S_1 + S_2 + S_3 + S_4 + S_5.......$

For Example: What is the perimeter of a pentagon whose sides are 5, 7, 10, 17, and 19 units?
Solution: Perimeter of Polygon $\Rightarrow$ Add all the sides
$$\Rightarrow 5 + 7 + 10 + 17 + 19$$
$$\Rightarrow 58 \text{ units}$$

Alternate Method to Find Perimeter of Regular Polygons: To find the perimeter of regular polygons, simply multiply the length of one side times the number of sides.

PERIMETER OF REGULAR POLYGON $\Rightarrow$ *Length of Side × Number of Sides*

For Instance: Perimeter of a regular triangle with side 10 is $\Rightarrow 10 \times 3 = 30$
                   Perimeter of a regular quadrilateral with side 10 is $\Rightarrow 10 \times 4 = 40$
                   Perimeter of a regular pentagon with side 10 is $\Rightarrow 10 \times 5 = 50$
                   Perimeter of a regular hexagon with side 10 is $\Rightarrow 10 \times 6 = 60$
                   Perimeter of a regular heptagon with side 10 is $\Rightarrow 10 \times 7 = 70$
                   Perimeter of a regular octagon with side 10 is $\Rightarrow 10 \times 8 = 80$

For Example: If the side of a regular hexagon (6-sided) is 15 units, what is its perimeter?
Solution: Perimeter of Polygon $\Rightarrow$ Length of Side × No. of Sides   [Write the appropriate formula]
$$\Rightarrow 6 \times 15 \qquad \text{[Substitute the known values]}$$
$$\Rightarrow 90 \text{ units} \qquad \text{[Do the multiplication]}$$

2.5: AREA OF REGULAR POLYGON:

The area of a regular polygon equals one-half the product of the length of its apothem and perimeter.

AREA OF REGULAR POLYGON $\Rightarrow$ **½ apothem × perimeter** $\Rightarrow$ **½ × a × p**

Where: **Apothem:** Apothem of a regular polygon is the line segment from the center of the polygon perpendicular to any side of the polygon.

Radius: Radius of a regular polygon is the line segment connecting any vertex of a regular polygon with the center of the polygon.

For Example: What is the area of a regular pentagon whose side is 2 units and apothem is 5 units?

Solution:

Perimeter of Polygon	$\Rightarrow$ *Length of Side × No. of Sides*	[Write the appropriate formula]
	$\Rightarrow 2 \times 5$	[Substitute the known values]
	$\Rightarrow 10$ units	[Do the multiplication]
Area of Regular Polygon	$\Rightarrow$ *½ ap*	[Write the appropriate formula]
	$\Rightarrow \frac{1}{2}(5)(10)$	[Substitute the known values]
	$\Rightarrow 25$ unit^2	[Do the multiplication]

ALTERNATE METHOD TO FIND AREA OF POLYGONS:

All polygons can be divided into some combination of rectangles and/or triangles. Therefore, if you ever forget the area formula for a particular shape, the area of a polygon can also be found by simply breaking up the polygon into smaller figures such as triangles, rectangles, and squares. Find the area of each individual piece and add them to get the area of the given polygon.

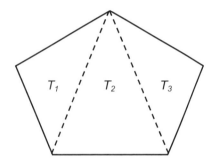

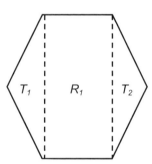

Area = Area of Triangle$_1$ + Triangle$_2$ + Triangle$_3$
Area of Polygon = $T_1 + T_2 + T_3$

Area = Area of Triangle$_1$ + Rectangle$_1$ + Triangle$_2$
Area of Polygon = $T_1 + R_1 + T_2$

PRACTICE EXERCISE – QUESTIONS AND ANSWERS WITH EXPLANATIONS: REGULAR POLYGON:

Question #1: What is the measure of each angle of a regular 12-sided polygon?

Solution:

Sum of the Angles	$\Rightarrow (n - 2) \times 180°$	[Write the appropriate formula]
	$\Rightarrow (12 - 2) \times 180°$	[Substitute the known values]
	$\Rightarrow 10 \times 180°$	[Do the subtraction]
	$\Rightarrow 1800°$	[Do the multiplication]
Each Interior Angle	$\Rightarrow$ Sum of Angles ÷ No. of Sides	[Write the appropriate formula]
	$\Rightarrow 1800° \div 12$	[Substitute the known values]
	$\Rightarrow 150°$	[Do the division]

Question #2: If each interior angle of a polygon measures 150°, how many sides does the polygon have?

Solution: Since each Interior Angle = 150°; each Exterior Angle = 30°

EZ Problem Set-Up $\Rightarrow$ Each exterior angle of a regular polygon = 360° ÷ n

$$\Rightarrow \frac{30^0}{1} = \frac{360^0}{n} \qquad \text{[Set up the equation]}$$

$\Rightarrow 30°n = 360°$ [Cross-multiply]

$\Rightarrow n = 12°$ [Divide both sides by 30°]

Therefore, the polygon has 12 sides.

Question #3: How many sides does a polygon have if the measure of each interior angle is 11 times the measure of each exterior angle?

Solution: Let, the measure of each exterior angle of the polygon $\Rightarrow x$

The, the measure of each interior angle of the polygon $\Rightarrow 11x$

EZ Problem Set-Up $\Rightarrow$ Measure of an exterior angle + Measure of an interior angle in polygon = 180°

$\Rightarrow 1x + 11x = 180°$ [Set up the equation]

$\Rightarrow 12x = 180°$ [Combine like-terms]

$\Rightarrow x = 15°$ [Divide both sides by 12]

Measure of each exterior angle of the polygon $\Rightarrow 15°$

Sum of the measure of all exterior angles of a polygon $\Rightarrow 360°$

Number of angles in the polygon $\Rightarrow 360° \div 15° = 24$

Therefore, the polygon has 24 angles or 24 sides.

Question #4: If the side of a regular hexagon (6-sided) is 16 units, what is its perimeter?

Solution:

Perimeter of Regular Polygon $\Rightarrow$ Length of Side × No. of Sides		[Write the appropriate formula]
	$\Rightarrow 6 \times 16$	[Substitute the known values]
	$\Rightarrow 96$ units	[Do the multiplication]

Question #5: If the side of a regular pentagon is 12 units and apothem is 7 units, what is its area?

Solution:

Perimeter of Regular Polygon $\Rightarrow$ Length of Side × No. of Sides		[Write the appropriate formula]
	$\Rightarrow 12 \times 5$	[Substitute the known values]
	$\Rightarrow 60$ units	[Do the multiplication]
Area of Regular Polygon	$\Rightarrow \frac{1}{2}ap$	[Write the appropriate formula]
	$\Rightarrow \frac{1}{2}(7)(60)$	[Substitute the known values]
	$\Rightarrow 210$ unit^2	[Do the multiplication]

THIS PAGE HAS BEEN INTENTIONALLY LEFT BLANK

PART 3.0: TRIANGLES:

TABLE OF CONTENTS:

EZ REFERENCE: -To practice easy-to-medium level questions, please refer to our EZ Practice Basic Workbook.
                   -To practice medium-to-difficult level questions, please refer to our EZ Practice Advanced Workbook.

3.1: BASICS ABOUT TRIANGLES:

The term *"triangle"* is formed from the word *"tri,"* which means *"three"* and *"angles"* means *"angles"*; hence, *"triangle,"* then quite literally means *"three angles"* figure. A triangle is a three-sided polygon with an enclosed three-sided geometric figure. Triangles have three angles and three straight sides. Triangle is a polygon that has the fewest number of sides.
Symbol of Triangle: Δ

3.1.1: PARTS OF TRIANGLE:

(A) SIDES:
- A side of a triangle is the line segment connecting vertices of two angles of the triangle, or whose endpoints are the vertices of two angles of the triangle.

(B) ANGLE:
- An Angle of a triangle is formed by the intersection or union of any two of its sides.

(C) VERTEX:
- The point-of-intersections of the sides of a triangle are called the vertices of the triangle.
- The vertices of a triangle measure its angles. (Vertex – singular; Vertices – plural)

(D) DEGREE:
- The Degree is a unit of angular measure.

Symbol: The raised small circle (°) is the symbol to represent degrees.

DIFFERENT WAYS OF WRITING TRIANGLE:
(A) By a capital letter that names its vertex, i.e., Δ*A*.
(B) By three capital letters, all of which are the vertices of the triangle, in any order, i.e., Δ*ABC*, Δ*BAC*, or Δ*ACB*, all of which represent the same triangle illustrated in the figure below.

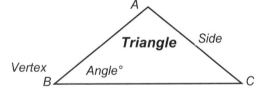

3.1.2: TERMS USED IN TRIANGLES:

(A) BASE:
The base of a triangle can be any one of three sides; hence, every triangle can have any of the three sides as its base.

(B) ALTITUDE:
An altitude (or height) of a triangle is the line segment connecting one of the vertices of the triangle to the opposite side and is perpendicular to that opposite side. In other words, it's the perpendicular distance from a vertex to its opposite side.
Altitudes in Different Types of Triangle: Since there are three vertices of every triangle, there can be three altitudes and three bases where it intersects. The altitude can fall inside the triangle, outside the triangle, or on one of its sides.
(A) In case of an acute triangle   ⇒ the height/altitude falls inside the triangle.
(B) In case of a right triangle   ⇒ the height/altitude is one of the legs that is perpendicular to the base.
(C) In case of an obtuse triangle   ⇒ the height/altitude falls outside the triangle.

EZ HINT: In order to find the height of a triangle, visualize it as a hill, and think how high is the tip of the hill from the ground level. You'll see that the height of the tip is the perpendicular distance from the base and not the slant distance.

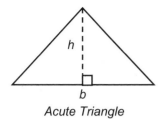
Acute Triangle

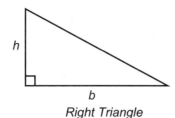
Right Triangle

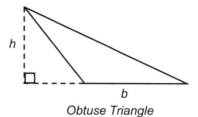
Obtuse Triangle

(C) MEDIAN:

A median of a triangle is the line segment connecting one of the vertices of the triangle to the midpoint of the opposite side, that is, it intersects the opposite side at its midpoint and divides it into two halves.

For Example: In the figure below, in $\triangle ABC$, AE is the Median and E is the midpoint of $BC \Rightarrow BE = EC$

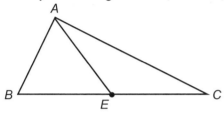

(D) PERPENDICULAR BISECTOR:

A perpendicular bisector of a triangle is the line segment that bisects and is perpendicular to one of the sides of a triangle, that is, it intersects one of the sides of the triangle at its midpoint and at 90°.

For Example: In the figure below, in $\triangle ABC$, PQ is the perpendicular bisector $\Rightarrow PQ \perp BC$ and $BQ = QC$

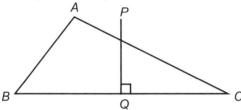

(E) ANGLE BISECTOR:

An angle bisector of a triangle is the line segment connecting one of the sides of the triangle to the opposite vertex bisecting that angle into two halves, that is, it bisects one of the angles of the triangle into two equal angles.

For Example: In the figure below, in $\triangle ABC$, AD is the angle bisector $\Rightarrow \angle x = \angle y$

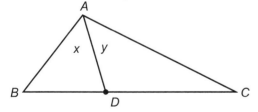

(F) MIDLINE:

A midline of a triangle is the line segment that connects the midpoints of any two sides of a triangle.

For Example: In the figure below, in $\triangle ABC$, PQ is the midline $\Rightarrow BP = PC$ and $AQ = QC$

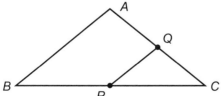

3.1.3: SUM OF ANGLES IN TRIANGLES:

EZ RULE #1: The sum of the measures of all three interior angles of any type of triangle equals exactly 180°.
For instance: In the figure given below $\Rightarrow \angle A + \angle B + \angle C = 180°$

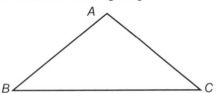

EZ RULE #2: The sum of the measures of all three exterior angles of any type of triangle equals exactly 360°.
For instance: In the figure given below $\Rightarrow \angle A_1 + \angle B_1 + \angle C_1 = 360°$

$\Rightarrow \angle A + \angle A_1 = 180°$	[Sum of supplementary angles equal 180°]
$\Rightarrow \angle B + \angle B_1 = 180°$	[Sum of supplementary angles equal 180°]
$\Rightarrow \angle C + \angle C_1 = 180°$	[Sum of supplementary angles equal 180°]
$\Rightarrow \angle A + \angle B + \angle C + \angle A_1 + \angle B_1 + \angle C_1 = 540°$	[Add up all angles]
$\Rightarrow \angle A_1 + \angle B_1 + \angle C_1 + 180° = 540°$	[Substitute $\angle A + \angle B + \angle C = 180°$]
$\Rightarrow \angle A_1 + \angle B_1 + \angle C_1 = 360°$	[Subtract 180° form both sides]

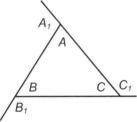

EZ RULE #3: If two triangles share a common angle, the sums of the other two angles are equal.
For instance: In the figure given below $\Rightarrow \angle APQ + \angle AQP = \angle ARS + \angle ASR$

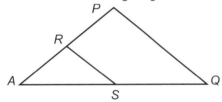

3.1.4: TRIANGLE INEQUALITY THEOREM:

The triangle inequality states the following relationships between sides and angles of a triangle:

EZ RULE:
$\Rightarrow$ Larger the angle of a triangle – Longer the opposite side
$\Rightarrow$ Smaller the angle of a triangle – Smaller the opposite side
$\Rightarrow$ If two sides of a triangle are unequal, then the angles opposite these sides are unequal.
$\Rightarrow$ If one angle in a triangle is larger than another angle, the side opposite the larger angle is longer than the side opposite the smaller angle. Therefore, in any triangle:
$\Rightarrow$ Largest angle of a triangle is always opposite the longest side.
$\Rightarrow$ Smallest angle of a triangle is always opposite the shortest side.
$\Rightarrow$ Angles with the same measure are opposite sides with the same length.

For Example: In the figure below, if a, b, & c are the lengths of three sides opposite angle A, B, & C respectively of a triangle, and:
$\Rightarrow$ if $A > B > C$, then $a > b > c$
$\Rightarrow$ If $b > c$, then $\angle B > \angle C$ and $\Rightarrow$ If $c < b$, then $\angle C < \angle B$

CONVERSELY:
$\Rightarrow$ Larger the side of a triangle – Larger the opposite angle
$\Rightarrow$ Smaller the Side of a triangle – Smaller the opposite angle

⇒ If two angles of a triangle are unequal, then the sides opposite these angles are unequal.
⇒ If one side in a triangle is longer than another side, then the angle opposite the longer side is larger than the angle opposite the shorter side. Therefore, in any triangle:
⇒ Longest side of a triangle is always opposite the largest angle.
⇒ Shortest side of a triangle is always opposite the smallest angle.
⇒ Sides with the same length are opposite angles with the same measure.

For Example: In the figure below, if a, b, & c are the lengths of three sides opposite angle A, B, & C respectively of a triangle, and:
⇒ If $a > b > c$, then $A > B > C$
⇒ If $\angle B > \angle C$, then $b > c$ and   ⇒ If $\angle C < \angle B$, then $c < b$

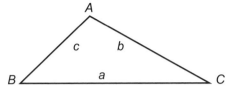

RELATIONSHIP #1: Sum of Two Sides > Third Side
The sum of the lengths of any two sides of a triangle is always greater than the length of the third side.
⇒ If a, b, & c are the lengths of three sides of a triangle, Then $b + c > a$, or $a + c > b$, or $a + b > c$
Conversely: The length of any one side of a triangle is always less than the sum of the lengths of the remaining two sides.

RELATIONSHIP #2: Difference of Two Sides < Third Side
The difference between the lengths of any two sides of a triangle is less than the length of the third side.
⇒ If a, b, & c are the lengths of three sides of a triangle, Then $b - c < a$, or $a - c < b$, or $a - b < c$
Conversely: The length of any one side of a triangle is greater than the positive difference between the lengths of the remaining two sides.

RANGE OF THIRD SIDE: Maximum and Minimum Lengths of a Side:
Sum of Two Sides > Third Side > Difference of Two Sides
⇒ If a, b, and c are the lengths of three sides of a triangle ⇒ Then, $b + c > a > b - c$
⇒ Then, $a + c > b > a - c$
⇒ Then, $a + b > c > a - b$
The length of any one side is less than the sum of the lengths of the two other sides and greater than the difference of the length of the two other sides. In other words, the length of the third side is somewhere in between the difference and sum of the other two sides.

EZ HINT: The best way to understand the concept explained above is to realize the fact that $a + c$, the length of the path from A to C through B, is greater than b, the length of the direct path from A to C. Consider the figure above.
⇒ $a + c > b$
⇒ $a > b - c$ or $b - c < a$ [Subtract "c" from both sides]

EZ TIP: One side of a triangle can never be longer than the sum of the lengths of the other two sides of the triangle, or less than their difference. Consider the figures below.

If we make $\angle ABC$ smaller and smaller, at some point, when $\angle ABC = 0°$, the figure ceases to be a triangle. So $\angle ABC$ becomes 0° when side AC equals the difference of the other two sides, in this case $7 - 5$. So in reality, AC can never quite reach 2, for the figure to exist. Likewise, if we make $\angle ABC$ bigger and bigger, at some point when $\angle ABC = 180°$, the figure again ceases to be a triangle. So $\angle ABC$ becomes 180° when side AC equals the sum of the other two sides, in this case $5 + 7$. So in reality, side AC can never quite reach 12.

Consider the following triangle that is impossible to have, and note what it tells us about the relationship between the three sides of any triangle:

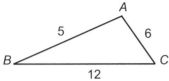

The triangle above can never be drawn with the given measurements. We already know that the shortest distance between any two points is a straight line. Now according to the triangle shown above, the direct straight line distance between point B and point C is 12; however, the indirect path from point B to C (the path that goes from B to A to C) is 5 + 6, or 11, which is shorter than the direct path, which is obviously not possible. Therefore, the maximum integer distance for side BC in the triangle above is 10. Alternatively, if side BC is actually 12, then either side AB has to be at least 7, or side AC has to be at least 8.

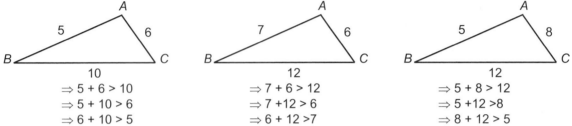

$\Rightarrow 5 + 6 > 10$

$\Rightarrow 5 + 10 > 6$

$\Rightarrow 6 + 10 > 5$

$\Rightarrow 7 + 6 > 12$

$\Rightarrow 7 + 12 > 6$

$\Rightarrow 6 + 12 > 7$

$\Rightarrow 5 + 8 > 12$

$\Rightarrow 5 + 12 > 8$

$\Rightarrow 8 + 12 > 5$

Therefore, in the above three cases, we have tested each combination of sides and proved that the measurements of the sides of these triangles are possible. Note that in all the above three cases, the sum of two sides is not equal to or less than the third side; in fact, the sum of two sides is greater than the third side.

3.1.5: RELATIONSHIPS BETWEEN INTERIOR & EXTERIOR ANGLES OF TRIANGLE:

2 INTERIOR – 1 EXTERIOR ANGLE PHENOMENON:

Interior Angles: An Interior Angle of a triangle is the interior angle formed inside the triangle by two sides. Every triangle has three interior angles.

Exterior Angles: A Supplementary Exterior Angle of a triangle is an exterior angle formed outside the triangle by one of the sides of the triangle and the extension of an adjacent side.

RELATIONSHIP #1: The degree measure of an exterior angle of a triangle is equal to 180° minus the measure of the adjacent interior angle; that is, each interior angle is supplementary to an adjacent exterior angle.

⇒ **Exterior Angle + Adjacent Interior Angle = 180°.**

For Example: In the diagram below: $c + x = 180°$

RELATIONSHIP #2: The degree measure of an exterior angle of a triangle is equal to the sum of the measure of the two opposite (remote) interior angles that are not adjacent to it.

⇒ **Exterior Angle = Sum of measure of two opposite interior angles.**

For Example: In the diagram below: $x = a + b$

$\Rightarrow a + b + c = 180$ [Sum of the interior angles of a triangle is 180]

$\Rightarrow c + x = 180$ [According to above rule, c is supplementary to x]

$\Rightarrow c + x = a + b + c$ [Equate first two equations since they both are equal to 180]

$\Rightarrow x = a + b$ [Subtract c from both sides]

Therefore, the exterior angle x is equal to sum of two remote or opposite interior angles, a and b.

RELATIONSHIP #3: Measure of exterior angle of a triangle is greater than either of the opposite/remote interior angles.

⇒ **Exterior Angle > Either of Opposite Interior Angles**

For Example: In the diagram below: $x > a$ and $x > b$

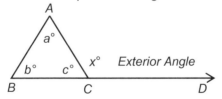

3.2: TYPES OF TRIANGLES:

Triangles can be classified by the lengths of their sides or by the measures of their angles. Note that sides or angles with the same number of marks are equal.

(A) EQUILATERAL TRIANGLE:

The word **"equi"** means, **"equal,"** **"lateral"** means **"sides"**; therefore, **"equilateral"** literally means **"equal sides"**. An equilateral triangle, also known as a regular triangle, is a triangle in which all three sides are of equal length and all three angles are of equal measure. equilateral triangles are also equiangular, since all three sides are equal.

$\Rightarrow$ In an equilateral triangle, all three sides are equal in length $\Rightarrow a = b = c$

$\Rightarrow$ In an equilateral triangle, all three angles are equal in measure $\Rightarrow A = B = C = 60°$.

Each angle in an equilateral triangle measures exactly 60° $\Rightarrow x + x + x = 180°$ $\Rightarrow 3x = 180°$ $\Rightarrow x = 60°$

Note: All equilateral triangles are acute triangles.

For Example: In the figure below, ΔABC is an equilateral triangle.

CONVERSELY: If the lengths of all three sides of a triangle are equal OR if all three angles in a triangle are of equal measure $\Rightarrow$ then the triangle must be an equilateral triangle.

Relationship Between Angles and Sides in an Equilateral Triangle:

#1: If all sides of a triangle are equal, then it can be deduced that all the angles of the triangle are also equal.
   If $AB = BC = AC$, then $\angle ABC = \angle ACB = \angle BAC$.

#2: If all angles of a triangle are equal, then it can be deduced that all the sides of the triangle are also equal.
   If $\angle ABC = \angle ACB = \angle BAC$, then $AB = BC = AC$.

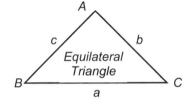

(B) ISOSCELES TRIANGLE:

An Isosceles triangle is a triangle in which at least two sides are of equal length and the two angles opposite to these sides are of equal measure. In an isosceles triangle, the two equal sides are called legs, the third side is called base.

$\Rightarrow$ In an isosceles triangle, two sides are equal in length $\Rightarrow x = y$

$\Rightarrow$ In an isosceles triangle, two angles are equal in measure $\Rightarrow B = C$

For Example: In the figure below, ΔABC is an isosceles triangle.

CONVERSELY: If the lengths of any two sides of a triangle are equal OR if any two angles in a triangle are of equal measure $\Rightarrow$ then the triangle must be an Isosceles Triangle.

Relationships Between Angles and Sides in an Isosceles Triangle:

#1: If two sides of a triangle are equal, then it can be deduced that the two angles opposite the two equal sides are also equal. If $AB = AC$, then $\angle ABC = \angle ACB$.

#2: If two angles of a triangle are equal, then it can be deduced that the lengths of the two sides opposite the equal angles are also equal. If $\angle ABC = \angle ACB$, then $AB = AC$.

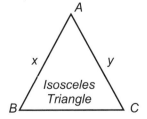

(C) SCALENE TRIANGLE:

A Scalene triangle is a triangle in which none of its sides are equal in length and none of the angles are equal in measure. All the sides have different lengths and all the angles have different measures.
Note: All scalene triangles are always obtuse triangles.
For Example: In the figure below, $\triangle ABC$ is scalene triangle.

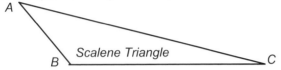

(D) ACUTE TRIANGLE:

An acute triangles is a triangle in which all of its three angles are acute angles, i.e., each angle measures less than 90°.
Note: All equilateral triangles are acute triangles. Acute triangle can be equilateral or isosceles.
For Example: In the figure below, $\triangle ABC$ is an acute triangle.

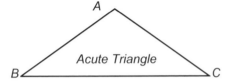

(E) OBTUSE TRIANGLE:

An obtuse triangles is a triangle in which one of the angles is an obtuse angle, that is, it measures greater than 90°, and the rest of the two angles are acute angles.
Note: An obtuse triangle can be isosceles or scalene.
For Example: In the figure below, $\triangle ABC$ is an obtuse triangle in which $\angle B > 90°$.

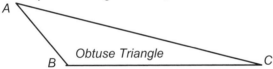

(F) RIGHT TRIANGLE:

A right triangles is a triangle in which one of the interior angles is a right angle, that is, it measures exactly 90°, and the rest of the two angles are acute angles.
For Example: In the figure below, in $\triangle ABC$, AC is the hypotenuse and AB & BC are the legs.

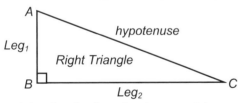

In any right triangle, the other two remaining acute angles opposite the two legs are complementary angles, i.e., sum of the measures of the two acute angles is 90°. If x & y are the measures of the two acute angles of a right triangle, then:
$\Rightarrow 90° + x + y = 180° \Rightarrow x + y = 90°$

(G) ISOSCELES RIGHT TRIANGLE:

An isosceles right triangle is a triangle in which one of the angles is a right angle, i.e., it measures exactly 90°; and the other two acute angles are equal and measure exactly 45° each, i.e., the two legs of the triangle are of equal measure.
For Example: In the figure below, $\triangle ABC$ is an isosceles right triangle in which $\angle B = 90°$, and $\angle A = \angle C = 45°$

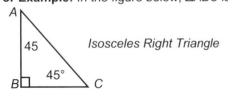

3.3: SPECIAL TRIANGLES:

Always be on the lookout for special right triangles in geometry problems that involve triangles as they contain a lot of hidden information that can be easily deduced. Many right triangles are special right triangles in which the measures of its sides always appear in predefined ratios. If you are able to recognize such special right triangles, you won't have to use the Pythagorean Theorem to find the value of its missing measure of side. Moreover, unlike regular right triangles in which you need to know the measure of two of its sides to figure out the measure of its third side, in some of the special right triangles, even if you know the measure of just one side, you can find the measure of its other two sides. Most right triangles on standardized tests are **"special"** right triangles.

3.3.1: PYTHAGOREAN THEOREM:

The **"Pythagorean Theorem"** states that in a right triangle, the square of the length of the hypotenuse (the longest side) is equal to the sum of the squares of the lengths of the other two sides (the two short sides). If the lengths of any two sides of a right triangle are given, the length of the third side can be found by using the Pythagorean Theorem.

PARTS OF A RIGHT TRIANGLE:

(A) Hypotenuse: The side opposite the right angle in a right triangle is called the hypotenuse. It is the longest side that lies opposite the right angle, the largest angle of a right triangle.
(B) Legs: The remaining two sides are usually referred to as arms or legs of the right triangle.

PYTHAGOREAN THEOREM STATES: $\Rightarrow (Leg_1)^2 + (Leg_2)^2 = (Hypotenuse)^2$
$$\Rightarrow a^2 + b^2 = c^2 \qquad \text{Where "}a\text{", "}b\text{", and "}c\text{" are the sides of right triangle } \triangle ABC$$

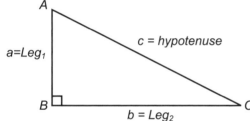

EZ TIP: Pythagorean Theorem is widely tested on standardized tests and if a question tells you that a triangle is a right triangle, you can be almost sure that you'll need to use that information to find the length of a side or a measure of an angle by using Pythagorean Theorem.

EZ NOTE: The Pythagorean Theorem is very useful whenever you're given the lengths of two sides of a right triangle; you can easily find the length of the third side by using the Pythagorean Theorem.

For Example: If the length of the two legs in a right triangle is 6 and 8, what is the length of its hypotenuse?
Solution:
$$\Rightarrow 6^2 + 8^2 = c^2$$
$$\Rightarrow 36 + 64 = c^2$$
$$\Rightarrow c = \sqrt{100} = 10$$

CONVERSE OF PYTHAGOREAN THEOREM: Conversely, If the lengths of the three sides of a triangle are a, b, and c, and $a^2 + b^2 = c^2$, then according to the Pythagorean Theorem, the triangle must be a right triangle, where "c" is the length of the hypotenuse.
For Example: If the three sides of a triangle are 5, 12, and 13, is it a right triangle?
Solution: Since $5^2 + 12^2 = 13^2 \Rightarrow$ it has to be a right triangle.

Let, a, b, and c be the Sides of Triangle $\triangle ABC$, With $a \le b \le c$, Then:
(A) If ABC is a right triangle & $\angle C$ is a right angle, then $a^2 + b^2 = c^2$ Example: $6^2 + 8^2 = 10^2$
(B) If ABC is an acute triangle & $\angle C$ is acute angle, then $a^2 + b^2 > c^2$ Example: $6^2 + 8^2 > 9^2$
(C) If ABC is an obtuse triangle & $\angle C$ is obtuse angle, then $a^2 + b^2 < c^2$ Example: $6^2 + 8^2 < 11^2$

PYTHAGOREAN TRIPLES: 3–4–5 PHENOMENON:

Remember, you can always use the Pythagorean Theorem to find the lengths of the sides in a right triangle; however, there are some special kinds of right triangles that always have the same ratios. There are some sets of integers that happen to satisfy the Pythagorean Theorem. These sets of integers are commonly referred to as *"Pythagorean Triples"*.

Pythagorean Triples are one of the most common sides in right triangles, in at least the ones that show up on your test. The most common right triangles whose sides are integers are 3-4-5 right triangles and its multiples. Since $3^2 + 4^2 = 5^2$, you can have a right triangle with legs of lengths 3 and 4, and hypotenuse of length 5. You should be familiar with these numbers, so that whenever you see a right triangle with legs of 3 and 4, without wasting any time you will immediately know the hypotenuse must have a length of 5. In addition, any multiple of these lengths makes other Pythagorean Triplets. For instance, $6^2 + 8^2 = 10^2$, so 6, 8, and 10 also make a right triangle. Therefore, the sides of a 3-4-5 right triangle are in the ratio of 3:4:5.

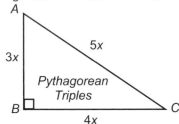

EZ RULE: For any positive number "*x*," there is a right triangle whose sides are in the ratio of 3*x*, 4*x*, 5*x*. Such triangles are known as the Pythagorean triples.

EZ TIP: The following are some unique types of special triangles that you must know in order to bypass Pythagorean Theorem and save time. These special types of right triangles are probably the most common kind of right triangle as they appear most often on the tests. You should be able to recognize them immediately whenever they show up in the problems. Remember, the less often you have to calculate using the Pythagorean Theorem, the more time you save.

TABLE OF EXAMPLES OF PYTHAGOREAN TRIPLES (3 – 4 – 5):

If $x = 1$	$3^2 + 4^2 = 5^2$	$\Rightarrow$ Measure of sides = 3, 4, 5.
If $x = 2$	$6^2 + 8^2 = 10^2$	$\Rightarrow$ Measure of sides = 6, 8, 10.
If $x = 3$	$9^2 + 12^2 = 15^2$	$\Rightarrow$ Measure of sides = 9, 12, 15.
If $x = 4$	$12^2 + 16^2 = 20^2$	$\Rightarrow$ Measure of sides = 12, 16, 20.
If $x = 5$	$15^2 + 20^2 = 25^2$	$\Rightarrow$ Measure of sides = 15, 20, 25.
If $x = 10$	$30^2 + 40^2 = 50^2$	$\Rightarrow$ Measure of sides = 30, 40, 50.
If $x = 25$	$75^2 + 100^2 = 125^2$	$\Rightarrow$ Measure of sides = 75, 100, 125.
If $x = 50$	$150^2 + 200^2 = 250^2$	$\Rightarrow$ Measure of sides = 150, 200, 250.
If $x = 75$	$225^2 + 300^2 = 375^2$	$\Rightarrow$ Measure of sides = 225, 300, 375.
If $x = 100$	$300^2 + 400^2 = 500^2$	$\Rightarrow$ Measure of sides = 300, 400, 500.
If $x = 0.5$	$1.5^2 + 2^2 + 2.5^2$	$\Rightarrow$ Measure of sides = 1.5, 2, 2.5
If $x = 2.5$	$7.5^2 + 10^2 = 12.5^2$	$\Rightarrow$ Measure of sides = 7.5, 10, 12.5
If $x = \pi$	$3\pi^2 + 4\pi^2 = 5\pi^2$	$\Rightarrow$ Measure of sides = 3π, 4π, 5π

EZ TIP: The above fact applies even when *x* is not an integer, as long as they are in the ratio of 3*x* : 4*x* : 5*x*

Some other most recognizable right triangle triplets that appear occasionally are triangles whose measures of sides are in the following ratio:

(i) 5–12–13 Triangles: **(ii)** 8–15–17 Triangles: **(iii)** 7–24–25 Triangles:
$\Rightarrow 5^2 + 12^2 = 13^2$ $\Rightarrow 8^2 + 15^2 = 17^2$ $\Rightarrow 7^2 + 24^2 = 25^2$
$\Rightarrow 25 + 144 = 169$ $\Rightarrow 64 + 225 = 289$ $\Rightarrow 49 + 576 = 625$

EZ TIP: If you ever come across a right triangle with two sides of 5 and 12 or 8 and 15, you can instantly predict that the third side is 13 or 17, respectively.

3.3.2: 45°–45°–90° TRIANGLE PHENOMENON:

A 45°–45°–90° triangle is called an isosceles right triangle, since it's both isosceles and right. A 45°–45°–90° triangle has a hypotenuse opposite 90° angle, and the other two legs opposite 45° angles are of equal measure. In a 45°–45°–90° triangle, the ratio between the lengths of sides is constant. Therefore, if we know the length of any one of the three sides, we can figure out the length of the other sides. So, in a 45°–45°–90° isosceles right triangle, the lengths of the sides are in the ratio of $1 : 1 : \sqrt{2}$.

For instance: In a 45°-45°-90° triangle, if length of each leg = x, and length of hypotenuse = h; Then, according to Pythagorean Theorem: ($a^2 + b^2 = c^2$):

$\Rightarrow x^2 + x^2 = h^2$

$\Rightarrow 2x^2 = h^2$

$\Rightarrow h = \sqrt{2x^2} = x\sqrt{2}$

EZ RULE: In a 45°–45°–90° triangle, also known as the "Isosceles Right Triangle", the lengths of the sides are in the constant ratio of $x : x : x\sqrt{2}$ where x is the length of each leg.

ANGLE – SIDE PROPORTION IN 45°–45°–90° TRIANGLES:

Length of side opposite 45° angle = Leg $\Rightarrow x$
Length of side opposite 45° angle = Leg $\Rightarrow x$
Length of side opposite 90° angle = Hypotenuse $\Rightarrow x\sqrt{2}$

(A) If the length of the leg, "x", is given $\Rightarrow$ Then Hypotenuse = Leg times $\sqrt{2}$ = $x\sqrt{2}$
(B) If the hypotenuse is given $\Rightarrow$ Then the Length of each leg = hypotenuse $\div \sqrt{2}$ = $x\sqrt{2} \div \sqrt{2}$ = x

EZ NOTE: The diagonal of a square divides the square into two equal isosceles right triangles. Two 45°–45°–90° triangles joined at a side opposite 90° angle form a square. So, a 45°–45°–90° triangle is half of a square. Two 45°–45°–90° triangles joined at a side opposite 45° angle form another 45°–45°–90° triangle.

3.3.3: 30°–60°–90° TRIANGLE PHENOMENON:

A 30°–60°–90° triangle has a hypotenuse opposite 90° angle, one smaller leg opposite 30° angle, and the other longer leg opposite 60° angle. In a 30°–60°–90° triangle, the ratio between the lengths of sides is constant. Therefore, if we know the length of any one of the three sides, we can figure out the length of the other sides. So, in a 30°–60°–90° triangle, the lengths of the sides are in the ratio of $1 : \sqrt{3} : 2$.

For instance: In a 30°-60°-90° triangle, if length of short leg = x, then the length of hypotenuse = $2x$; Then, according to Pythagorean Theorem: ($a^2 + b^2 = c^2$):

$\Rightarrow x^2 + b^2 = (2x)^2$

$\Rightarrow x^2 + b^2 = 4x^2$

$\Rightarrow b^2 = 3x^2$

$\Rightarrow b = \sqrt{3}x$

So, the length of long leg = $\sqrt{3}x$

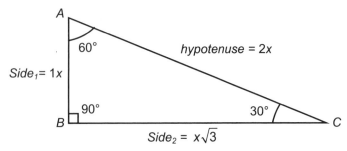

EZ RULE: In a 30°–60°–90° triangle, the sides are in the constant ratio of $x : x\sqrt{3} : 2x$, where x is the length of the shorter leg.

ANGLE – SIDE PROPORTION IN 30°–60°–90° TRIANGLES:

Length of side opposite 30° angle = Short Leg $\Rightarrow x$

Length of side opposite 60° angle = Long Leg $\Rightarrow \sqrt{3}x$

Length of side opposite 90° angle = Hypotenuse $\Rightarrow 2x$

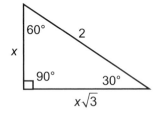   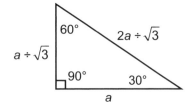   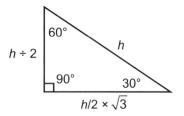

(A) If the length of the Shorter Leg (x) is given $\Rightarrow$ Then, the length of Longer Leg = Shorter Leg $\times \sqrt{3}$ = $\sqrt{3}x$

$\Rightarrow$ And, the Hypotenuse = Shorter Leg $\times$ 2 = $2x$

(B) If the length of the Longer Leg, "a", is given $\Rightarrow$ Then, the length of the Shorter Leg = Longer Leg $\div \sqrt{3}$ = $\dfrac{a}{\sqrt{3}}$

$\Rightarrow$ And, the Hypotenuse = Shorter leg $\times$ 2 = $\dfrac{2a}{\sqrt{3}}$

(C) If the length of the Hypotenuse, "h", is given $\Rightarrow$ Then, the length of the Shorter Leg = Hypotenuse $\div$ 2 = $\dfrac{h}{2}$

$\Rightarrow$ And, the length of the Longer Leg = Shorter Leg $\times \sqrt{3}$ = $\dfrac{h}{2}\sqrt{3}$

ALTERNATE METHOD USING TRIGONOMETRIC RATIOS:

If you know some basic trigonometry, it is possible to use the trigonometric (sine, cosine, and tangent) ratios to solve questions involving 30-60-90 triangles and 45-45-90 triangles. However, you should try not to; in fact, you should stay away from using any trigonometry for such types of questions, instead, you should use the method explained above. Using trigonometry to solve such problems may take more time than solving without using trigonometry. Moreover, you'll be more likely to make a mistake while using trigonometry. Use the trigonometric ratios as the last option because most of these problems can be solved by using Pythagorean Theorem or the special right triangle theorems.

Therefore, try to adopt a non-trigonometric approach while solving any geometry question that involves special triangles. Make sure to memorize the special triangle ratios, and know how to use them to find the missing sides.

Following are the trigonometric ratios:

Sine = $\dfrac{opposite}{hypotenuse}$ (soh)   Cosine = $\dfrac{adjacent}{hypotenuse}$ (cah)   Tangent = $\dfrac{opposite}{adjacent}$ (toa)

Mnemonic: SOH-CAH-TOA (a simple way to remember which sides correspond to each ratio)

ALTITUDE IN AN EQUILATERAL TRIANGLE DIVIDES IT INTO TWO 30–60–90 RIGHT TRIANGLES:

Two 30°–60°–90° triangles joined at the side opposite the 60° angle form an equilateral triangle. So, a 30°–60°–90° triangle is half of an equilateral triangle.

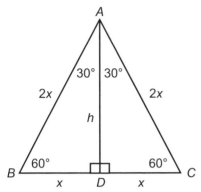

If $\triangle ABC$ is an equilateral triangle in which the length of each side is $2x$, and the length of drawn altitude AD is h. Then, $\angle ADB$ and $\angle ADC$ are both equal 30-60-90 right triangles with sides x, $2x$, and h.
Now, according to the Pythagorean Theorem: $\Rightarrow x^2 + h^2 = (2x)^2 = 4x^2$
$$\Rightarrow h^2 = 4x^2 - x^2 = 3x^2$$
$$\Rightarrow h = \sqrt{3x^2} = \sqrt{3}\,x$$

Therefore, the height of the equilateral triangle is $= \frac{1}{2} \times side \times \sqrt{3} = \sqrt{3}\,x$

For Example: What is the altitude of an equilateral triangle whose side is 50 units?

Solution: Height of Equilateral Triangle $\Rightarrow \frac{1}{2} \times side \times \sqrt{3}$ [Write the appropriate formula]

$$\Rightarrow \frac{1}{2} \times 50 \times \sqrt{3}$$ [Substitute the known values]

$$\Rightarrow 25\sqrt{3} \text{ units}$$ [Simplify the expression]

EZ NOTE: If you have some knowledge about basic trigonometry, you could use the sine, cosine, and tangent ratios to solve questions involving 45-45-90 and 30-60-90 triangles; however, we recommend that you don't. Instead, you should use the method shown above. Using trigonometry to solve these types of problems takes more time, and you are more likely to make a mistake. Hence, try to avoid using trigonometry as all questions on your test can be solved without it, by using our methods.

3.4: PERIMETER OF TRIANGLES:

The perimeter of any type of triangle is the distance around the triangle, i.e., the perimeter of a triangle is equal to the sum of the lengths of all the sides of the triangle.

PERIMETER OF TRIANGLE $\Rightarrow Side_1 + Side_2 + Side_3 \Rightarrow S_1 + S_2 + S_3$

For Example: What is the perimeter of a triangle whose sides are 2 units, 7 units, and 9 units?
Solution: Perimeter of Triangle $\Rightarrow Side_1 + Side_2 + Side_3$ [Write the appropriate formula]
$$\Rightarrow 2 + 7 + 9$$ [Substitute the known values]
$$\Rightarrow 18 \text{ units}$$ [Do the addition]

3.5: AREA OF TRIANGLES:

3.5.1: AREA OF ANY TRIANGLE:

The area of a triangle is equal to one-half the product of its base and height.

AREA OF TRIANGLE $\Rightarrow$ ½ (***Base × Height***) $\Rightarrow$ ½ ***BH***

Where: **Base:** Base of a triangle can be any one of the sides.

Height: Height of a triangle is the altitude, the perpendicular distance from the opposite vertex to the base, forming a right triangle at the base. Therefore, the height (or altitude) is perpendicular to the base = Height $\perp$ Base

How to Pick Base & Height of a Triangle:

You can start with any vertex of the triangle. The side opposite the vertex you choose becomes the base and the perpendicular line segment from that vertex to the base becomes the height. In other words, the base of a triangle is any one of the sides, and the height is the altitude measured at a right angle to the base. Be careful while determining the altitude of a triangle.

In all the cases, base and height are perpendicular to each other $\Rightarrow$ **Base $\perp$ Height**

For example: In the figure below: $\Rightarrow$ If *AB* is the base, then *CE* is the height.

$\Rightarrow$ If *AC* is the base, then *BD* is the height.

$\Rightarrow$ If *BC* is the base, then *AF* is the height.

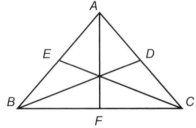

EZ TIP: When any two sides of a triangle are perpendicular to each other, the area is quite easy to calculate. If none of the sides of a triangle are perpendicular, then you will have to find the perpendicular distance from one of its vertices to the opposite side, unless it's already given in the problem.

For Example: What is the area of a triangle whose base is 20 and height is 5?
Solution: Area of Triangle $\Rightarrow$ ½ × base × height = ½ × (20) (5) = 50

BASE & ALTITUDE IN DIFFERENT TYPES OF TRIANGLE:

(A) Acute Triangles: In case of acute triangles, the base is any one of the sides, and the height is perpendicular to the base starting from the opposite vertex and the height falls inside the triangle.
(B) Right Triangles: In case of right triangles, the base can be either one of the legs and the height is the other leg that is automatically perpendicular to the base, and the height falls on one of the sides of the triangle.
(C) Obtuse Triangles: In case of obtuse triangles, the base is usually the shortest side, and the height is perpendicular to the base starting from the opposite vertex, and the height falls outside the triangle.

EZ HINT: In order to find the height of a triangle, visualize it as a mountain, and then think how high the tip of the mountain from the ground level is. You will realize that the height of the tip is the perpendicular distance from the base and not the slanting distance.

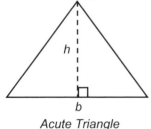
Acute Triangle

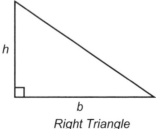
Right Triangle

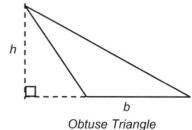
Obtuse Triangle

3.5.2: AREA OF RIGHT TRIANGLE:

In a right triangle, the two sides that form the 90° angle are called legs. Since the legs of a right triangle are perpendicular to each other, the area of a right triangle is one-half the product of the lengths of its legs.

AREA OF RIGHT TRIANGLE $\Rightarrow$ ½ (Leg_1 × Leg_2) $\Rightarrow$ ½ (L_1 × L_2)

Example #1:   What is the area of the ΔABC below?

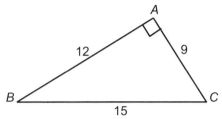

Solution: In the triangle above, the first thing that comes to mind is to treat BC, the hypotenuse as the base of the triangle, since that is the way the figure is drawn. It's fine to think in that way; however, in this case, you would need to know the perpendicular distance from BC, the hypotenuse to the opposite vertex in order to determine the area of the triangle. Now that would be darn hard to figure out, and probably based on the limited information given in the problem, it may even be impossible to do so. If you look at the diagram closely, you'll notice that this is a right triangle with AB & AC as its two legs. If you still can't notice it, then you may want to turn around the book so that you can see AB as your base. Therefore, now the base is 12 and height is 9 or the two legs are 12 and 9; and you can now calculate the area of the triangle by using the formula:
Area of a Right Triangle $\Rightarrow$ ½ (Leg_1 × Leg_2) = ½ (L_1 × L_2) = ½ (12) (9) = 54 sq. in.

Example #2:   What is the area of a right triangle whose hypotenuse is 25 units and one of whose legs is 15 units?
Solution: Apply Pythagorean Theorem $\Rightarrow$ (Leg_1)^2 + (Leg_2)^2 = (Hypotenuse)^2 [Write the Pythagorean Theorem]
$\Rightarrow$ (Leg_1)^2 + (15)^2 = (25)^2 [Substitute the known values]
$\Rightarrow$ (Leg_1)^2 + 225 = 625   [Solve the exponents]
$\Rightarrow$ (Leg_1)^2 = 400   [Subtract 225 from both sides]
$\Rightarrow$ (Leg_1) = 20 units   [Square root both sides]
Area of a Right Triangle $\Rightarrow$ ½ (Leg_1 × Leg_2)   [Write the appropriate formula]
$\Rightarrow$ ½ (15) (20)   [Substitute the known values]
$\Rightarrow$ 150 unit^2 [Do the multiplication]

3.5.3: AREA OF ISOSCELES TRIANGLE:

In an isosceles right triangle, we call the two sides that form the 90° angle its legs, both of which are equal. So Leg_1 = Leg_2. Since the legs of an isosceles right triangle are perpendicular and equal to each other, the area of an isosceles right triangle is one-half the product of the square of its one of the legs.

AREA OF ISOSCELES RIGHT TRIANGLE $\Rightarrow$ ½ (Leg_1 × Leg_2) $\Rightarrow$ ½ (Leg)^2

Example #1:   What is the area of an isosceles right triangle with a hypotenuse of 2 units?
Solution: Apply Pythagorean Theorem $\Rightarrow$ Leg^2 + Leg^2 = Hypotenuse^2 [Write the Pythagorean Theorem]
$\Rightarrow$ 2Leg^2 = Hypotenuse^2 [Combine like-terms]
$\Rightarrow$ 2Leg^2 = 2^2 [Substitute the known values]
$\Rightarrow$ Leg^2 = 2   [Divide both sides by 2]
$\Rightarrow$ Leg = $\sqrt{2}$ units   [Square root both sides]
Area of Isosceles Right Triangle $\Rightarrow$ ½ (leg)^2 [Write the appropriate formula]
$\Rightarrow$ ½$\left(\sqrt{2}\right)^2$ [Substitute the known values]
$\Rightarrow$ ½(2)   [Solve the exponent]
$\Rightarrow$ 1 unit^2 [Simplify the expression]

Example #2:   What is the length of the hypotenuse of an isosceles right triangle with an area of 12.5 unit^2?
Solution: Area of Isosceles Right Triangle $\Rightarrow$ ½ (leg)^2 = 12.5

Apply Pythagorean Theorem
$$\Rightarrow (\text{leg})^2 = 25$$
$$\Rightarrow \text{leg} = 5 \text{ units}$$
$$\Rightarrow leg^2 + leg^2 = hypotenuse^2 \quad \text{[Write the Pythagorean Theorem]}$$
$$\Rightarrow 5^2 + 5^2 = h^2 \quad \text{[Substitute the known values]}$$
$$\Rightarrow 25 + 25 = h^2 \quad \text{[Solve the exponents]}$$
$$\Rightarrow 50 = h^2 \quad \text{[Do the addition]}$$
$$\Rightarrow h = 5\sqrt{2} \text{ units} \quad \text{[Square root both sides]}$$

EZ HINT: Don't expect the triangle to be right side up.
For instance, all triangles in the figure below are right angles.

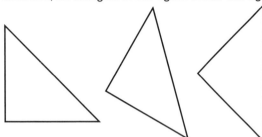   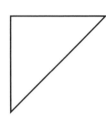

For Example: If the lengths of the sides of a triangle are 5 feet, 12 feet, and 13 feet, what is the area of the triangle?
Solution: Since $5^2 + 12^2 = 25 + 144 = 169 = 13^2 \Rightarrow$ the triangle is a right triangle and the legs are the sides with lengths 5 feel and 12 feet, and hypotenuse with length 13.
Area of Triangle = ½ × base × height = ½ × 5 × 12 = 30 square feet.

3.5.4: AREA OF EQUILATERAL TRIANGLE:

AREA OF EQUILATERAL TRIANGLE $\Rightarrow \dfrac{s^2\sqrt{3}}{4}$ Where, "s" is the side of the equilateral triangle.

Example #1: What is the area of an equilateral triangle whose sides are 10 units?

Solution: Area of Equilateral Triangle $\Rightarrow \dfrac{s^2\sqrt{3}}{4}$ [Write the appropriate formula]

$$\Rightarrow \frac{10^2\sqrt{3}}{4} \quad \text{[Substitute the known values]}$$

$$\Rightarrow \frac{100\sqrt{3}}{4} \quad \text{[Solve the exponent]}$$

$$\Rightarrow 25\sqrt{3} \text{ unit}^2 \quad \text{[Simplify the expression]}$$

Example #2: What is the side of an equilateral triangle whose area is $25\sqrt{3}$ unit²?

Solution: EZ Problem Set-Up $\Rightarrow$ Area of Equilateral Triangle $= 25\sqrt{3}$

$$\Rightarrow \frac{s^2\sqrt{3}}{4} = 25\sqrt{3} \quad \text{[Set up the equation]}$$

$$\Rightarrow \frac{s^2}{4} = 25 \quad \text{[Divide both sides by } \sqrt{3}\text{]}$$

$$\Rightarrow s^2 = 100 \quad \text{[Multiply both sides by 4]}$$

$$\Rightarrow s = 10 \text{ units} \quad \text{[Square root both sides]}$$

3.6: TRIANGLE CONGRUENCY:

Two triangles are said to be **"congruent"** when their corresponding parts – the angles and sides are congruent, i.e., corresponding angles have the same measure and corresponding sides have the same length. In other words, congruent triangles always have the exact same size and shape. If two triangles are congruent, they coincide exactly when superimposed or placed over each other. You may even want to think of two congruent figures as identical twins. You can usually determine that two triangles are congruent just by looking at them. However, in geometry, you can't make that assumption just by looking at the figures; instead, you must be able to prove that figures are congruent.

Symbol for Congruency: The symbol for "is congruent to" is $\cong$

For instance: $\triangle ABC$ is congruent to $\triangle XYZ \Rightarrow \triangle ABC \cong \triangle XYZ$

3.6.1: CHARACTERISTICS OF TRIANGLE CONGRUENCY:

- Must have Same Shape.
- Must have Same Size.
- Corresponding Angles have the same Measure.
- Corresponding Sides have the same Length.

For instance, in the figure below:

(A) Each side of $\triangle ABC$ has the same length as the corresponding side of $\triangle DEF$ $\Rightarrow AB = DE$
$\Rightarrow AC = DF$
$\Rightarrow BC = EF$

(B) Each angle of $\triangle ABC$ has the same measure as the corresponding angle of $\triangle DEF$ $\Rightarrow \angle A = \angle D$
$\Rightarrow \angle B = \angle E$
$\Rightarrow \angle C = \angle F$

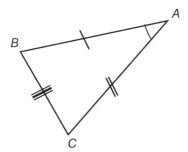　　　　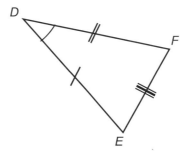

3.6.2: CONDITIONS OF TRIANGLE CONGRUENCY:

Two triangles are congruent under one of the following conditions:

CONDITION #1: SIDE-ANGLE-SIDE (S.A.S.):

Two triangles are congruent if two pairs of corresponding sides are of equal lengths, and the corresponding included angles (formed by these sides) between them are of equal measure. This is known as the Side-Angle-Side or S.A.S method of determining congruency.

For Example: In the figure below: Since $AB = DE$, $\angle BAC = \angle EDF$, and $AC = DF$
$\Rightarrow$ it implies that $\triangle ABC \cong \triangle DEF$

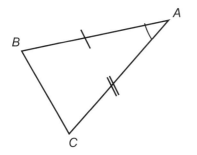 $\cong$ 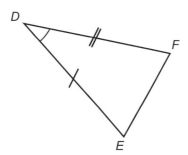

CONDITION #2: ANGLE-SIDE-ANGLE (A.S.A.):

Two triangles are congruent if two pairs of corresponding angles are of equal measure, and the corresponding included sides between them are of equal measure. This is known as the Angle-Side-Angle or A.S.A method of determining congruency.

For Example: In the figure below, Since $\angle ABC = \angle DEF$, $BC = EF$, and $\angle ACB = \angle DFE$
⇒ it implies that $\triangle ABC \cong \triangle DEF$

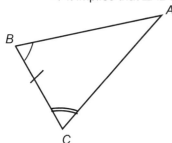 ≅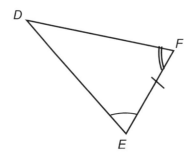

CONDITION #3: SIDE-SIDE-SIDE (S.S.S.):

Two triangles are congruent if all three pairs of corresponding sides of two triangles are of equal lengths. This is known as the Side-Side-Side or S.S.S method of determining congruency.

For Example: In the figure below, Since $AB = DE$, $AC = DF$, and $BC = EF$
⇒ it implies that $\triangle ABC \cong \triangle DEF$

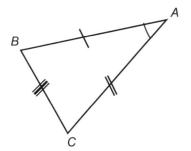 ≅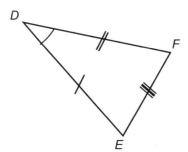

CONDITION #4: CONGRUENCY IN RIGHT TRIANGLES:

Because of the Pythagorean Theorem, if any two corresponding legs of two right triangles are equal, then the third sides are equal and hence the triangles are congruent.

For Example: In the figure below: Since $AB = DF$, $BC = EF$, and ⇒ $\angle ABC = \angle DFC$
⇒ it implies that $\triangle ABC \cong \triangle DEF$

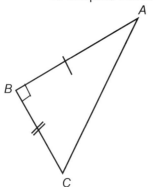 ≅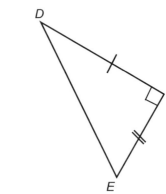

EZ NOTE: In general, if two corresponding sides of two non-right triangles are equal, that is not enough information to conclude that the triangles are congruent, and hence we cannot infer that the triangles are congruent.

For Example: In the figure below: Even though $AB = DE$, $BC = EF$

⇒ it DOES NOT imply that ΔABC ≅ ΔDEF

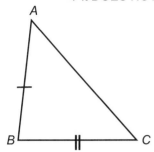

≅

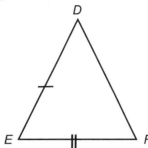

CONDITION #5: CONGRUENCY IN ISOSCELES TRIANGLES:

In an isosceles triangle, meaning if two sides of a triangle are equal, then the altitude to the third side divides the original triangle into two congruent triangles.

For Example: In the figure below: Even though AB = AC and AD ⊥ BC
⇒ it implies that ΔABD ≅ ΔACD

Since, ∠BAD = ∠CAD ⇒ AD bisects ∠BAC
Since BD = DC ⇒ D is the midpoint of BC ⇒ AD is the median from A to BC
A median is the line segment from a vertex to the midpoint of the side opposite the vertex.

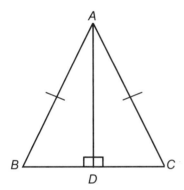

TWO TRIANGLES ARE CONGRUENT, IF ONE OF THE FOLLOWING CONDITIONS HOLDS TRUE:

(A) Two triangles are congruent if two pairs of corresponding sides and the corresponding included angles are equal.
(B) Two triangles are congruent if two pairs of corresponding angles and the corresponding included sides are equal.
(C) Two triangles are congruent if all three pairs of corresponding sides of two triangles are equal.
(D) Two right triangles that have any two equal corresponding sides.
(E) In an isosceles triangle, the altitude to the third side divides the original triangle into two congruent triangles.

3.7: TRIANGLE SIMILARITY:

Two triangles are said to be **"similar"** when all of their corresponding pair of angles are congruent (equal) and the corresponding sides are proportional, i.e., they are in the same ratio. In other words, similar triangles always have the same shape, but they do not necessarily have to be the same size. You may be able to determine that two triangles are similar just by looking at them. However, in geometry, you can't make that assumption just by looking at the figures; instead, you must be able to prove that figures are similar.

For instance, any two triangles whose angles measure 30°, 60°, 90° and 50°, 60°, 70° are not similar.

Symbol for Similarity: The symbol for "is similar to" is ≈

For instance: $\triangle ABC$ is similar to $\triangle XYZ \Rightarrow \triangle ABC \approx \triangle XYZ$

3.7.1: CHARACTERISTICS OF SIMILAR TRIANGLES:
- Must have the same shape.
- May or may not have the same size.
- Corresponding angles are identical. i.e., they have the same Measure.
- Corresponding sides are proportional, i.e., they have the same Ratio.

3.7.2: CONDITIONS OF TRIANGLE SIMILARITY:
Two triangles are similar under one of the following conditions:

CONDITION #1: ANGLE-ANGLE-ANGLE (A.A.A.):
Two triangles are similar if all three pairs of corresponding angles are of equal measure. This is called Angle-Angle-Angle, and is denoted by A.A.A.

EZ HINT: Since the sum of the angles in a triangle is 180°, it follows that if two corresponding angles are equal, the third angle must be equal. Therefore, if two angle measures in the first triangle are equal to two angle measures in the second triangle, the triangles are similar.

For Example: In the figure below: Since $\angle A = \angle D$, $\angle B = \angle E$, and $\angle C = \angle F$
                    $\Rightarrow$ it implies that $\triangle ABC \approx \triangle DEF$

CONDITION #2: CORRESPONDING SIDES IN SAME RATIO:
Two triangles are similar if the length of all the three pair of corresponding sides is in the same ratio. (In other words, the lengths of corresponding sides are in proportion).

For Example: In the figure below: Since $AB:DE = BC:EF = AC:DF$
                    $\Rightarrow$ it implies that $\triangle ABC \approx \triangle DEF$

CONDITION #3: SIDE-ANGLE-SIDE (S.A.S.):
Two triangles are similar if two pairs of corresponding sides are in the same ratio, and the corresponding included angles (formed by these sides) between them are of equal measure. In other words, two triangles are similar if any one pair of corresponding angles are of equal measure, and the pair of corresponding sides that form those angles have lengths that are in the same ratio.

For Example: In the figure below: Since $AB:DE = AC:DF$ and $\angle BAC = \angle EDF$
                    $\Rightarrow$ it implies that $\triangle ABC \approx \triangle DEF$

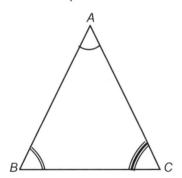 ≈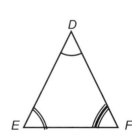

CONDITION #4: SIMILARITY IN RIGHT TRIANGLES:

For Right Triangles: Two triangles are similar if even one other pair of corresponding angles are of equal measure. This means all three corresponding angles are equal and the two right triangles are similar triangles.

For Example: In the figure below: If $\angle A = \angle D$ OR   if $\angle C = \angle F$
                    $\Rightarrow$ it implies that $\triangle ABC \approx \triangle DEF$

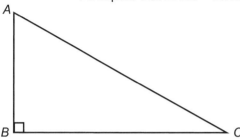 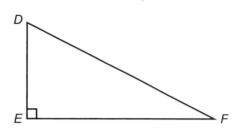

CONDITION #5: SIMILARITY WITHIN A TRIANGLE:

If we draw a line that passes through a triangle and is parallel to any one of the sides of the triangle, then the new triangle formed is similar to the original triangle.

For Example: In the figure below, in $\triangle ABC$, if $BC \parallel PQ$, then $\triangle ABC \approx \triangle APQ$
                    In the figure below, in $\triangle DEF$, if $DE \parallel RS$, then $\triangle DEF \approx \triangle RSF$

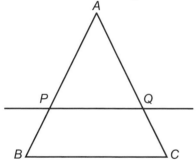 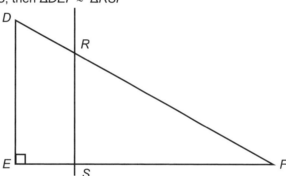

TWO TRIANGLES ARE SIMILAR, IF ONE OF THE FOLLOWING CONDITIONS HOLDS TRUE:

(A) Two triangles are similar if all three pairs of corresponding angles are equal.

(B) Two triangles are similar if all the three pairs of corresponding sides has the same ratio.

(C) If we draw a line that passes through a right triangle and is parallel to any one of its legs, the new triangle formed is similar to the original triangle.

EZ TIP: If a question tells you that triangles are similar, you will probably need that information to find the length of a side and/or the measure of an angle.

PRACTICE EXERCISE – QUESTIONS AND ANSWERS WITH EXPLANATIONS: TRIANGLES:

Question #1: In the figure given below, in $\triangle ABC$, what is the value of x?

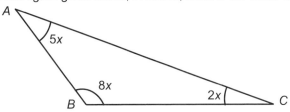

Solution: EZ Problems Set-Up $\Rightarrow$ Sum of all the interior angles of any type of triangle equals 180°
$\Rightarrow 2x + 5x + 8x = 180°$ [Set up the equation]
$\Rightarrow 15x = 180°$ [Combine like-terms]
$\Rightarrow x = 12°$ [Divide both sides by 15]

Question #2: In the figure given below, in $\triangle ABC$, what is the value of x?

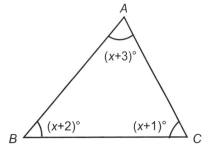

Solution: EZ Problems Set-Up $\Rightarrow$ Sum of all the interior angles of any type of triangle equals 180°
$\Rightarrow (x + 1) + (x + 2) + (x + 3) = 180°$ [Set up the equation]
$\Rightarrow 3x + 6 = 180°$ [Combine like-terms]
$\Rightarrow 3x = 174°$ [Subtract 6 from both sides]
$\Rightarrow x = 58°$ [Divide both sides by 3]

Question #3: In the figure given below, in $\triangle ABC$, what is the value of $\angle x$?

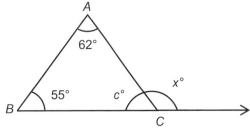

Solution: EZ Problem Set-Up $\Rightarrow$ Measure of exterior angle of triangle equals sum of opposite interior angles
$\Rightarrow \angle x = \angle A + \angle B$ [Set up the equation]
$\Rightarrow \angle x = 55° + 62°$ [Substitute $\angle A = 55°$ and $\angle B = 62°$]
$\Rightarrow \angle x = 117°$ [Combine like-terms]

Question #4: In the figure given below, in $\triangle ABC$, what is the value of $\angle A$?

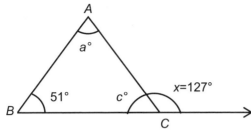

Solution: EZ Problem Set-Up ⇒ Measure of exterior angle of triangle equals sum of opposite interior angles
                                    ⇒ $\angle A + \angle B = \angle x$ [Set up the equation]
                                    ⇒ $\angle A + 51° = 127°$ [Substitute $\angle B = 51°$]
                                    ⇒ $\angle A = 76°$ [Subtract 51° from both sides]

Question #5:   In the figure given below, if $\triangle ABC$ is an isosceles triangle, then what is the value of $\angle B$?

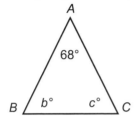

Solution: EZ Problem Set-Up ⇒ Sum of all the interior angles of a triangle equals 180°
                                    ⇒ $\angle a + \angle b + \angle c = 180°$ [Set up the equation]
                                    ⇒ $68° + \angle b + \angle c = 180°$ [Substitute the values of the known angles]
                                    ⇒ $\angle b + \angle c = 112°$ [Subtract 68° from both sides]
                                    ⇒ $\angle b + \angle b = 112°$ [Opposite angles in isosceles triangles are equal]
                                    ⇒ $2\angle b = 112°$ [Combine like-terms]
                                    ⇒ $\angle b = 56°$ [Divide both sides by 2]

Question #6:   In the figure given below, in $\triangle ABC$ what is the value of AC?

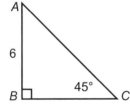

Solution: The sides in a 45°-45°-90° triangle are in the ratio of $x : x : x\sqrt{2}$
                     Measure of side opposite 45° angle   ⇒ AB $= x$ = 6 units
                     Measure of side opposite 45° angle   ⇒ BC $= x$ = 6 units
                     Measure of side opposite 90° angle   ⇒ AC $= x\sqrt{2}$ $= 6\sqrt{2}$ units

Question #7:   In the figure given below, in $\triangle ABC$ what is the value of AC?

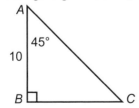

Solution: The sides in a 45°-45°-90° triangle are in the ratio of $x : x : x\sqrt{2}$
                     Measure of side opposite 45° angle   ⇒ AB $= x$ = 10 units

Measure of side opposite 45° angle $\Rightarrow BC = x = 10$ units
Measure of side opposite 90° angle $\Rightarrow AC = x\sqrt{2} = 10\sqrt{2}$ units

Question #8: In the figure given below, in ΔABC what is the value   of AC?

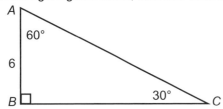

Solution: The sides in a 30°-60°-90° triangle are in the ratio of $x : x\sqrt{3} : 2x$
Measure of side opposite 30° angle $\Rightarrow AB = x = 6$ units
Measure of side opposite 60° angle $\Rightarrow BC = x\sqrt{3} = 6\sqrt{3}$ units
Measure of side opposite 90° angle $\Rightarrow AC = 2x = 12$ units

Question #9: In the figure given below, in ΔABC what is the value of AC?

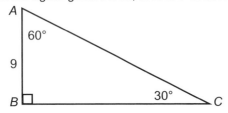

Solution: The sides in a 30°-60°-90° triangle are in the ratio of $x : x\sqrt{3} : 2x$
Measure of side opposite 30° angle $\Rightarrow AB = x = 9$ units
Measure of side opposite 60° angle $\Rightarrow BC = x\sqrt{3} = 9\sqrt{3}$ units
Measure of side opposite 90° angle $\Rightarrow AC = 2x = 18$ units

Question #10: What is the altitude of an equilateral triangle whose side is 20?
Solution: Altitude of Equilateral Triangle $\Rightarrow \frac{1}{2} \times$ side $\times \sqrt{3}$ [Write the appropriate formula]
$\Rightarrow \frac{1}{2} \times 20 \times \sqrt{3}$ [Substitute the known values]
$\Rightarrow 10\sqrt{3}$ units   [Do the multiplication]

PERIMETER OF TRIANGLE:

Question #11: If the sides of a triangle are 15 units, 19 units, and 25 units, what is the perimeter of the triangle?
Solution: Perimeter of Triangle $\Rightarrow S_1 + S_2 + S_3$ [Write the appropriate formula]
$\Rightarrow 15 + 19 + 25 = 59$ units   [Substitute the known values and simplify]

Question #12: If the side of an equilateral triangle is 7 units, what is the perimeter of the equilateral triangle?
Solution: Perimeter of Equilateral Triangle $\Rightarrow 3S$ [Write the appropriate formula]
$\Rightarrow 3(7) = 21$ units   [Substitute the known values and simplify]

AREA OF TRIANGLE:

Question #13: In the figure given below, what is the area of ΔABC?

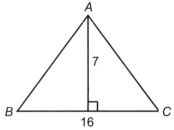

Solution: Area of Triangle $\Rightarrow \frac{1}{2}bh$ [Write the appropriate formula]
                                $\Rightarrow \frac{1}{2}$ (16) (7) = 56 unit^2 [Substitute the known values and simplify]

Question #14:   In the figure given below, what is the area of ΔABC?

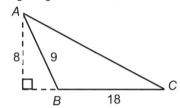

Solution: Area of Triangle $\Rightarrow \frac{1}{2}bh$ [Write the appropriate formula]
                                $\Rightarrow \frac{1}{2}$ (18) (8) = 72 unit^2 [Substitute the known values and simplify]

Question #15:   In the figure given below, what is the area of ΔABC?

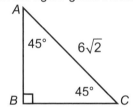

Solution: Let, the measure of $AB = x$ [Assumption]
                                Then, the measure of $BC = x$ [In isosceles right triangle sides opposite 45° are equal]
                                In ΔABC (45°-45°-90°) $\Rightarrow AB^2 + BC^2 = AC^2$ [Apply Pythagorean Theorem]
                                                                $\Rightarrow x^2 + x^2 = (6\sqrt{2})^2$ [Substitute the values of the known sides]
                                                                $\Rightarrow 2x^2 = 72$ [Simplify both sides]
                                                                $\Rightarrow x^2 = 36$ [Divide both sides by 2]
                                                                $\Rightarrow x = 6$ units   [Square root both sides]
                                Base = 6   &   Height = 6   [Base = Height = x = 6]
                                Area of Triangle $\Rightarrow \frac{1}{2}bh$ [Write the appropriate formula]
                                                                $\Rightarrow \frac{1}{2}$ (6) (6) =18 unit^2 [Substitute the known values and simplify]

Question #16:   In the figure given below, what is the area of ΔABC?

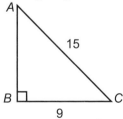

Solution: In ΔABC $\Rightarrow AB^2 + BC^2 = AC^2$ [Apply Pythagorean Theorem]
                                                $\Rightarrow AB^2 + 9^2 = 15^2$ [Substitute the values of the known sides]
                                                $\Rightarrow AB^2 = 15^2 - 9^2$ [Subtract 9^2 from both sides]
                                                $\Rightarrow AB^2 = 225 - 81$ [Solve the exponents]
                                                $\Rightarrow AB^2 = 144$ [Do the subtraction]

$\Rightarrow AB$ = 12 units   [Square root both sides]

Area of Triangle $\Rightarrow \frac{1}{2}bh$ [Write the appropriate formula]

$\Rightarrow \frac{1}{2}$ (9)(12) = 54 unit^2 [Substitute the known values and simplify]

Question #17: In the figure given below, what is the area of equilateral ΔABC?

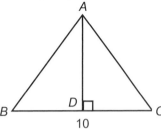

Solution: Any side can be the base of the equilateral triangle; therefore, base = 10

Height/altitude will divide the equilateral triangle into two equal 30°-60°-90° triangles, base = 5

In ΔADC $\Rightarrow AC^2 = AD^2 + DC^2$ [Apply Pythagorean Theorem]

$\Rightarrow 10^2 = AD^2 + 5^2$ [Substitute the values of the known sides]

$\Rightarrow AD^2 = 10^2 - 5^2$ [Subtract 5^2 from both sides]

$\Rightarrow AD^2 = 100 - 25$ [Solve the exponents]

$\Rightarrow AD^2 = 75$ [Do the subtraction]

$\Rightarrow AD = \sqrt{75} = 5\sqrt{3}$ units   [Square root both sides]

Area of Equilateral Triangle $\Rightarrow \frac{1}{2}bh$ [Write the appropriate formula]

$\Rightarrow \frac{1}{2}$ (10) ($5\sqrt{3}$) = $25\sqrt{3}$ unit^2 [Substitute the known values and simplify]

Question #18: In the figure given below, what is the area of equilateral ΔABC?

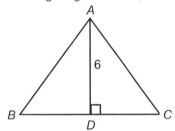

Solution: The altitude divides an equilateral triangle into two 30°-60°-90° triangles whose sides are in the ratio of $x : x\sqrt{3} : 2x$.

Measure of Side opposite 60° $\Rightarrow AD$ $\Rightarrow x\sqrt{3}$ = 6 units

$\Rightarrow x$ $= \dfrac{6}{\sqrt{3}} = \dfrac{6}{\sqrt{3}} \times \dfrac{\sqrt{3}}{\sqrt{3}} = \dfrac{6\sqrt{3}}{3} = 2\sqrt{3}$ units

Measure of Side opposite 30° $\Rightarrow DC$ $\Rightarrow x$ $= 2\sqrt{3}$ units

Measure of Side opposite 90° $\Rightarrow AC$ $\Rightarrow 2x$ $= 4\sqrt{3}$ units

Area of Equilateral Triangle $\Rightarrow \frac{1}{2}bh$ [Write the appropriate formula]

$\Rightarrow \frac{1}{2}$ ($4\sqrt{3}$) (6) = $12\sqrt{3}$ unit^2 [Substitute the known values and simplify]

PART 4.0: QUADRILATERALS:

TABLE OF CONTENTS:

EZ REFERENCE: -To practice easy-to-medium level questions, please refer to our EZ Practice Basic Workbook.
                      -To practice medium-to-difficult level questions, please refer to our EZ Practice Advanced Workbook.

4.1: BASICS ABOUT QUADRILATERALS:

Quadrilateral is formed from the word *"quad"*, which means *"four"* and *"lateral"* means *"side"*; hence, *"quadrilateral"*, then quite literally means *"four sided figure"*.

A Quadrilateral is a type of polygon with exactly four sides and four angles.

4.1.1: PARTS OF QUADRILATERALS:

(A) Sides of Quadrilateral:
Length: The Length of any Quadrilateral is the measure of the longer or longest side.
Width: The Width of any Quadrilateral is the measure of the shorter or shortest side.

(B) Diagonals of Quadrilateral:
Diagonals of any Quadrilateral are the line segments connecting any two non-subsequent vertices. Every Quadrilateral has two diagonals, either one divides the Quadrilateral into two triangles.

(C) Altitude of Quadrilateral:
Altitude of any Quadrilateral is the perpendicular distance between the two parallel sides.

(D) Angles of Quadrilateral:
  (i) **Sum of the Interior Angles in Quadrilateral:** Since the sum of the measures of the three angles in each of the triangle is 180°, the sum of the measures of the four angles in the quadrilateral is 360°. Therefore, in any type of Quadrilateral, the sum of the measures of all four interior angles is always exactly equal to 360°.
  (ii) **Sum of the Exterior Angles in Quadrilateral:** In any Quadrilateral, the sum of the measures of all exterior angles is always exactly equal to 360°.

4.1.2: TYPES OF QUADRILATERALS:

The following are the main types of quadrilaterals:
(A) Square
(B) Rectangle
(C) Parallelogram
(D) Rhombus
(E) Trapezoid

4.2: SQUARE:

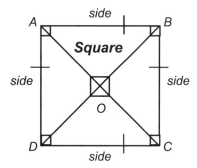

4.2.1: ABOUT SQUARES:

PROPERTIES OF SQUARES:

- Opposite sides of a Square are parallel. ($AB \parallel DC$ & $AD \parallel BC$)
- All four sides of a Square have equal measure of length. ($AB = DC = AD = BC$)
- All four angles of a Square have equal measure and are right angles ($\angle A = \angle B = \angle C = \angle D = 90°$)
- The two diagonals of a Square are perpendicular to each other, i.e., they intersect at 90°. ($AC \perp BD$)
- Both diagonals of a Square have equal measure of length. ($AC = BD$)
- Each diagonal of a Square bisects the interior angles into two 45°–45° angles.
- Each diagonal of a Square bisects each other at the point of intersection into two halves. ($AO = OC = BO = OD$)
- Each diagonal of a Square divides the square into two equal 45°–45°–90° isosceles right triangles. We can use Pythagorean Theorem to figure out the length of its side from its diagonal or the length of its diagonal from its side.
- Both diagonals of a Square divide the square into four equal 45°–45°–90° right triangles.
- Subsequent/Adjacent angles of a Square are supplementary ⇒ they add up to 180°.

EZ TIP: All Squares are also Rectangle, Parallelogram, and Rhombus.
Note: Square is a regular or equilateral quadrilateral with exactly four equal sides and exactly four equal angles.

4.2.2: PERIMETER OF SQUARE:

PERIMETER OF SQUARE   ⇒ **Side + Side + Side + Side** ⇒ $S + S + S + S$ ⇒ $4S$

4.2.3: AREA OF SQUARE:

FORMULA #1: AREA OF SQUARE   ⇒ **Side × Side** ⇒ $S × S$ ⇒ S^2
Note: Since all sides of a square are equal, length and width of squares are often both referred to as the measure of a side, so we label all the sides of a square as "s" (side).

FORMULA #2: AREA OF SQUARE   ⇒ **½ Diagonal^2** ⇒ **½ D^2**
Area of a square is also half of the square of its diagonal; following is the explanation:
⇒ $s^2 + s^2 = d^2$ [According to Pythagorean Theorem]
⇒ $2s^2 = d^2$ [Combine like-terms]
⇒ $s^2 = ½d^2$ [Divide both sides by 2]
⇒ $A = ½d^2$ [Replace s^2 with the area of a square]

FINDING THE AREA OF A SQUARE BY DIVIDING IT INTO TWO TRIANGLES:
Another way of looking at the area of a square is by drawing one of the two diagonals in the square and dividing it into two equal triangles. Draw the diagonal BD that divides the square into two equal triangles $\triangle ABD$ and $\triangle BCD$. Now, the area of the square is twice the area of one of the triangles.
Area of Square $ABCD$ ⇒ Area of $\triangle ABD$ + Area of $\triangle BCD$
                        ⇒ $½s^2 + ½s^2 = s^2$

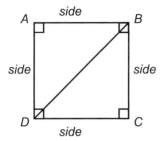

4.2.4: RELATIONSHIP BETWEEN SIDE & DIAGONAL OF SQUARE:

If you know the measure of any side of a square, you can also know the measure of its diagonal, and vice versa. Each diagonal of a square divides the square into two equal 45°-45°-90° isosceles right triangles. So, a diagonal makes two 45°-45°-90° triangles whose legs are the same as the sides of the square and the hypotenuse is the same as the diagonal of the square. You can use Pythagorean Theorem to figure out the measure of the sides from the measure of a diagonal or the measure of the diagonals from the measure of a side. In other words, we have two components here: sides and diagonal; if you know any one of these two, you can figure out the other one.

$\Rightarrow$ Side^2 + Side^2 = Diagonal^2

$\Rightarrow$ 2(Side)^2 = Diagonal^2

$\Rightarrow$ **$D^2 = 2S^2$**

$\Rightarrow$ **$D = S\sqrt{2}$**   or   **$S = \dfrac{D}{\sqrt{2}}$**

Example #1:	What is the perimeter of a square whose side is 5 units?		
Solution:	Perimeter of Square $\Rightarrow 4s$		[Write the appropriate formula]
		$\Rightarrow 4 \times 5$	[Substitute the known values]
		$\Rightarrow 20$ units	[Do the multiplication]

Example #2:   What is the perimeter of a square whose diagonal is 10 units?

Solution: Side of Square $\Rightarrow \dfrac{d}{\sqrt{2}}$ [Write the appropriate formula]

$\Rightarrow \dfrac{10}{\sqrt{2}}$ [Substitute the known values]

$\Rightarrow 5\sqrt{2}$ units   [Do the division]

Perimeter of Square $\Rightarrow 4s$ [Write the appropriate formula]

$\Rightarrow 4 \times 5\sqrt{2}$ [Substitute the known values]

$\Rightarrow 20\sqrt{2}$ units   [Do the multiplication]

Example #3:   If the perimeter of a square is 20 units, what is its side?

Solution: EZ Problem Set-Up $\Rightarrow$ Perimeter of Square = 20

$\Rightarrow 4s = 20$ [Se up the equation]

$\Rightarrow s = 5$ units   [Divide both sides by 4]

Example #4:   If the perimeter of a square is 20 units, what is its diagonal?

Solution: EZ Problem Set-Up $\Rightarrow$ Perimeter of Square = 20

$\Rightarrow 4s = 20$ [Set up the equation]

$\Rightarrow s = 5$ units   [Divide both sides by 4]

Apply Pythagorean Theorem $\Rightarrow side^2 + side^2 = diagonal^2$

$\Rightarrow 2(5)^2 = d^2$ [Substitute the known values]

$\Rightarrow 50 = d^2$ [Solve the left side]

$\Rightarrow d = 5\sqrt{2}$ units   [Square root both sides]

Example #5:   What is the area of square whose side is 5 units?

Solution: Area of Square $\Rightarrow$ side^2 [Write the appropriate formula]
                                   $\Rightarrow 5^2$ [Substitute the known values]
                                   $\Rightarrow 25$ unit^2 [Solve the exponent]

Example #6:   What is the area of a square whose diagonal is 10 units?
Solution: Area of Square $\Rightarrow$ ½ diagonal^2 [Write the appropriate formula]
                                   $\Rightarrow$ ½ $(10)^2$ [Substitute the known values]
                                   $\Rightarrow$ ½ (100) [Solve the exponent]
                                   $\Rightarrow 50$ unit^2 [Simplify the expression]

Example #7:   If the area of a square is 25 unit^2, what is its side?
Solution: EZ Problem Set-Up $\Rightarrow$ Area of Square = 25
                                   $\Rightarrow s^2 = 25$ [Set up the equation]
                                   $\Rightarrow s = 5$ units   [Square root both sides]

Example #8:   If the area of a square is 25 unit^2, what is its diagonal?
Solution: EZ Problem Set-Up $\Rightarrow$ Area of Square = 25
                                   $\Rightarrow \frac{1}{2}d^2 = 25$ [Set up the equation]
                                   $\Rightarrow d^2 = 50$ [Multiply both sides by 2]
                                   $\Rightarrow d = 5\sqrt{2}$ units   [Square root both sides]

Example #9:   What is the length of each side of a square whose diagonals are $5\sqrt{2}$ units?

Solution: Side of Square $\Rightarrow \dfrac{d}{\sqrt{2}}$ [Write the appropriate formula]

                                   $\Rightarrow \dfrac{5\sqrt{2}}{\sqrt{2}}$ [Substitute the known values]

                                   $\Rightarrow 5$ units   [Do the division]

Example #10: If the side of a square is 5 units, what is its diagonal?
Solution: Apply Pythagorean Theorem $\Rightarrow$ side^2 + side^2 = diagonal^2
                                   $\Rightarrow 5^2 + 5^2 = d^2$ [Substitute the known values]
                                   $\Rightarrow 25 + 25 = d^2$ [Solve the exponents]
                                   $\Rightarrow d^2 = 50$ [Do the addition]
                                   $\Rightarrow d = 5\sqrt{2}$ units   [Square root both sides]

Example #11: If the area of a square is 25 unit^2, what is its perimeter?
Solution: EZ Problem Set-Up $\Rightarrow$ Area of Square = 25
                                   $\Rightarrow s^2 = 25$ [Set up the equation]
                                   $\Rightarrow s = 5$ units   [Square root both sides]
                  Perimeter of Square $\Rightarrow 4s$ [Write the appropriate formula]
                                   $\Rightarrow 4 \times 5$ [Substitute the known values]
                                   $\Rightarrow 20$ units   [Do the multiplication]

Example #12: If the perimeter of a square is 20 units, what is its area?
Solution: EZ Problem Set-Up $\Rightarrow$ Perimeter of Square = 20
                                   $\Rightarrow 4s = 20$ [Set up the equation]
                                   $\Rightarrow s = 5$ units   [Divide both sides by 4]
                  Area of Square $\Rightarrow$ side^2 [Write the appropriate formula]
                                   $\Rightarrow 5^2$ [Substitute the known values]
                                   $\Rightarrow 25$ unit^2 [Solve the exponent]

4.3: RECTANGLE:

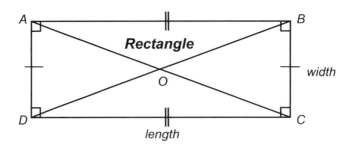

4.3.1: ABOUT RECTANGLES:

PROPERTIES OF RECTANGLES:
- Opposite sides of a Rectangle are parallel and equal. ($AB = DC$ & $AD = BC$)
- All four angles of a Rectangle have equal measures and are right angles, i.e., each angle measures 90° ($\angle A = \angle B = \angle C = \angle D = 90°$)
- Both diagonals of a Rectangle have equal measure of length. ($AC = BD$)
- Each diagonal of a Rectangle bisects each other at the point of intersection into two halves. ($AO = OC = BO = OD$)
- Each diagonal of a Rectangle divides the Rectangle into two exact equal right triangles. ($\triangle ADC = \triangle ABC = \triangle ADB = \triangle BCD$) We can use Pythagorean Theorem to figure out the length of its sides from its diagonal or the length of its diagonal from its sides.
- Both diagonals of a Rectangle divide the Rectangle into four equal opposite right triangles. ($\triangle AOB = \triangle DOC$ & $\triangle AOD = \triangle BOC$)
- Subsequent/Adjacent angles of a Rectangle are supplementary, that is they add up to 180°. ($\angle A + \angle B = \angle B + \angle C = \angle C + \angle D = \angle D + \angle A = 180°$)

EZ TIP: All Rectangles are Parallelogram.
Two adjacent sides of a rectangle are usually called its length (*L*) and its width (*W*). Note that the length does not necessarily have to be greater than the width and vice versa.

4.3.2: PERIMETER OF RECTANGLE:
PERIMETER OF RECTANGLE $\Rightarrow$ *Length + Length + Width + Width* $\Rightarrow$ *2L + 2W* $\Rightarrow$ *2(L + W)*

4.3.3: AREA OF RECTANGLE:
AREA OF RECTANGLE $\Rightarrow$ *Length × Width* $\Rightarrow$ *L × W*

FINDING THE AREA OF A RECTANGLE BY DIVIDING IT INTO TWO TRIANGLES:
Another way of looking at the area of a rectangle is by drawing one of the two diagonals in the rectangle and dividing it into two equal triangles. Draw the diagonal *BD* which divides the rectangle into two equal triangles $\triangle ABD$ and $\triangle BCD$. Now, the area of the rectangle is twice the area of one of the triangles.
Area of Rectangle *ABCD* $\Rightarrow$ Area of $\triangle ABD$ + Area of $\triangle BCD \Rightarrow$ ½*LW* + ½*LW* $\Rightarrow$ *LW*

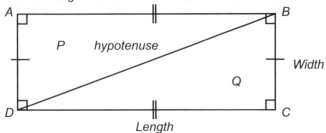

4.3.4: RELATIONSHIP BETWEEN SIDES & DIAGONAL OF RECTANGLE:

If you know the length and width of a rectangle, you can also know the length of its diagonal. Each diagonal of a rectangle divides the rectangle into two equal right triangles. So, a diagonal makes two equal right triangles whose legs are the same as the sides of the rectangle and the hypotenuse is the same as the diagonal of the rectangle. You can use Pythagorean Theorem to figure out the diagonal from the length and width; or the length from the diagonal and width; or the width from the diagonal and length. In other words, you have three components here: length, width, and diagonal; if you know any two of these three, we can figure out the third one.

$\Rightarrow \text{Length}^2 + \text{Width}^2 = \text{Diagonal}^2$ $\Rightarrow \text{Length}^2 = \text{Diagonal}^2 - \text{Width}^2$ $\Rightarrow \text{Width}^2 = \text{Diagonal}^2 - \text{Length}^2$

Example #1: What is the perimeter of a rectangle whose length is 2 units and width is 5 units?
Solution: Perimeter of Rectangle $\Rightarrow 2(L + W)$ [Write the appropriate formula]
                                        $\Rightarrow 2(2 + 5)$ [Substitute the known values]
                                        $\Rightarrow 2(7)$ [Do the addition within parentheses]
                                        $\Rightarrow 14$ units   [Do the multiplication]

Example #2: If fencing costs $9 per unit, what would be the total cost of the fencing a rectangular region whose length is 2 units and width is 5 units?
Solution: Perimeter of Rectangle $\Rightarrow 2(L + W)$ [Write the appropriate formula]
                                        $\Rightarrow 2(2 + 5)$ [Substitute the known values]
                                        $\Rightarrow 2(7)$ [Do the addition within parentheses]
                                        $\Rightarrow 14$ units   [Do the multiplication]
               Cost of fencing $\Rightarrow 14$ units $\times$ \$9 = \$126   [Multiply the perimeter by cost per unit]

Example #3: What is the area of a rectangle whose length is 2 units and width is 5 units?
Solution: Area of Rectangle $\Rightarrow LW$ [Write the appropriate formula]
                                    $\Rightarrow 2 \times 5$ [Substitute the known values]
                                    $\Rightarrow 10$ unit^2 [Do the multiplication]

Example #4: If carpeting costs $5 per unit^2, what would be the total cost of carpeting a rectangular floor whose length is 2 units and width is 5 units?
Solution: Area of Rectangle $\Rightarrow LW$ [Write the appropriate formula]
                                    $\Rightarrow 2 \times 5$ [Substitute the known values]
                                    $\Rightarrow 10$ unit^2 [Do the multiplication]
               Cost of carpeting $\Rightarrow 10$ unit$^2 \times$ \$5 = \$50   [Multiply the area by cost per square unit]

Example #5: If a rectangle has a length of 5 and a width of 12, what is the measure of its diagonal?
Solution: Diagonal^2 $\Rightarrow \text{Length}^2 + \text{Width}^2$ [Write the relationship between sides and diagonal]
                                $\Rightarrow 5^2 + 12^2$ [Substitute the given values]
                                $\Rightarrow 25 + 144$ [Solve the exponents]
                                $\Rightarrow 169$ [Do the addition]
               Diagonal $\Rightarrow 13$ [Square root both sides]

Example #6: If a rectangle has a diagonal of 13 and a width of 5, what is the measure of its length?
Solution: Length$^2 \Rightarrow \text{Diagonal}^2 - \text{Width}^2$ [Write the relationship between sides and diagonal]
                            $\Rightarrow 13^2 - 5^2$ [Substitute the given values]
                            $\Rightarrow 169 - 25$ [Solve the exponents]
                            $\Rightarrow 144$ [Do the subtraction]
               Length $\Rightarrow 12$ [Square root both sides]

Example #7: If a rectangle has a diagonal of 13 and a length of 12, what is the measure of its width?
Solution: Width$^2 \Rightarrow \text{Diagonal}^2 - \text{Length}^2$ [Write the relationship between sides and diagonal]
                            $\Rightarrow 13^2 - 12^2$ [Substitute the given values]
                            $\Rightarrow 169 - 144$ [Solve the exponents]
                            $\Rightarrow 25$ [Do the subtraction]
               Width $\Rightarrow 5$ [Square root both sides]

4.3.5: FACTS ABOUT RECTANGLE'S DIMENSIONS, AREA, AND PERIMETER:

FACT #1: Two or more rectangles with the same area can have different dimensions (length and width).

For Example: In the figure below, all rectangles have the same area, but different dimensions.

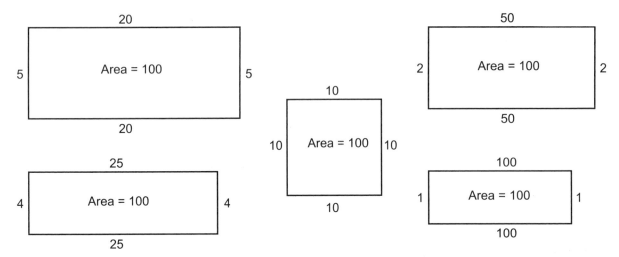

Note: Two or more squares with the same area can have different dimensions; they do not necessarily need to have the same dimensions in order to have the same areas.

FACT #2: Two or more rectangles with the same perimeter can have different dimensions (length and width)

For Example: In the figure below, all rectangles have the same perimeter, but different dimensions.

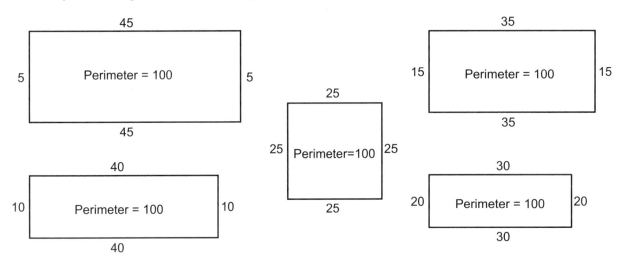

Note: Two or more squares with the same perimeter can have different dimensions; they do no necessarily need to have the same dimensions in order to have the same perimeters.

FACT #3: Two rectangles with the same perimeter can have different areas.

For Example: In the figure below, all rectangles have the same perimeter, but different areas.

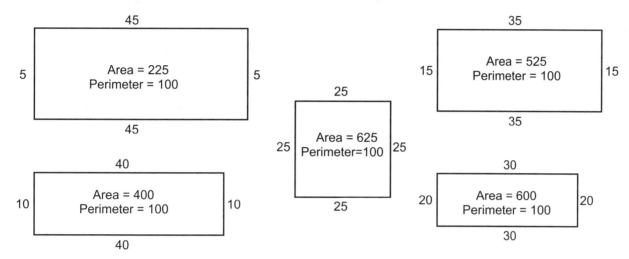

FACT #4: Two rectangles with the same area can have different perimeters.

For Example: In the figure below, all rectangles have the same area but different perimeters.

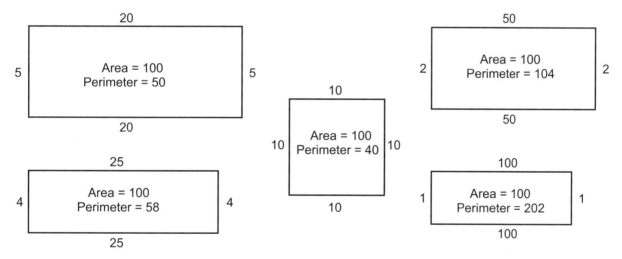

4.3.6: RELATIONSHIP BETWEEN AREAS & PERIMETERS OF SQUARE & RECTANGLE:

EZ FACT #1: For a given perimeter, the rectangle with the largest area is a square.

For Example: In the figure below, both, the square and the rectangle have the same perimeter, but the square has a larger area than the rectangle.

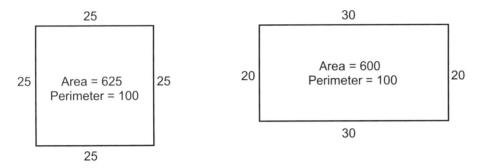

EZ FACT #2: For a given area, the rectangle with the smallest perimeter is a square.

For Example: In the figure below, both, the square and the rectangle have the same area, but the square has a smaller perimeter than the rectangle.

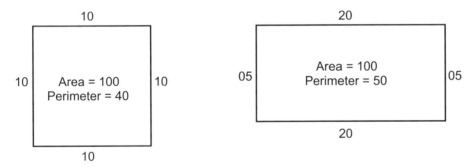

4.4: PARALLELOGRAM:

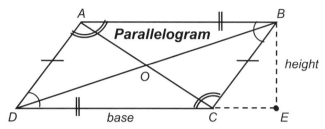

4.4.1: ABOUT PARALLELOGRAMS:

PROPERTIES OF PARALLELOGRAMS:

- Opposite sides of a Parallelogram are parallel and equal. (*AB* || *DC* and *AB* = *DC*; *AD* || *BC* and *AD* = *BC*)
- Opposite angles (the angles diagonally across from each other) of a Parallelogram are equal in measure. ($\angle A$ = $\angle C$ & $\angle B$ = $\angle D$)
- Each diagonal of a Parallelogram bisects each other at the point of intersection into two halves. (*AO* = *OC* & *BO* = *OD*)
- Each diagonal of a Parallelogram divides the Parallelogram into two congruent triangles that have exactly the same size and shape. (ΔABC = ΔACD and ΔABD = ΔBDC)
- Both diagonals of a Parallelogram divide the Parallelogram into four equal opposite triangles. (ΔABO = ΔDOC & ΔAOD = ΔBOC)
- Consecutive angles of a Parallelogram are supplementary, that is, they add up to 180°. ($\angle A$ + $\angle B$ = $\angle B$ + $\angle C$ = $\angle C$ + $\angle D$ = $\angle D$ + $\angle A$ = 180°)

EZ TIP: Some parallelograms are Rhombus. All Rhombuses are parallelograms.

Altitude of Parallelogram: An Altitude or Height of a Parallelogram is the line segment connecting one side of the parallelogram to the opposite side of the parallelogram and is perpendicular to both the sides, that is, it meets both the sides at 90°, and that either side can be the base of the parallelogram.

4.4.2: PERIMETER OF PARALLELOGRAM:

PERIMETER OF PARALLELOGRAM ⇒ *Length + Length + Width + Width* ⇒ *2L + 2W* ⇒ *2(L + W)*

4.4.3: AREA OF PARALLELOGRAM:

AREA OF PARALLELOGRAM ⇒ *Base × Height* ⇒ *BH*

FINDING THE AREA OF A PARALLELOGRAM BY CONVERTING IT INTO A RECTANGLE:
To find the area of a parallelogram, we "square up" the slanted sides of the parallelogram by dropping perpendiculars – line *AE* and *BF* in the figure shown below. This makes two identical right triangles ΔAED and ΔBFC.
Next, if we take the ΔAED away or subtract from the parallelogram and place or add it to the other side, i.e., ΔBFC, we have formed a rectangle with the same area as the original parallelogram.

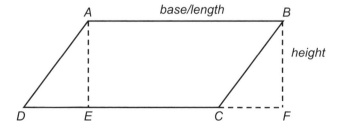

Now, we have transformed the parallelogram *ABCD* into rectangle *ABFE*, both with same areas.
⇒ The width of the new rectangle is the same as the height of the parallelogram.
⇒ The length of the new rectangle is the same as the base of the parallelogram.

So the formula for the area of a parallelogram or the rectangle is:
Area of Parallelogram = base × height = *bh*

FINDING THE AREA OF A PARALLELOGRAM BY DIVIDING IT INTO TWO TRIANGLES:

Another way of looking at the area of a parallelogram is by drawing one of the two diagonals in the parallelogram and dividing it into two equal triangles. Draw the diagonal *BD* that divides the parallelogram into two equal triangles Δ*ABD* and Δ*BCD*. Now, the area of the parallelogram is twice the area of one of the triangles.

Area of Parallelogram *ABCD* ⇒ Area of Δ*ABD* + Area of Δ*BCD*
$$\Rightarrow \tfrac{1}{2}bh + \tfrac{1}{2}bh$$
$$\Rightarrow bh$$

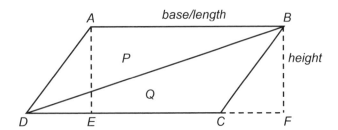

Example #1: What is the perimeter of a parallelogram whose length is 5 units and width is 2 units?
Solution:

Perimeter of Parallelogram	⇒ 2(*L* + *W*)	[Write the appropriate formula]
	⇒ 2(5 + 2)	[Substitute the known values]
	⇒ 2(7)	[Do the addition within parentheses]
	⇒ 14 units	[Do the multiplication]

Example #2: What is the area of a parallelogram whose base is 5 units and height is 2 units?
Solution:

Area of Parallelogram	⇒ *bh*	[Write the appropriate formula]
	⇒ 5 × 2	[Substitute the known values]
	⇒ 10 unit^2	[Do the multiplication]

4.5: RHOMBUS:

4.5.1: ABOUT RHOMBUS:

PROPERTIES OF RHOMBUS:
- All four sides of a Rhombus are equal. ($AB = DC = AD = BC$)
- Opposite sides of a Rhombus are parallel to each other. ($AB \parallel DC$ & $AD \parallel BC$)
- Opposite angles of a Rhombus are equal. ($\angle A = \angle C$ & $\angle B = \angle D$)
- The two diagonals of a Rhombus are perpendicular to each other, that is, they intersect at 90°. ($AC \perp BD$)
- Each diagonal of a Rhombus bisects the angles into two equal angles.
- Each diagonal of a Rhombus bisects each other at the point of intersection into two halves. ($AO = OC$ & $BO = OD$)
- Each diagonal of a Rhombus divides the Rhombus into two exact equal isosceles triangles. ($\triangle ADC = \triangle ABC$ and $\triangle ABD = \triangle BDC$)
- Both diagonals of a Rhombus divide the Rhombus into four equal opposite triangles. ($\triangle ABO = \triangle DOC$ & $\triangle AOD = \triangle BOC$)
- Subsequent/Adjacent angles of a Rhombus are supplementary, that is, they add up to 180°.

EZ TIP: All Rhombuses are Parallelograms.

Altitude of Rhombus: An Altitude or Height of a Rhombus is the line segment connecting one side of the rhombus to the opposite side of the rhombus and is perpendicular to both the sides, that is, it meets both the sides at 90°, and either side can be the base.

4.5.2: PERIMETER OF RHOMBUS:

PERIMETER OF RHOMBUS $\Rightarrow$ **Side + Side + Side + Side** $\Rightarrow$ **S + S + S + S** $\Rightarrow$ **4S**

4.5.3: AREA OF RHOMBUS:

FORMULA #1: AREA OF RHOMBUS $\Rightarrow$ **Base × Height** $\Rightarrow$ **BH**
FORMULA #2: AREA OF RHOMBUS $\Rightarrow$ **½(Diagonal$_1$ × Diagonal$_2$)** $\Rightarrow$ **½(D$_1$ × D$_2$)**

Example #1:   What is the perimeter of a rhombus whose side is 5 units?
Solution: Perimeter of Rhombus $\Rightarrow 4s$ [Write the appropriate formula]
                                       $\Rightarrow 4 \times 5$ [Substitute the known values]
                                         $\Rightarrow 20$ units   [Do the multiplication]

Example #2:   What is the area of a rhombus whose base is 5 units and height is 2 units?
Solution: Area of Rhombus $\Rightarrow bh$ [Write the appropriate formula]
                                         $\Rightarrow 5 \times 2$ [Substitute the known values]
                                         $\Rightarrow 10$ unit^2 [Do the multiplication]

Example #3:   What is the area of a rhombus whose one diagonal is 12 units and the other diagonal is 15 units?
Solution: Area of Rhombus $\Rightarrow ½ (d_1 \times d_2)$ [Write the appropriate formula]
                                         $\Rightarrow ½ (12 \times 15)$ [Substitute the known values]
                                         $\Rightarrow 90$ unit^2 [Do the multiplication]

4.6: Trapezoid:

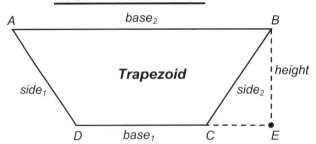

4.6.1: About Trapezoids:

Properties of Trapezoids:
- One pair of opposite sides is parallel but not equal in all trapezoids.
- Other pair of opposite sides is non-parallel but equal in only isosceles trapezoids.
- The diagonals of an isosceles trapezoid are equal.
- The base angles of an isosceles trapezoid are equal.
- The opposite angles of an isosceles trapezoid are supplementary, that is they add up to 180°

Bases: Pair of parallel sides $\Rightarrow$ **$base_1$** & **$base_2$**
Sides: Pair of non-parallel sides $\Rightarrow$ **$side_1$** & **$side_2$**

Median of Trapezoid: The median of a trapezoid is the line segment joining the midpoints of the two non-parallel sides.

Altitude of Trapezoid: An Altitude or Height of a Trapezoid is the line segment connecting one base of the trapezoid to the opposite base of the trapezoid and is perpendicular to both the bases, that is, it meets both the bases at 90°.

4.6.2: Perimeter of Trapezoid:
Perimeter of Trapezoid $\Rightarrow$ **$Base_1$ + $Base_2$ + $Side_1$ + $Side_2$** $\Rightarrow$ **B_1 + B_2 + S_1 + S_2**

4.6.3: Area of Trapezoid:
Area of Trapezoid $\Rightarrow$ (Average of parallel sides) × Height/Altitude
$\Rightarrow$ **½ ($Base_1$ + $Base_2$) × Height** $\Rightarrow$ **½ (B_1 + B_2) H**

EZ Alternate Method: You can also drop a line or two to break the trapezoid into a rectangle and a triangle or two triangles, and then use the area formulas of those familiar shapes. First find the area of those shapes separately and then add them together to find the area of the whole trapezoid.

Example #1:   What is the perimeter of an isosceles trapezoid whose one base is 5 units and the other base is 7 units, and the side is 2 units?
Solution: Perimeter of Trapezoid $\Rightarrow b_1 + b_2 + s_1 + s_2$ [Write the appropriate formula]
                                            $\Rightarrow 5 + 7 + 2 + 2$ [Substitute the known values]
                                              $\Rightarrow 16$ units   [Do the addition]

Example #2:   What is the area of a trapezoid whose one base is 5 and other base is 7, and the height is 2?
Solution: Area of Trapezoid $\Rightarrow ½(b_1 + b_2)h$ [Write the appropriate formula]
                                    $\Rightarrow ½ (5 + 7) × 2$ [Substitute the known values]
                                    $\Rightarrow ½ (12) × 2$ [Do the addition within parentheses]
                                    $\Rightarrow 12$ unit^2 [Do the multiplication]

PRACTICE EXERCISE – QUESTIONS AND ANSWERS WITH EXPLANATIONS:
QUADRILATERALS:

Question #1: If the side of a square is 9 units, what is its area?
Solution: Area of Square $\Rightarrow side^2$ [Write the appropriate formula]
                                  $\Rightarrow 9^2 = 81$ unit^2 [Substitute the known values and simplify]

Question #2: If the diagonal of a square is 12 units, what is its area?
Solution: Area of Square $\Rightarrow \frac{1}{2} diagonal^2$ [Write the appropriate formula]
                                  $\Rightarrow \frac{1}{2}(12)^2 = \frac{1}{2}(144) = 72$ unit^2 [Substitute the known values and simplify]

Question #3: If the area of a square is 64 unit^2, what is its side?
Solution: Area of Square $\Rightarrow s^2 = 64$ [Equate the area formula with the given area]
                               $\Rightarrow s = 8$ units   [Square root both sides]

Question #4: If the area of a square is 50 unit^2, what is its diagonal?
Solution: Area of Square $\Rightarrow \frac{1}{2}d^2 = 50$ [Equate the area formula with the given area]
                               $\Rightarrow d^2 = 100$ [Multiply both sides by 2]
                               $\Rightarrow d = 10$ units   [Square root both sides]

Question #5: If the side of a square is 6 units, what is its perimeter?
Solution: Perimeter of Square $\Rightarrow 4s$ [Write the appropriate formula]
                               $\Rightarrow 4 \times 6 = 24$ units   [Substitute the known values and simplify]

Question #6: If the diagonal of a square is $\sqrt{50}$ units, what is its perimeter?
Solution: Apply Pythagorean Theorem $\Rightarrow side^2 + side^2 = diagonal^2$ [Write the Pythagorean Theorem]
$$\Rightarrow 2s^2 = \left(\sqrt{50}\right)^2 \quad\quad \text{[Substitute the known values]}$$
$$\Rightarrow 2s^2 = 50 \quad\quad \text{[Solve the exponent]}$$
$$\Rightarrow s^2 = 25 \quad\quad \text{[Divide both sides by 2]}$$
$$\Rightarrow s = 5 \text{ units} \quad\quad \text{[Square root both sides]}$$
        Perimeter of Square $\Rightarrow 4s$ [Write the appropriate formula]
                               $\Rightarrow 4 \times 5 = 20$ units   [Substitute the known values and simplify]

Question #7: If the perimeter of a square is 28 units, what is its side?
Solution: Perimeter of Square $\Rightarrow 4s = 28$ [Equate the perimeter formula with the given perimeter]
                               $\Rightarrow s = 7$ units   [Divide both sides by 4]

Question #8: If the perimeter of a square is 8 units, what is its diagonal?
Solution: Perimeter of Square $\Rightarrow 4s = 8$ [Equate the perimeter formula with the given perimeter]
                               $\Rightarrow s = 2$ units   [Divide both sides by 4]
        Diagonal of Square $\Rightarrow d = 2\sqrt{2}$ units   [Diagonal is hypotenuse of 45°-45°-90° triangle]

Question #9: If the perimeter of a square is 60 units, what is its area?
Solution: Perimeter of Square $\Rightarrow 4s = 60$ [Equate the perimeter formula with the given perimeter]
                               $\Rightarrow s = 15$ units   [Divide both sides by 4]
        Area of Square $\Rightarrow s^2$ [Write the appropriate formula]
                               $\Rightarrow 15^2 = 225$ unit^2 [Substitute the known values and simplify]

Question #10: If the area of a square is 625 unit^2, what is its perimeter?
Solution: Area of Square $\Rightarrow s^2 = 625$ [Equate the area formula with the given area]
                               $\Rightarrow s = 25$ units   [Square root both sides]
        Perimeter of Square $\Rightarrow 4s$ [Write the appropriate formula]
                               $\Rightarrow 4 \times 25 = 100$ units   [Substitute the known values and simplify]

Question #11: If the side of a square is 2 units, what is its diagonal?
Solution: Apply Pythagorean Theorem $\Rightarrow side^2 + side^2 = diagonal^2$ [Write the Pythagorean Theorem]
$$\Rightarrow 2s^2 = d^2 \qquad \text{[Combine like-terms]}$$
$$\Rightarrow 2(2)^2 = d^2 \qquad \text{[Substitute the known values]}$$
$$\Rightarrow d^2 = 8 \qquad \text{[Solve the left side]}$$
$$\Rightarrow d = 2\sqrt{2} \text{ units} \qquad \text{[Square root both sides]}$$

Question #12: If the diagonal of a square is 2 units, what is its side?
Solution: Apply Pythagorean Theorem $\Rightarrow side^2 + side^2 = diagonal^2$ [Write the Pythagorean Theorem]
$$\Rightarrow 2s^2 = d^2 \qquad \text{[Combine like-terms]}$$
$$\Rightarrow 2s^2 = 2^2 \qquad \text{[Substitute the known values]}$$
$$\Rightarrow s^2 = 2 \qquad \text{[Divide both sides by 2]}$$
$$\Rightarrow s = \sqrt{2} \text{ units} \qquad \text{[Square root both sides]}$$

Question #13: If a rectangle has a length of 9 units and width of 8 units, what is its area?
Solution: Area of Rectangle $\Rightarrow LW$ [Write the appropriate formula]
$$\Rightarrow 9 \times 8 = 72 \text{ unit}^2 \qquad \text{[Substitute the known values and simplify]}$$

Question #14: If a rectangle has a length of 12 units and diagonal of 15 units, what is its area?
Solution: Apply Pythagorean Theorem $\Rightarrow Diagonal^2 = Lenght^2 + Width^2$ [Write the Pythagorean Theorem]
$$\Rightarrow 15^2 = 12^2 + W^2 \qquad \text{[Substitute the known values]}$$
$$\Rightarrow 225 = 144 + W^2 \qquad \text{[Solve the exponents]}$$
$$\Rightarrow W^2 = 81 \qquad \text{[Subtract 144 from both sides]}$$
$$\Rightarrow W = 9 \text{ units} \qquad \text{[Square root both sides]}$$
Area of Rectangle $\Rightarrow LW$ [Write the appropriate formula]
$$\Rightarrow 9 \times 12 = 108 \text{ unit}^2 \qquad \text{[Substitute the known values and simplify]}$$

Question #15: If a man is wall-to-wall carpeting a rectangular room whose length is 15 units and width is 6 units, how much carpet is required in order to completely carpet the room?
Solution: Area of Rectangle $\Rightarrow LW$ [Write the appropriate formula]
$$\Rightarrow 15 \times 6 = 90 \text{ unit}^2 \qquad \text{[Substitute the known values and simplify]}$$

Question #16: If a rectangle has a length of 6 units and width of 5 units, what is its perimeter?
Solution: Perimeter of Rectangle $\Rightarrow 2(L + W)$ [Write the appropriate formula]
$$\Rightarrow 2(6 + 5) = 2(11) = 22 \text{ units} \qquad \text{[Substitute the known values and simplify]}$$

Question #17: If a rectangle has a length of 16 units and diagonal of 20 units, what is its perimeter?
Solution: Apply Pythagorean Theorem $\Rightarrow Diagonal^2 = Length^2 + Width^2$ [Write the Pythagorean Theorem]
$$\Rightarrow 20^2 = 16^2 + W^2 \qquad \text{[Substitute the known values]}$$
$$\Rightarrow 400 = 256 = W^2 \qquad \text{[Solve the exponents]}$$
$$\Rightarrow W^2 = 144 \qquad \text{[Subtract 256 from both sides]}$$
$$\Rightarrow W = 12 \text{ units} \qquad \text{[Square root both sides]}$$
Perimeter of Rectangle $\Rightarrow 2(L + W)$ [Write the appropriate formula]
$$\Rightarrow 2(16 + 12) = 2(28) = 56 \text{ units} \qquad \text{[Substitute the known values and simplify]}$$

Question #18: If a man is fencing his yard, whose length is 27 units and width is 22 units, what is the length of fencing that would be required?
Solution: The perimeter of the yard is required to find the whole yard is supposed to be fenced. Now since the yard is in a rectangular shape, simply find the perimeter of the rectangular yard.
Perimeter of Rectangle $\Rightarrow 2(L + W)$ [Write the appropriate formula]
$$\Rightarrow 2(27 + 22) = 2(49) = 98 \text{ units} \qquad \text{[Substitute the known values and simplify]}$$

Question #19: If a rectangle has a length of 8 units and a width of 15 units, what is the measure of its diagonal?
Solution: $Diagonal^2 \Rightarrow Length^2 + Width^2$ [Write the relationship between sides and diagonal]
$$\Rightarrow 8^2 + 15^2 \qquad \text{[Substitute the given values]}$$

	$\Rightarrow 64 + 225$	[Solve the exponents]
	$\Rightarrow 289$	[Do the addition]
Diagonal	$\Rightarrow 17$ units	[Square root both sides]

Question #20: If a rectangle has a diagonal of 20 units and a width of 12 units, what is the measure of its length?
Solution:

$\text{Length}^2 \Rightarrow \text{Diagonal}^2 - \text{Width}^2$ [Write the relationship between sides and diagonal]
$\Rightarrow 20^2 - 12^2$ [Substitute the given values]
$\Rightarrow 400 - 144$ [Solve the exponents]
$\Rightarrow 256$ [Do the subtraction]
$\text{Length} \Rightarrow 16$ units   [Square root both sides]

Question #21: What is the perimeter of a parallelogram whose length is 16 units, width is 12 units, and height is 10 units?
Solution:

Perimeter of Parallelogram $\Rightarrow 2(L + W)$ [Write the appropriate formula]
$\Rightarrow 2(16 + 12) = 2(28) = 56$ units   [Substitute the known values/simplify]

Question #22: What is the area of a parallelogram whose base is 11 units, width is 2 units, and height is 5 units?
Solution:

Area of Parallelogram $\Rightarrow bh$ [Write the appropriate formula]
$\Rightarrow 11 \times 5 = 55$ unit^2 [Substitute the known values and simplify]

Question #23: In the figure given below, quadrilateral *ABCD* is a parallelogram. If $\angle A = (7x + 1)°$ and $\angle C = (2x + 26)°$, what is the value of *x*?

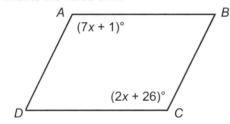

Solution:

EZ Problem Set-Up $\Rightarrow$ Opposite angles in a parallelogram are equal to each other
$\Rightarrow \angle A = \angle C$ [Set up the equation]
$\Rightarrow 7x + 1 = 2x + 26$ [Substitute the values of the angles]
$\Rightarrow 5x + 1 = 26$ [Subtract 2x from both sides]
$\Rightarrow 5x = 25$ [Subtract 1 from both sides]
$\Rightarrow x = 5$ [Divide both sides by 5]

Question #24: In the figure given below, quadrilateral *ABCD* is a parallelogram. If $\angle A = (x + 5)°$ and $\angle B = (x + 17)°$, what is the value of *x*?

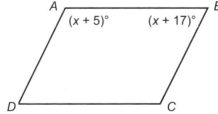

Solution:

EZ Problem Set-Up $\Rightarrow$ Subsequent angles in a parallelogram add up to 180°
$\Rightarrow \angle A + \angle B = 180°$ [Set up the equation]
$\Rightarrow x + 5 + x + 17° = 180°$ [Substitute the known values]
$\Rightarrow 2x + 22° = 180°$ [Combine like-terms]
$\Rightarrow 2x = 158°$ [Subtract 22° from both sides]
$\Rightarrow x = 79°$ [Divide both sides by 2]

Question #25: If the side of a rhombus is 19 units, what is its perimeter?
Solution:

Perimeter of Rhombus $\Rightarrow 4s$ [Write the appropriate formula]
$\Rightarrow 4 \times 19 = 76$ units   [Substitute the known values and simplify]

Question #26: What is the area of a rhombus whose sides are 6 units and height is 2 units?
Solution: Area of Rhombus $\Rightarrow bh$ [Write the appropriate formula]
$\Rightarrow 6 \times 2 = 12$ unit^2 [Substitute the known values and simplify]

Question #27: What is the area of a rhombus whose sides are 6 units, and the two diagonals are 7 units and 8 units?
Solution: Area of Rhombus $\Rightarrow \frac{1}{2}(d_1 \times d_2)$ [Write the appropriate formula]
$\Rightarrow \frac{1}{2}(7 \times 8) = 28$ unit^2 [Substitute the known values and simplify]

Question #28: What is the perimeter of an isosceles trapezoid whose two bases are 7 units and 9 units, two sides are 5 units each, and the height is 2 units?
Solution: Perimeter of Trapezoid $\Rightarrow b_1 + b_2 + s_1 + s_2$ [Write the appropriate formula]
$\Rightarrow 7 + 9 + 5 + 5 = 26$ units   [Substitute the known values and simplify]

Question #29: What is the area of an isosceles trapezoid whose two bases are 12 units and 16 units, two sides are 10 units each, and the height is 8 units?
Solution: Area of Trapezoid $\Rightarrow \frac{1}{2}(b_1 + b_2)h$ [Write the appropriate formula]
$\Rightarrow \frac{1}{2}(12 + 16) \times 8 = \frac{1}{2}(28) \times 8 = 112$ unit^2 [Substitute the known values/simplify]

Question #30: In the figure given below, in trapezoid *ABCD*, what is the value of *n*?

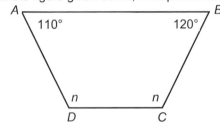

Solution: EZ Problem Set-Up $\Rightarrow$ Sum of all angles of Trapezoid = 360°
$\Rightarrow 120° + 110° + n + n = 360°$ [Set up the equation]
$\Rightarrow 230° + 2n = 360°$ [Combine like-terms]
$\Rightarrow 2n = 130°$ [Subtract 230° from both sides]
$\Rightarrow n = 65°$ [Divide both sides by 2]

PART 5.0: CIRCLES:

TABLE OF CONTENTS:

EZ REFERENCE: -To practice easy-to-medium level questions, please refer to our EZ Practice Basic Workbook.
                     -To practice medium-to-difficult level questions, please refer to our EZ Practice Advanced Workbook.

5.1: BASICS ABOUT CIRCLES:

A *"circle"* is a closed linear figure that consists of a set or series of all the points in the same plane that are all located at the same distance (equidistant) from one fixed point, called the center of the circle. So if you draw multiple lines from the center of a circle out to its edge, they'll all be of the same length no matter where they're drawn. That distance or length is also called the radius of the circle. The degree measure of any complete circle is 360°.

Naming a Circle: A circle is denoted or labeled by a single letter, which is usually its center point. For example: circle *O* means the circle with center point *O*.

5.1.1: PARTS OF CIRCLE:

RADIUS:

The distance between the center of the circle and any point on the circle is called the *"radius"* of a circle. In other words, radius is any line segment that connects or joins the center of the circle to any point on the circle. It extends from the center of the circle to any point on the circle. Note: *radius* – singular; *radii* – plural

- Radius' one endpoint lies in the center of the circle and the other anywhere on the circle.
- All radii of the same circle have equal lengths.

Length of Radius: Since a radius is made up of half of diameter, the radius is half as long as a diameter. In other words, the length of a radius is half the length of a diameter.

Radius ⇒ Half of Diameter = ½ (Diameter)

$r = \frac{1}{2}d$ ⇒ Where "*r*" is the radius and "*d*" is the diameter of the circle.

For Example: In the figure below, *OA*, *OB*, *OC*, *OD*, and *OE* are all radii of circle *O*. The figure below is a circle of radius 1 unit whose center is at the point *O*. *A*, *B*, *C*, *D*, and *E*, which are each 1 unit from *O*, are all points on circle *O*. If the circle below has radius *r*, each of the radii is *r* units long.

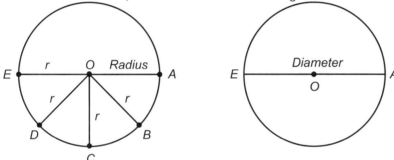

DIAMETER:

The distance between any two points on the circle passing through the center is called the *"diameter"* of a circle. In other words, diameter is any line segment or chord connecting two points on the circle that passes through the center of the circle.

- Diameter's endpoints lie on the circle.
- Diameter divides the circle into two congruent halves which are called semicircles.
- Diameter is the longest possible line-segment/chord that can be drawn inside a circle.
- All diameters of the same circle have equal lengths.

Length of Diameter: Since a diameter is made up of two radii, the diameter is twice as long as a radius. In other words, the length of a diameter is twice the length of a radius.

Diameter ⇒ Twice Radius = 2(Radius)

$d = 2r$ ⇒ Where "*d*" is the diameter and "*r*" is the radius of the circle.

For Example: In the figure below, *EA* is the diameter made up of two radii, *OA* and *OE*.

CHORD:

A *"chord"* is any line segment joining any two points on the circle. In other words, a chord is a line segment whose both endpoints lie on the circle. The diameter of the circle is the longest chord in a circle.

For Example: In the figure below, *AB* is the chord.

Chord & Diameter: A diameter that is perpendicular to a chord bisects that chord into two congruent halves.

For Example: In the figure below, if *CD* is the diameter and *AB* is a chord in the circle, such that, $AB \perp CD \Rightarrow AE = EB$

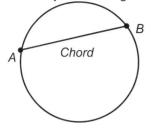

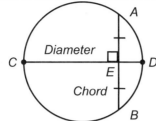

INSCRIBED TRIANGLES:

(A) Triangle Inscribed in Semicircle: A triangle inscribed in a semicircle is always a right triangle. That is, if a triangle is inscribed in a circle, such that, one of its sides coincides with the diameter of the circle, then that triangle must be a right triangle.

Conversely: Any right triangle inscribed in a circle must have one of its sides coincide with the diameter of the circle, thus splitting the circle in two semicircles.

For Example: In the figure below, *AB* is the diameter & $\angle ACB$ is inscribed in the semicircle, therefore, $\angle ACB = 90°$
Alternately: Triangle *ABC* must be a right triangle, since *AB* is a diameter of the circle.

(B) Triangle Formed by Two Radii: Any triangle formed at the center of a circle by connecting the endpoints of any two radii always results in an isosceles triangle.

For Example: In the figure below, the triangle formed at the center of the circle, *O*, by connecting the endpoints of the two radii, *OP* and *OQ* results in an isosceles triangle $\triangle OPQ$, where $OP = OQ$ and $\angle P = \angle Q$.

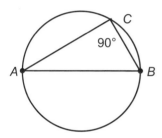

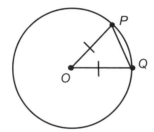

SECANT:

Any line or line segment that cuts through a circle by intersecting the circle at any two points is called a **"secant"**.

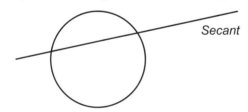

TANGENT:

Line Tangent to a Circle: A line tangent to a circle is any line or line segment outside the circle that intersects or touches the circle at exactly one and only one point on the circumference of the circle. In other words, the line and circle has only one point in common with each other.

Two Circles Tangent to Each Other: Two circles are tangent if they only intersect or touch each other at any one and only one point.

In other words, a line and a circle or two circles are tangent if they have only one point of intersection.

Point-of-Tangency: The point common to a circle and a tangent to the circle or two circles is called the point of tangency. It's the point of intersection of the tangent and the circle or two circles.

(A) Radius of a Circle is Perpendicular to its Tangent: The radius from the center of the circle to the point of tangency is perpendicular to the tangent. In other words, the radius that springs from the point of tangency forms a right angle (90°) on the tangent. Therefore, a line drawn tangent to a circle is always perpendicular to the radius drawn from the circle's center to the point of tangency at the point of contact. If a line is tangent to a circle, a radius (or diameter) drawn to the point where the tangent touches the circle is perpendicular to the tangent line. Conversely, a line that is perpendicular to a radius at one of its endpoints is tangent to the circle at that endpoint.

⇒ Radius ⊥ Tangent

For Example: In the figure below: AC is tangent to circle O at point B ⇒ AC is tangent to the circle with center O
⇒ B is the point of tangency
⇒ $OB \perp AC$

(B) Two Tangents to a Circle are Equal: Two tangent segments drawn to the same circle from the same external point are congruent. In other words, the length (distance between the origin of the two tangents and the point of tangency) of the two tangents that springs from the same fixed point to the same circle are equal to each other. There can only be a maximum of two tangents that can be drawn from any point outside a given circle.

For Example: In the figure below: AC and AE are both tangent to circle O at point B and D ⇒ $AB = AD$

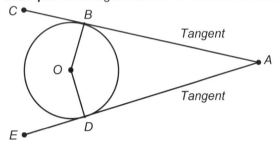

LINE OF CENTERS:

The line or line segment passing through the centers of two or more circles is called the ***"line-of-centers"***.

For Example: In the figure below, the line segment "L" passes the centers of circle A, B, C, and D.

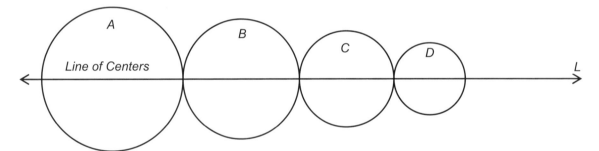

SECTOR:

A section of a circle between any two of its radii is called a ***"sector"*** of the circle. In other words, the portion of the circle bounded by two radii and an arc is called a sector of the circle.

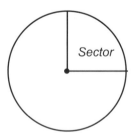

DEGREE MEASURE AROUND A CIRCLE:

The degree measure of a complete circle is 360°.

5.1.2: TYPES OF CIRCLES:

(A) FULL CIRCLE:
- A full circle is a complete circle.
- The degree measure of a full/complete circle is 360°.

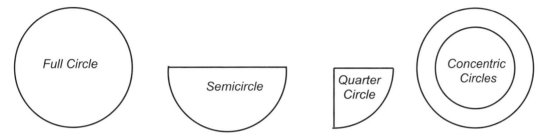

(B) SEMICIRCLE:
- A semicircle is a half-circle.
- The degree measure of a semi circle is 180°.
- Two equal semicircles form a complete circle.
- An arc which is exactly half the circumference of the circle is called a semicircle.

(C) QUARTER CIRCLE:
- A quarter-circle is a one fourth of a circle.
- The degree measure of a quarter-circle is 90°.
- Four equal quarter circles forms a complete circle.
- An arc which is exactly quarter the circumference of the circle is called a quarter-circle.

(D) CONCENTRIC CIRCLE:
- Concentric circles are two circles that have the exact same center but unequal radii.

5.1.3: TYPES OF ANGLES IN CIRCLE:

(A) CENTRAL ANGLE:
A *"central angle"* is defined as an angle whose vertex lies exactly at the center point of the circle and its two sides are the radii of the circle. In other words, it's any angle formed inside the circle by any two radii. A central angle defines both an arc and a sector of a circle. The concept of a central angle is important while dealing with arcs and sectors
For Example: In the figure below: $\angle AOB$ is the central angle

(B) INSCRIBED ANGLE:
An *"inscribed angle"* is defined as an angle whose vertex lies at any point on the circle itself and the two sides are chords of the circle. In other words, it's any angle formed by any two chords originating from a single point on the circle.
For Example: In the figure below: $\angle APB$ is the inscribed angle.

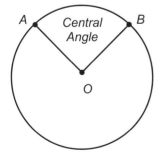 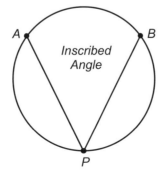

5.2: CIRCUMFERENCE:

The perimeter of a circle is called the **"circumference"** of the circle. Circumference (perimeter) of a circle is the total distance around the circle. Circumference can be found without measuring the distance around the circle if the length of the radius or if the diameter is known.

Pi or (π): The number π (pi) is the ratio of the circle's circumference to its diameter, which is always exactly the same, i.e., it's constant, and is known as or denoted by the symbol π (pi), the Greek letter π.
Approximate Value of π = 22/7 = 3.1415926....... (for approximation purposes, remember that pi is a little more than 3)
Note: There is no fraction that is exactly equal to π; that is why π is called an irrational number.
"pi" = π $\Rightarrow$ **C**ircumference ÷ **d**iameter = **C ÷ d**
CIRCUMFERENCE $\Rightarrow \pi d$ OR $\Rightarrow 2\pi r$

DIAMETER = d $\Rightarrow \dfrac{C}{\pi}$ **RADIUS = r** $\Rightarrow \dfrac{C}{2\pi}$

Example #1:   If the radius of a circle is 5 units, then what is its circumference?
Solution: Circumference $\Rightarrow 2\pi r$ [Write the appropriate formula]
                             $\Rightarrow 2 \times \pi \times 5$ [Substitute the known values]
                             $\Rightarrow 10\pi$ units   [Do the multiplication]

Example #2:   If the diameter of a circle is 5 units, then what is its circumference?
Solution: Circumference $\Rightarrow \pi d$ [Write the appropriate formula]
                             $\Rightarrow \pi \times 5$ [Substitute the known values]
                             $\Rightarrow 5\pi$ units   [Do the multiplication]

Example #3:   If the circumference of a circle is 10π units, then what is its radius?
Solution: Circumference $\Rightarrow 2\pi r = 10\pi$ [Equate the circumference formula with the given circumference]
                             $\Rightarrow r = 5$ units   [Divide both sides by 2π]

Example #4:   If the circumference of a circle is 5π units, then what is its diameter?
Solution: Circumference $\Rightarrow \pi d = 5\pi$ [Equate the circumference formula with the given circumference]
                             $\Rightarrow d = 5$ units   [Divide both sides by π]

CIRCUMFERENCE & REVOLUTION OF WHEEL:

The distance covered by a wheel in one complete revolution is equal to the circumference of the wheel. In making one revolution, every point on the rim of the wheel comes in contact with the surface. The distance covered in one complete revolution is then the same as stretching or cutting the rim of the wheel out into a straight line.

Example #1:   How far will a wheel of outer diameter 5 meters travel in 250 revolutions?
Solution: Diameter $\Rightarrow d = 5$
              Radius $\Rightarrow r = ½(5) = 2.5$ meters
              Circumference $\Rightarrow C = 2\pi r = 2 \times \pi \times 2.5 = 5\pi$ meters
              Distance traveled in 1 revolution $\Rightarrow 5\pi$ meters
              Distance traveled in 250 revolutions $\Rightarrow 5\pi \times 250 = 1,250\pi$

Example #2:   In a certain machine, a gear makes 15 revolutions per minutes. If the diameter of the gear is 10 meters, approximately how many meters will the gear turn in an hour?
Solution: Diameter $\Rightarrow d = 10$
              Radius $\Rightarrow r = ½(10) = 5$ meters
              Circumference $\Rightarrow C = 2\pi r = 2 \times \pi \times 5 = 10\pi$ meters
              Distance traveled in 1 revolution $\Rightarrow 10\pi$ meters
              No. of Revolutions in one hour $\Rightarrow 15 \times 60 = 900$
              No. of meters the gear will turn in 1 hr $\Rightarrow 10\pi \times 900 = 9,000\pi = 9,000 \times 3.14 = 28,000$ meters

5.3: ARC OF CIRCLE:

A part or portion of the circumference of a circle is called an ***"arc"***. It consists of two endpoints on a circle and all the points between them. It is the rounded portion of the circle between two points.

5.3.1: TYPES OF ARCS:

(A) Minor Arc: It is the shorter distance between two points on the circle along the circle. Minor Arc is the arc formed by the central angle. The measure of the minor arc is the same as the measure of the inner central angle.
For Example: In the figure below: *PYQ* is the Minor Arc.

(B) Major Arc: It is the longer distance between two points on the circle along the circle. Major arc is the arc formed outside the central angle. The measure of the major arc is the same as the measure of outer central angle.
For Example: In the figure below: *PXQ* is the Major Arc.

How to Denote Arcs: If two letters are used to denote an arc, they always represent the smaller of the two possible arcs unless specified otherwise.

For example, in the figure below, arc *PQ* refers to the small arc joining *P* and *Q*, going from *P* to *Q* through *Y*. If you want to refer to the large arc joining *P* and *Q*, going from *P* to *Q* through *X*, it would say arc *PXQ*.

Semicircular Arcs: If two points on a circle are the endpoints of a diameter, they divide the circle into two equal arcs called semicircular arcs. In other words, this arc will be half the circumference of the circle.

For example, in the figure below, if two points, such as *A* and *B* in circle O, are the endpoints of a diameter, they divide the circle into two arcs called semicircles.

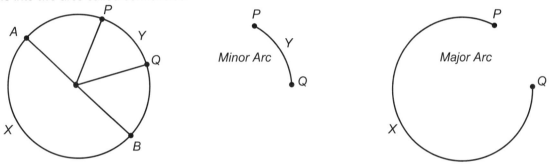

5.3.2: MEASURE OF ARC:

You may be asked to solve for the distance of a portion of a circle known as an arc of the circle, instead of the circumference of the entire circle. To find the length of an arc of a circle, think of the arc as a fraction or part of the circumference of the whole circle and determine what fraction the arc is of the entire circumference, which can be done by looking at the central angle that defines the arc. An arc is measured in degrees. Since the entire circle is 360°, an arc of 120° would be 1/3rd of a circle and an arc of 72° would be 1/5th of a circle.

If an inscribed angle and a central angle cut out the same arc in a circle, the central angle will be twice as large as the inscribed angle. In the figure given above, there is a central angle and an inscribed angle, both of which intercept arc *AQB*.

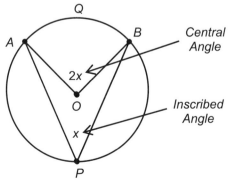

5.3.2.1: ARC MEASURE – CENTRAL ANGLE:

Arcs formed by the Central Angle have the same degree measure as the degree measure of the central angle. In other words, if we form an angle by drawing two radii from the ends of the arc to the center of the circle, the number of degrees contained in the arc equals the number of degrees contained in the angle formed by the two radii at the center of the circle. To find the length of an arc, think of the arc as a fraction or part of the circumference of the circle.

(A) ARC DEGREE MEASURE = Degree Measure of the Central Angle

The length of an arc is the same fraction of a circle's circumference as its degree measure is of the degree measure of the circle ($360°$). The degree measure of an arc is equal to the degree measure of the central angle that intercepts it, or the degree measure of the central angle is equal to the degree measure of the arc it intercepts.

For Example: In the figure above, $\angle AOB$ = Arc AQB

EZ NOTE: Degree measure of an arc is not the same as the measure of its length – both are two different things and are calculated differently.

(B) ARC LENGTH MEASURE

$$\Rightarrow \frac{\textbf{Degrees of Central Angle}}{360^0} \times \textbf{Circumference}$$

$$\Rightarrow \frac{n°}{360°} \times 2\pi r$$

Where: $n°$ is the degree measure of the central angle of a circle
r is the radius of the circle

For Example: If the radius of a circle is 10 units, then what is the measure of an arc in degree and in length formed by a 90° central angle?

Solution: Arc Degree Measure = degree measure of the central angle = 90°

Arc Length Measure $\Rightarrow \dfrac{Degrees\ of\ Central\ Angle}{360^0} \times$ Circumference

$$\Rightarrow \frac{90}{360} \times 2\pi r = ¼ \times 2 \times \pi \times 10 = ¼ \times 20\pi = 5\pi \text{ units}$$

5.3.2.2: ARC MEASURE – INSCRIBED ANGLE:

Arcs formed by Inscribed Angles are twice the degree measure of the inscribed angle. Or if we form an angle by drawing chords from the ends of the arc to any point outside the arc on the circle, the number of degrees contained in the arc is double the number of degrees contained in the angle formed by the two chords at that point on the circle.

(A) ARC MEASURE IN DEGREES = 2 × degree measure of the inscribed angle

The measure of an arc is twice the measure of the inscribed angle, or an inscribed angle is equal in measure to ½ of the arc it intercepts.

For Example: In the figure above: $\Rightarrow \angle APB$ = ½ Arc AQB or,
$\Rightarrow$ Arc $AQB = 2(\angle APB)$

(B) ARC LENGTH

$$\Rightarrow \frac{\textbf{2} \times \textbf{Degrees of Inscribed Angle}}{360^0} \times \textbf{Circumference}$$

$$\Rightarrow \frac{2n°}{360°} \times 2\pi r \quad \text{(where } n \text{ is the degree measure of the inscribed angle)}$$

For Example: If the radius of a circle is 10 units, then what is the measure of an arc in degree and in length formed by a 90° inscribed angle?

Solution: Arc Degree Measure = 2 × degree measure of the inscribed angle = 2 × 90° = 180°

Arc Length $\Rightarrow \dfrac{2 \times Degrees\ of\ Inscribed\ Angle}{360^0} \times$ Circumference.

$$\Rightarrow \frac{2 \times 90}{360} \times 2\pi r = 2 \times ¼ \times 2 \times \pi \times 10 = ½ \times 20\pi = 10\pi \text{ units}$$

5.3.2.3: ARC MEASURE – INTERSECTING CHORDS:

An angle inside a circle formed by two chords intersecting is equal in degrees to one-half the sum of its intercepted arcs.

$$\Rightarrow \angle P = \angle Q = \frac{\overparen{AC} + \overparen{BD}}{2}$$

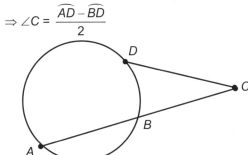

For instance: If arc $AC = 70°$ and arc $BD = 50°$; then $\angle P = \angle Q = \dfrac{70+50}{2} = \dfrac{120}{2} = 60°$

5.3.2.4: ARC MEASURE – INTERSECTING SECANTS/TANGENTS:

An angle outside the circle formed by two secants, two tangents, or a secant and a tangent, is equal in degrees to one-half the difference of its intercepted arcs.

$$\Rightarrow \angle C = \frac{\overparen{AD} - \overparen{BD}}{2}$$

For instance: If arc $AD = 160°$ and arc $BD = 20°$; then $\angle C = \dfrac{160-20}{2} = \dfrac{140}{2} = 70°$

5.3.2.5: PERIMETER OF SECTOR OF CIRCLE:

The boundaries of a sector of a circle are formed by an arc and two radii. Therefore, if we know the length of the radius and the central (or inscribed) angle, we can find the perimeter of the sector.

PERIMETER OF SECTOR OF CIRCLE ⇒ Arc Measure + 2r

For Example: If the radius of the circle is 6 units, what is the perimeter of the sector formed by 60° central angle?

Solution:

Circumference of Circle	$\Rightarrow 2\pi r$	[Write the appropriate formula]
	$\Rightarrow 2(6)\pi$	[Substitute the known values]
	$\Rightarrow 12\pi$ units	[Do the multiplication]
Arc Measure of Circle	$\Rightarrow \dfrac{\textit{Degrees of Central Angle}}{360^0} \times C$	[Write the appropriate formula]
	$\Rightarrow \dfrac{60^0}{360^0} \times 12\pi$	[Substitute the known values]
	$\Rightarrow 2\pi$ units	[Simplify the expression]
Perimeter of Sector of Circle	$\Rightarrow$ Arc Measure + 2r	[Write the appropriate formula]
	$\Rightarrow 2\pi + 2(6)$	[Substitute the known values]
	$\Rightarrow 2\pi + 12$ units	[Simplify the expression]

5.4: AREA OF CIRCLE:

5.4.1: AREA OF FULL CIRCLE:

The area of a circle can be found by multiplying pi (π) times the radius squared.

AREA OF FULL CIRCLE $\Rightarrow \pi \times r \times r = \pi r^2$

$$\Rightarrow \pi \left(\tfrac{1}{2}d\right)^2 = \pi \left(\frac{d}{2}\right)^2 = \pi \frac{d^2}{4}$$

Where: r = length of the radius
d = length of the diameter

Area of 1/2 (half) of the Circle $\Rightarrow \tfrac{1}{2}(\pi r^2)$ Area of 1/3 (third) of the Circle $\Rightarrow 1/3(\pi r^2)$
Area of 1/4 (quarter) of the Circle $\Rightarrow \tfrac{1}{4}(\pi r^2)$ Area of 1/8 (eighth) of the Circle $\Rightarrow 1/8(\pi r^2)$

Example #1:   If the radius of a circle is 10 units, then what is its area?
Solution: Area of Circle $\Rightarrow \pi r^2$ [Write the appropriate formula]
                                    $\Rightarrow \pi(10)^2$ [Substitute the known values]
                                    $\Rightarrow 100\pi$ unit^2 [Solve the exponent]

Example #2:   If the area of a circle is 100π unit^2, then what is its radius?
Solution: Area of Circle $\Rightarrow \pi r^2 = 100\pi$ [Equate the area formula with the given area]
                                    $\Rightarrow r^2 = 100$ [Divide both sides by π]
                                    $\Rightarrow r = 10$ units   [Square root both sides]

Example #3:   If the diameter of a circle is 10 units, then what is its area?
Solution: Area of Circle $\Rightarrow \pi \left(\tfrac{1}{2}d\right)^2$ [Write the appropriate formula]
                                    $\Rightarrow \pi(10/2)^2$ [Substitute the known values]
                                    $\Rightarrow \pi(5)^2$ [Solve within parentheses]
                                    $\Rightarrow 25\pi$ unit^2 [Solve the exponent]

Example #4:   If the area of a circle is 25π unit^2, then what is its diameter?
Solution: Area of Circle $\Rightarrow \pi \left(\tfrac{1}{2}d\right)^2 = 25\pi$ [Equate the area formula with the given area]
                                    $\Rightarrow \left(\tfrac{1}{2}d\right)^2 = 25$ [Divide both sides by π]
                                    $\Rightarrow \left(\tfrac{1}{2}d\right) = 5$ [Square root both sides]
                                    $\Rightarrow d = 10$ units   [Multiply both sides by 2]

5.4.2: AREA OF SECTOR OF CIRCLE:

Area of a sector of circle formed by an arc and two radii can be found by multiplying the fraction of the area of the circle that the sector represents (360° that is contained in the degree measure of central angle of sector) by the area of the circle. To find the area of a sector of a circle, think of the sector as a fraction or part of the area of the whole circle and determine what fraction it is of the entire area, which can be done by looking at the central angle that defines the sector.

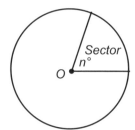

AREA OF SECTOR OF CIRCLE $\Rightarrow \dfrac{\textbf{Degrees of Central Angle}}{\textbf{360}^0} \times \textbf{\textit{Area of Circle}} \Rightarrow \dfrac{n^\circ}{360^\circ} \times \pi r^2$

Where: n° is the degree measure of the central angle of a circle
r is the radius of the circle

For Example: If the radius of the circle is 10 units, then what is the area of the sector formed by 90° central angle?
Solution: Area of Circle $\Rightarrow \pi r^2$ [Write the appropriate formula]

$\Rightarrow \pi (10)^2$ [Substitute the known values]

$\Rightarrow 100\pi$ unit^2 [Solve the exponent]

Area of Sector of Circle $\Rightarrow \dfrac{n°}{360°} \times \pi r^2$ [Write the appropriate formula]

$\Rightarrow \dfrac{90°}{360°} \times 100\pi$ [Substitute the known values]

$\Rightarrow 25\pi$ unit^2 [Simplify the expression]

5.4.3: AREA AND CIRCUMFERENCE OF CIRCLE:

Area and Circumference of a circle are interrelated and if you know one, you can find the other. Look at the following two types:

Example #1:   If the circumference of a circle is 16π units, what is its area?
Solution: Circumference $\Rightarrow 2\pi r = 16\pi$ [Equate the circumference formula with the given circumference]

$\Rightarrow r = 8$ units   [Divide both sides by 2π]

Area of Circle $\Rightarrow \pi r^2$ [Write the appropriate formula]

$\Rightarrow \pi(8)^2$ [Substitute the known values]

$\Rightarrow 64\pi$ unit^2 [Solve the exponent]

Example #2:   If the area of a circle is 64π unit^2, what is its circumference?
Solution: Area of Circle $\Rightarrow \pi r^2 = 64\pi$ [Equate the area formula with the given area]

$\Rightarrow r^2 = 64$ [Divide both sides by π]

$\Rightarrow r = 8$ units   [Square root both sides]

Circumference $\Rightarrow 2\pi r$ [Write the appropriate formula]

$\Rightarrow 2\pi(8)$ [Substitute the known values]

$\Rightarrow 16\pi$ units   [Do the multiplication]

EZ TIP: In general, there are four major elements in a circle: the circumference, the radius, the diameter, and the area of a circle; if you know even one of these four components, you can use one to find any of the other measurements.

PRACTICE EXERCISE – QUESTIONS AND ANSWERS WITH EXPLANATIONS: CIRCLES:

Question #1: If the radius of circle O is 27 units, what is the degree measure and the length measure of arc AB made by a 60° central angle?

Solution: Arc Degree Measure $\Rightarrow$ Degree measure of central angle   [Write the appropriate formula]

$\Rightarrow 60°$ [Substitute the known values]

Arc Length Measure $\Rightarrow \dfrac{\text{Degrees of Central Angle}}{360^0} \times 2\pi r$ [Write the appropriate formula]

$\Rightarrow \dfrac{60^0}{360^0} \times (2 \times \pi \times 27) = 9\pi$ units   [Substitute the known values and simplify]

Question #2: If the radius of a circle is 10 units, what is the degree measure and the length measure of arc AB formed by a 45° inscribed angle?

Solution: Arc Degree Measure $\Rightarrow 2 \times$ Degree measure of inscribed angle   [Write the appropriate formula]

$\Rightarrow 2 \times 45° = 90°$ [Substitute the known values]

Arc Length Measure $\Rightarrow \dfrac{2 \times \text{Degrees of Inscribed Angle}}{360^0} \times 2\pi r$ [Write the appropriate formula]

$\Rightarrow 2 \times \dfrac{45^0}{360^0} \times (2 \times \pi \times 10) = 5\pi$ units   [Substitute the known values/simplify]

Question #3: In the figure given below, if arc $AC = 60°$ and arc $BD = 50°$, what is the measure of $\angle P$?

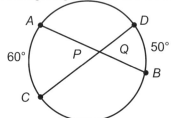

Solution: Measure of $\angle P \Rightarrow \dfrac{\overset{\frown}{AC} + \overset{\frown}{BD}}{2}$ [Write the appropriate formula]

$\Rightarrow \dfrac{60 + 50}{2} = 55°$ [Substitute the known values and simplfy]

Question #4: In the figure given below, if arc $AD = 150°$ and arc $BD = 20°$, what is the measure of $\angle C$?

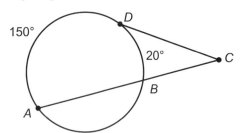

Solution: Measure of $\angle C \Rightarrow \dfrac{\overset{\frown}{AD} - \overset{\frown}{BD}}{2}$ [Write the appropriate formula]

$\Rightarrow \dfrac{150 - 20}{2} = 65°$ [Substitute the known values and simplify]

Question #5: If the radius of a circle is 11 units, what is its circumference?

Solution: Circumference $\Rightarrow 2\pi r$ [Write the appropriate formula]
                                       $\Rightarrow 2 \times \pi \times 11 = 22\pi$ units   [Substitute the known values and simplify]

Question #6:   If the diameter of a circle is 25 units, what is its circumference?
Solution: Circumference $\Rightarrow \pi d$ [Write the appropriate formula]
                                       $\Rightarrow \pi \times 25 = 25\pi$ units   [Substitute the known values and simplify]

Question #7:   If the circumference of a circle is 50π units, what is its radius?
Solution: Circumference $\Rightarrow 2\pi r = 50\pi$ [Equate the circumference formula with given circumference]
                                       $\Rightarrow r = 25$ units   [Divide both sides by 2π]

Question #8:   If the circumference of a circle is 50π units, what is its diameter?
Solution: Circumference $\Rightarrow \pi \times d = 50\pi$ [Equate the circumference formula with given circumference]
                                       $\Rightarrow d = 50$ units   [Divide both sides by π]

Question #9:   If the radius of a circle is 8 units, what is its area?
Solution: Area of Circle $\Rightarrow \pi r^2$ [Write the appropriate formula]
                                       $\Rightarrow \pi(8)^2 = 64\pi$ unit^2 [Substitute the known values and simplify]

Question #10:   If the diameter of a circle is 18 units, what is its area?
Solution: Area of Circle $\Rightarrow \pi(\frac{1}{2}d)^2$ [Write the appropriate formula]
                                       $\Rightarrow \pi(18/2)^2 = 81\pi$ unit^2 [Substitute the known values and simplify]

Question #11:   If the area of a circle is 121π unit^2, what is its radius?
Solution: Area of Circle $\Rightarrow \pi r^2 = 121\pi$ [Equate the area formula with given area]
                                       $\Rightarrow r^2 = 121$ [Divide both sides by π]
                                       $\Rightarrow r = 11$ units   [Square root both sides]

Question #12:   If the area of a circle is 144π unit^2, what is its diameter?
Solution: Area of Circle $\Rightarrow \pi(\frac{1}{2}d)^2 = 144\pi$ [Equate the area formula with given area]
                                       $\Rightarrow (\frac{1}{2}d)^2 = 144$ [Divide both sides by π]
                                       $\Rightarrow \frac{1}{2}d = 12$ [Square root both sides]
                                       $\Rightarrow d = 24$ units   [Multiply both sides by 2]

Question #13:   If the area of a circle is 81π unit^2, what is its circumference?
Solution: Area of Circle $\Rightarrow \pi r^2 = 81\pi$ [Equate the area formula with given area]
                                       $\Rightarrow r^2 = 81$ [Divide both sides by π]
                                       $\Rightarrow r = 9$ units   [Square root both sides]
                      Circumference $\Rightarrow 2\pi r$ [Write the appropriate formula]
                                       $\Rightarrow 2 \times \pi \times 9 = 18\pi$ units   [Substitute the known values and simplify]

Question #14:   If the circumference of a circle is 16π units, what is its area?
Solution: Circumference $\Rightarrow 2\pi r = 16\pi$ [Equate the circumference formula with given circumference]
                                       $\Rightarrow r = 8$ units   [Divide both sides by 2π]
                      Area of Circle $\Rightarrow \pi r^2$ [Write the appropriate formula]
                                       $\Rightarrow \pi(8)^2 = 64\pi$ unit^2 [Substitute the known values and simplify]

Question #15:   If the radius of the circle is 12 units, what is the area of the sector AOB formed by 20° central angle?
Solution: Area of Circle $\Rightarrow \pi r^2$ [Write the appropriate formula]
                                                  $\Rightarrow \pi(12)^2 = 144\pi$ unit^2 [Substitute the known values and simplify]

                      Area of Sector of Circle $\Rightarrow \dfrac{Degrees\ of\ Central\ Angle}{360^0} \times A$ [Write the appropriate formula]

                                                  $\Rightarrow \dfrac{20^0}{360^0} \times 144\pi = 8\pi$ unit^2 [Substitute the known values and simplify]

Question #16: If the radius of the circle is 60 units, what is the perimeter of the sector *AOB* formed by 60° central angle?

Solution:

Circumference	$\Rightarrow 2\pi r$	[Write the appropriate formula]
	$\Rightarrow 2(60)\pi = 120\pi$ units	[Substitute the known values and simplify]
Arc Measure	$\Rightarrow \dfrac{Degrees\ of\ Central\ Angle}{360^0} \times C$	[Write the appropriate formula]
	$\Rightarrow \dfrac{60^0}{360^0} \times 120\pi = 20\pi$ units	[Substitute the known values and simplify]
Perimeter of Sector	$\Rightarrow$ Arc Measure + $2r$	[Write the appropriate formula]
	$\Rightarrow 20\pi + 2(60) = 20\pi + 120$ units	[Substitute the known values and simplify]

PART 6.0: SOLID GEOMETRY:

TABLE OF CONTENTS:

EZ REFERENCE: -To practice easy-to-medium level questions, please refer to our EZ Practice Basic Workbook.
                    -To practice medium-to-difficult level questions, please refer to our EZ Practice Advanced Workbook.

6.1: BASICS ABOUT SOLID GEOMETRY:

The *"solid geometry"* is a study of shapes and figures, also known as *"solids"* that are drawn in more than one plane, and are three-dimensional, that is, they have: *length*, *width*, and *thickness* (which is the *height* or *depth*).

Since solid is a three-dimensional figure, it's rather difficult to express it accurately on a two-dimensional page. Therefore, figures are drawn in perspective, giving them the appropriate appearance of depth, the third dimension. For the purpose of your test, if a figure or diagram represents a three-dimensional figure, it will be specified in the problem or accompanying text. You will be told specifically in a question if a given figure does not lie in a plane, that is, if the figure is a three-dimensional solid. It needs to be noted that the dotted or dashed lines in a diagram indicate edges of the solid that are hidden from your view. However, just because you see a dotted or dashed line in a figure does not mean it is a solid. There could be other reasons for the use of the dotted or dashed lines. So make sure that given figure in a question is indeed a solid or not.

PROPERTIES OF SOLIDS:
- All points in solids do not lie in the same plane, i.e., they lie in different planes.
- Solid objects occupy space and have volume.
- Solids can be measured in three directions or dimensions – *length*, *width*, and *height*.

Three Dimensions: Shapes that have *three dimensions*, also known as *solids*, require the use of the principles of solid geometry.

TERMS USED IN SOLIDS:
(A) Vertex: The vertices of a solid are the points at its corners where its edges meet. For example, a rectangular solid has eight vertices.
(B) Edge: The edges of a solid are the line segments that connect the vertices and form the sides of each face of the solid. For example, a rectangular solid has twelve edges.
(C) Face: The faces of a solid are the polygons that form the outside boundaries of the solid. For example, a rectangular solid has six faces.

TYPES OF SOLIDS:
(A) Rectangular Solids: Solids that have rectangular or square faces are known as rectangular solids, such as, brick, closed shoe box, etc.
   Types of Rectangular Solids: Cubes, Rectangular Prisms

(B) Circular Solids: Solids that have circular or conical faces are known as circular solids, such as, soda cans, ice-cream cones, tennis balls, camping tents, etc.
   Types of Circular Solids: Cylinders, Cones, Spheres, Pyramids, Tetrahedrons

EZ TIP: The solids that most frequently appear on your test are rectangular solids, and sometimes cylinders. Other types of solids, such as cones and spheres, may appear on your test, but rarely, and even if they do appear, they would typically only involve understanding the solid's properties. The questions may require logic and your ability to apply your knowledge under different situations. They are not likely to involve use of any complicated formulas.

OTHER TYPES OF SOLIDS:
(A) Prisms: A rectangular solid is one example of a right prism, which is a solid in which two congruent polygons are joined by rectangular faces that are perpendicular to the polygons. The polygons are called the bases of the prism, and the length of an edge joining the polygons is called the height, even if the prism is not standing on its base. A prism may be named after its polygonal base: for example, triangular prism, and hexagonal prism. The volume of a prism is given by the product of its height and the area of its base.
(B) Pyramids: A pyramid has a base that is a polygon, which is connected by triangular faces to its vertex. If the base is a regular polygon and the triangular faces are all congruent isosceles triangles, then the pyramid is called a regular pyramid.

6.2: RECTANGULAR SOLIDS:

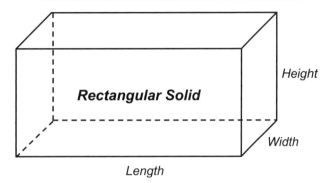

6.2.1: ABOUT RECTANGULAR SOLIDS:

PROPERTIES OF RECTANGULAR SOLID:
- A Rectangular Solid is a solid box that is formed by six rectangular lateral surfaces.
- Each surface of a Rectangular Solid is known as a face, there are 6 faces.
- Each face of a Rectangular Solid mirrors the rectangle exactly opposite it.
- All opposite rectangular faces in a Rectangular Solid are identical, and lie in parallel planes.
- Each rectangular face in a Rectangular Solid intersects at right angles.
- Each rectangular face is connected with an edge, and there are 12 edges.
- Each point at which the edges meet is called a vertex, and there are 8 vertices.

Examples of Rectangular Solid: cereal boxes, bricks.

Rectangular Solid is a Uniform Solid: A rectangular solid is a uniform or consistent solid; i.e., the horizontal cross sections are all rectangles of equal size. In other words, a slice of a rectangular solid from the middle is the same as a slice from the top or the bottom.

Similarity between Cubes and Rectangular Solids: Rectangular solids are just like cubes – the only difference is that in a cube, all the six faces are identical squares; where as in a rectangular solid, only opposite faces are identical rectangles.

DIMENSIONS OF RECTANGULAR SOLID:
The sides of the Rectangular Solid are called edges, and the edges are called:
▪ Length (*L*)   ▪ Width (*W*)   ▪ Height (*H*)
EZ NOTE: The labeling of the length, width, and height of a rectangle solid is quite arbitrary. It doesn't matter which side(s) you call which. In other words, you can label any of the sides as its length, width, and height.

FACES OF RECTANGULAR SOLID:
A Rectangular Solid consists of exactly six faces:
▪ Equal pair of the Front and the Back Faces $\Rightarrow$ Front Face = Back Face
▪ Equal pair of the Top and the Bottom Faces $\Rightarrow$ Top Face = Bottom Face
▪ Equal pair of the Right and the Left Faces $\Rightarrow$ Right Face = Left Face

6.2.2: SURFACE AREA OF RECTANGULAR SOLIDS:

Total Surface Area of a Rectangular Box	= Sum of the area of the six outside rectangular faces.
Area of Front and Back Faces	= 2(*Length* × *Height*) $\Rightarrow$ **2LH**
Area of Top and Bottom Faces	= 2(*Length* × *Width*) $\Rightarrow$ **2LW**
Area of Right and Left Faces	= 2(*Width* × *Height*) $\Rightarrow$ **2WH**

TOTAL SURFACE AREA OF RECTANGULAR BOX $\Rightarrow \Rightarrow \Rightarrow \Rightarrow \Rightarrow \Rightarrow \Rightarrow \Rightarrow$ **2LH + 2LW + 2WH**
$\Rightarrow$ **2 (LH + LW + WH)**

Note: To find the surface area of a rectangular solid, find the area of each of the six faces, and then add them together. Since the front and back faces are equal, the top and bottom faces are equal, and the left and right faces are equal, we can calculate the area of one face from each pair and then double the sum.

OPENED OUT RECTANGULAR SOLID:

If you cut and open up a rectangular solid and then flatten it out so that all its faces are clearly visible, the following is how it would look like. This picture will make it easier for you to image how a rectangular solid is made up using faces.

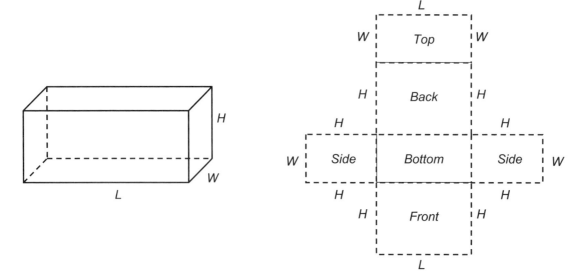

6.2.3: VOLUME OF RECTANGULAR SOLIDS:

The volume of any three-dimensional uniform solid is the area of the base times its height. In this case the base is rectangular. So think of the formula for the volume of a rectangular solid as the area of the rectangular base multiplied by the height.

VOLUME OF RECTANGULAR SOLID $\Rightarrow$ Area of Base × Height
$$\Rightarrow \textbf{\textit{Length × Width × Height}} = \textbf{\textit{LWH}}$$

6.2.4: DIAGONAL PHENOMENON OF RECTANGULAR SOLID:

A diagonal of a solid box is the longest line segment that can be drawn between any two points on the box. It connects any one vertex to its opposite vertex. A solid box has four diagonals, all of which are of the same length. For instance, one of the diagonal of a box is the line segment joining a vertex on the top of the box to the opposite vertex on the bottom. In the diagram given below, PS is one of the diagonals of the box.

If the dimensions of a box are L, W, and H, and if D is the measure of a diagonal, then:

Diagonal^2 = Length^2 + Width^2 + Height^2
$\boldsymbol{D^2}$ $= \boldsymbol{L^2 + W^2 + H^2}$
$\boldsymbol{D}$ $= \boldsymbol{\sqrt{L^2 + W^2 + H^2}}$

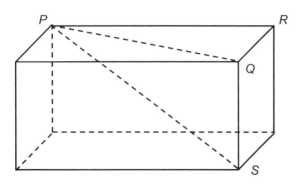

Alternately: The formula given above is actually just an extension of Pythagorean Theorem. You just have to use the Pythagorean Theorem twice. Apply the following steps:

STEP 1: First, find the diagonal of one of the faces of the rectangular solid by using the Pythagorean Theorem.
For instance in the top face, pick any two sides (*PR* & *QR*) which will form a right triangle (Δ*PQR*), and find the hypotenuse which will be the diagonal (*PQ*) of the top face.
$$\Rightarrow PR^2 + QR^2 = PQ^2$$

STEP 2: Next, use that diagonal (*PQ*) as one of the leg, and use one of the edges of the rectangular solid (*QS*) as the other leg in such a way that it makes a right triangle (Δ*PQS*).

STEP 3: Finally, the hypotenuse of the diagonal of one of the faces (*PQ*) and one of the edges (*QS*) will be the diagonal of the whole rectangular solid (*PS*). Again, apply the Pythagorean Theorem and find the length of the hypotenuse.
$$\Rightarrow PQ^2 + QS^2 = PS^2$$

Example #1:	If a rectangular box has, length = 2 units, width = 8 units, and height = 9 units, what is its surface area?		
Solution:	SA of Rectangular Solid	$\Rightarrow 2(LW + LH + WH)$	[Write the appropriate formula]
		$\Rightarrow 2[(2 \times 8) + (2 \times 9) + (8 \times 9)]$	[Substitute the known values]
		$\Rightarrow 2[16 + 18 + 72]$	[Solve within parentheses]
		$\Rightarrow 2(106)$	[Solve within brackets]
		$\Rightarrow 212 \text{ unit}^2$	[Do the multiplication]

Example #2:	If a rectangular box has, length = 2 units, width = 5 units, and height = 7 units, what is its volume?		
Solution:	Volume of Rectangular Solid	$\Rightarrow LWH$	[Write the appropriate formula]
		$\Rightarrow 2 \times 5 \times 7$	[Substitute the known values]
		$\Rightarrow 70 \text{ unit}^3$	[Do the multiplication]

Example #3: If a rectangular box has, length = 3 units, width = 4 units, and height = 5 units, what is the length of its diagonal?

Solution: EZ Problem Set-Up $\Rightarrow D^2 = L^2 + W^2 + H^2$ (According Diagonal Phenomenon of Rectangular Solids)

$$\Rightarrow D^2 = 3^2 + 4^2 + 5^2 \quad \text{[Set up the equation]}$$
$$\Rightarrow D^2 = 9 + 16 + 25 \quad \text{[Solve the exponents]}$$
$$\Rightarrow D^2 = 50 \quad \text{[Combine like-terms]}$$
$$\Rightarrow D = 5\sqrt{2} \text{ units} \quad \text{[Square root both sides]}$$

Alternately: This problem can also be solved by applying the alternative method given above by applying the Pythagorean Theorem twice.

6.3: CUBE:

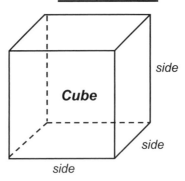

6.3.1: ABOUT CUBES:

PROPERTIES OF CUBE:
- A Cube is a type of rectangular solid that has six identical lateral faces.
- Each face in a Cube is a congruent square.
- Each square face in a Cube mirrors the square face exactly opposite it.
- All square faces in a Cube are identical and opposite faces lie in parallel planes.
- Each square face in a Cube intersects at right angles.
- All the edges of a Cube are of equal measures and are called its *length*, *width*, and *height* or simply *side*.

Examples of Cube: sugar cube, rubrics cube.

Cube is a Uniform Solid: A cube is a uniform or consistent solid; i.e., the horizontal cross sections are all squares of equal size. In other words, a slice of a cube from the middle is the same as a slice from the top or the bottom.

Similarity between Cubes and Rectangular Solids: Cubes are just like rectangular solids – the only difference is that in a cube, all the six faces are identical squares; whereas, in a rectangular solid, only opposite faces are identical.

FACES OF CUBE:
A Cube consists of exactly six equal square faces:
▪ Equal pair of the Front and the Back Faces   ⇒ Front Face = Back Face
▪ Equal pair of the Top and the Bottom Faces   ⇒ Top Face = Bottom Face
▪ Equal pair of the Right and the Left Faces   ⇒ Right Face = Left Face
▪ Front = Back = Top = Bottom = Right Face = Left Face

6.3.2: SURFACE AREA OF CUBES:
In a cube, since all six faces are identical, each of the six faces has the same area.
Area of each Square Face of a Cube   = side × side = side^2 = s^2

TOTAL SURFACE AREA OF CUBE   ⇒ Sum of the area of the six outside square faces
⇒ 6 × Area of each Square Face
⇒ **$6S^2$**

OPENED OUT CUBE:
If you cut and open up a cube and then flatten it out so that all its faces are clearly visible, the following is how it would look like. This picture will make it easier for you to image how a cube is made up using faces.

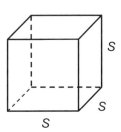

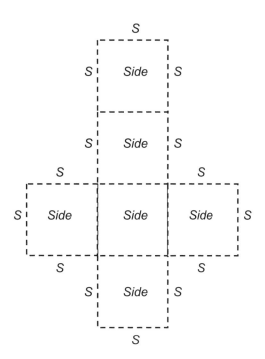

6.3.3: VOLUME OF CUBES:

The volume of any three-dimensional uniform solid is the area of the base times its height. In this case, the base is square. So think of the formula for the volume of a cube as the area of the square base multiplied by the height.

VOLUME OF CUBE $\Rightarrow$ Area of Base × Height
                   $\Rightarrow$ **Side × Side × Side = Side³ = S³**

6.3.4: DIAGONALS PHENOMENON OF CUBE:

A diagonal of a cube is the longest line segment that can be drawn between any two points on the cube. It connects any one vertex to its opposite vertex. A cube has four diagonals, all of which are of the same length. For instance, one of the diagonal of a cube is the line segment joining a vertex on the top of the cube to the opposite vertex on the bottom. In the diagram given below, *PS* is one of the diagonals of the box.

If the sides of a box are *S*, and if *D* is the measure of a diagonal, then:

Diagonal² $= \text{Side}^2 + \text{Side}^2 + \text{Side}^2$
$D^2 \qquad = S^2 + S^2 + S^2 = 3S^2$

$D \qquad = S\sqrt{3}$ and $S = \dfrac{D}{\sqrt{3}}$ Where: *S* is the side of the cube, and *D* is the diagonal of the cube

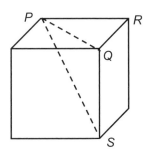

Example #1: If a cube has an edge of 5 units, what is its surface area?
Solution: SA of Cube $\Rightarrow 6s^2$ [Write the appropriate formula]
                              $\Rightarrow 6(5)^2$ [Substitute the known values]
                              $\Rightarrow 6(25)$ [Solve the exponent]
                              $\Rightarrow 150 \text{ unit}^2$ [Do the multiplication]

Example #2:   If a cube has a surface area of 150 unit^2, what is its edge?
Solution: SA of Cube $\Rightarrow 6s^2 = 150$ [Equate the SA formula with the given SA]
                                  $\Rightarrow s^2 = 25$ [Divide both sides by 6]
                                  $\Rightarrow s = 5$ units   [Square root both sides]

Example #3:   If a cube has an edge of 5 units, what is its volume?
Solution: Volume of Cube $\Rightarrow s^3$ [Write the appropriate formula]
                                  $\Rightarrow (5)^3$ [Substitute the known values]
                                  $\Rightarrow 125$ unit^3 [Solve the exponent]

Example #4:   If a cube has a volume of 125 unit^3, what is its edge?
Solution: Volume of Cube $\Rightarrow s^3 = 125$ [Equate the volume formula with the given volume]
                                  $\Rightarrow s = 5$ units   [Cube root both sides]

Example #5:   What is the surface area of a cube whose volume is 125 unit^3?
Solution: Volume of Cube $\Rightarrow s^3 = 125$ [Equate the volume formula with the given volume]
                                  $\Rightarrow s = 5$ units   [Cube root both sides]
                  SA of Cube $\Rightarrow 6s^2$ [Write the appropriate formula]
                                  $\Rightarrow 6(5)^2$ [Substitute the known values]
                                  $\Rightarrow 6(25)$ [Solve the exponent]
                                  $\Rightarrow 150$ unit^2 [Do the multiplication]

Example #6:   What is the volume of a cube whose surface area is 150 unit^2?
Solution: SA of Cube $\Rightarrow 6s^2 = 150$ [Equate the SA formula with the given SA]
                                  $\Rightarrow s^2 = 25$ [Divide both sides by 6]
                                  $\Rightarrow s = 5$ units   [Square root both sides]
                  Volume of Cube $\Rightarrow s^3$ [Write the appropriate formula]
                                  $\Rightarrow (5)^3$ [Substitute the known values]
                                  $\Rightarrow 125$ unit^3 [Solve the exponent]

Example #7:   If the length of an edge of a cube is 2 units, what is the length of its diagonal?
Solution: Diagonal/Side Phenomenon of Cube $\Rightarrow$ Diagonal $= s\sqrt{3}$ [Write the appropriate formula]
                                                    $\Rightarrow$ Diagonal $= 2\sqrt{3}$ units   [Substitute the known values]

Example #8:   If the length of a diagonal of a cube is $2\sqrt{3}$ units, what is the length of its edge?

Solution: Diagonal/Side Phenomenon of Cube $\Rightarrow$ Side $= \dfrac{d}{\sqrt{3}}$ [Write the appropriate formula]

                                                    $\Rightarrow$ Side $= \dfrac{2\sqrt{3}}{\sqrt{3}}$ [Substitute the known values]

                                                    $\Rightarrow$ Side $= 2$ units   [Simplify the fraction]

6.3.5: FACTS ABOUT RECTANGULAR SOLID'S DIMENSIONS, AREA, AND VOLUME:

FACT #1:   ⇒ Two or more rectangular solids with the same area can have different shapes/dimensions (*L*, *W*, *H*).
           ⇒ Two or more rectangular solids with the same area can have different volumes.

For Example: Rectangular Solid #1:   Rectangular Solid #2:

Rectangular Solid #1	Rectangular Solid #2
Dimensions ⇒ 10 by 5 by 5	Dimensions ⇒ 20 by 5 by 1
SA ⇒ 2[(*LW*) + (*LH*) + (*WH*)]	SA ⇒ 2[(*LW*) + (*LH*) + (*WH*)]
⇒ 2[(10 × 5) + (10 × 5) + (5 × 5)]	⇒ 2[(20 × 5) + (20 × 1) + (5 × 1)]
⇒ 2[50 + 50 + 25]	⇒ 2[100 + 20 + 5]
⇒ 2[125]	⇒ 2[125]
⇒ 250	⇒ 250
V ⇒ *L* × *W* × *H*	V ⇒ *L* × *W* × *H*
⇒ 10 × 5 × 5	⇒ 20 × 5 × 1
⇒ 250	⇒ 100

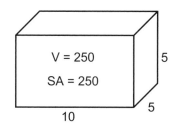

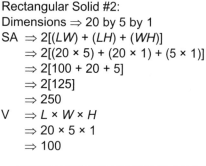

FACT #2:   ⇒ Two or more rectangular solids with the same volume can have different shapes/dimensions (*L*, *W*, *H*).
           ⇒ Two or more rectangular solids with the same volume can have different areas.

For Example: Rectangular Solid #1:   Rectangular Solid #2:

Rectangular Solid #1	Rectangular Solid #2
Dimensions ⇒ 10 by 2 by 5	Dimensions ⇒ 20 by 5 by 1
V ⇒ *L* × *W* × *H*	V ⇒ *L* × *W* × *H*
⇒ 10 × 2 × 5	⇒ 20 × 5 × 1
⇒ 100	⇒ 100
SA ⇒ 2[(*LW*) + (*LH*) + (*WH*)]	SA ⇒ 2[(*LW*) + (*LH*) + (*WH*)]
⇒ [(10 × 2) + (10 × 5) + (2 × 5)]	⇒ [(20 × 5) + (20 × 1) + (5 × 1)]
⇒ 2[20 + 50 + 10]	⇒ 2[100 + 20 + 5]
⇒ 2[80]	⇒ 2[125]
⇒ 160	⇒ 250

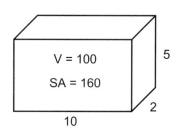

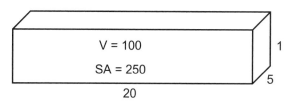

6.4: CYLINDER:

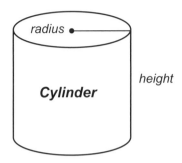

6.4.1: ABOUT CYLINDERS:

A right circular cylinder is a solid in which two identical (congruent) circular bases that are in parallel planes are connected (joined) to each other by a curved rectangular section that is perpendicular to the two circles, that is, it meets the circles at a right angle. Therefore, two circles of same size and a rectangle combine to form this three-dimensional shape called a right circular cylinder. A cylinder is similar to a rectangular solid except that the bases are circles instead of rectangles.

Cylinder is a Uniform Solid: A right circular cylinder is a uniform or consistent solid; i.e., the horizontal cross sections are all circles of equal radii or sizes. In other words, a slice of a cylinder from the middle is the same as a slice from the top or the bottom.

Examples of Cylinders: soft-drink cans, soup cans, pipes, barrels, tanks, stack of coins, stack of round coasters, etc.

The top and bottom part of the cylinder are circles, while the middle part of the cylinder is formed from a rolled-up rectangle, as shown in the diagram below:

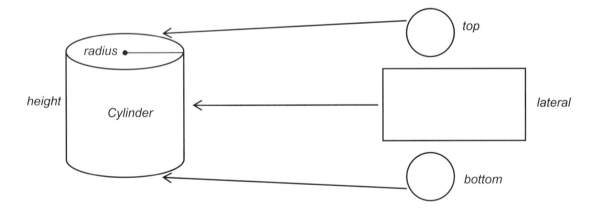

TERMS USED IN CYLINDERS:
(A) Radius of Cylinder: The radius of either of the circular bases is the radius of the cylinder.
(B) Height of Cylinder: The height of the cylinder is the horizontal distance connecting the two circular bases.

PARTS OF CYLINDERS: Cylinders have the following two parts:
(A) Circular Bases: The top & bottom parts are the circular bases of the cylinder.
(B) Lateral Surface: The lateral surface is the circular side of a cylinder.

6.4.2: SURFACE AREA OF CYLINDER:

In order to calculate the surface area of a cylinder, apply the following method:

(A) Area of the Top & Bottom Circular Bases: The area of both the top and the bottom circular bases is the area of the two circles or lids.
Area of the Top Circle $= \pi r^2$
Area of the Bottom Circle $= \pi r^2$
Area of the Top & Bottom Circle $= \pi r^2 + \pi r^2 = 2\pi r^2$

(B) Lateral Surface Area (LSA): The surface area around the circular side of a cylinder is called the lateral surface area.
Note: If we unroll the circular part of the cylinder that wraps around it and make it flat, it's actually in the shape of a rectangle whose dimensions are: one side is equal to the length of the rectangle which is the distance around the circle or circumference of the circular base; and the other side is equal to the width of the rectangle which is the height of the cylinder
Lateral Surface Area $\Rightarrow$ Length × Width = Circumference of the Circular Base × Height of the Cylinder
(Surface Area of Side) $\Rightarrow$ **$2\pi r × h = 2\pi rh$**

TOTAL SURFACE AREA OF CYLINDER: $\Rightarrow$ **(A)**   **+**   **(B)**
                                         $\Rightarrow$ **Area of the Top & Bottom**   **+**   **Lateral Surface Area**
                                              (Area of Circular Bases)   (Area of the side)
                                            $\Rightarrow$ $(\pi r^2 + \pi r^2)$ **+** $(2\pi r × h)$
                                            $\Rightarrow$ $2\pi r^2 + 2\pi rh$

Hollow or Solid Cylinder: The surface area of a cylinder depends on whether you are envisioning it to be a hollow tube like structure, such as a straw, which has no top or bottom, or a solid structure, such as a can, which has both a top and a bottom circular base.
EZ TIP: To calculate the surface area of a hollow tube like structure, only use the LSA formula. To calculate solid structure with top and bottom, use the total surface area formula.

6.4.3: VOLUME OF CYLINDER:

The volume of any three-dimensional uniform solid is the area of the base times its height. In this case, the base is circular. So think of the formula for the volume of a cylinder as the area of the circular base multiplied by the height, which is similar to the formula for the volume of a rectangular solid.
If a cylinder's circular base has radius "r" and its height is "h", then the volume, V, of the cylinder is given by the following formula.
VOLUME OF CYLINDER $\Rightarrow$ Area of the circular base × Height
                                   $\Rightarrow$ **$\pi r^2 h$**

Example #1:   If a right circular cylinder has a radius of 5 units and height of 2 units, what is its surface area?
Solution: SA of Cylinder $\Rightarrow 2\pi r^2 + 2\pi rh$ [Write the appropriate formula]
                                     $\Rightarrow 2\pi(5)^2 + 2\pi(5)(2)$ [Substitute the known values]
                                     $\Rightarrow 50\pi + 20\pi$ [Solve the exponents]
                                     $\Rightarrow 70\pi$ unit^2 [Combine like-terms]

Example #2:   If a right circular cylinder has a radius of 5 units and height of 2 units, what is its volume?
Solution: Volume of Cylinder $\Rightarrow \pi r^2 h$ [Write the appropriate formula]
                                     $\Rightarrow \pi(5)^2(2)$ [Substitute the known values]
                                     $\Rightarrow \pi(25)(2)$ [Solve the exponent]
                                     $\Rightarrow 50\pi$ unit^3 [Do the multiplication]

6.4.4: FACTS ABOUT CYLINDER'S DIMENSIONS, AREA, AND VOLUME:

FACT #1: ⇒ Two or more cylinders with the same area can have different shapes or dimensions (L, W, H).
⇒ Two or more cylinders with the same area can have different volumes.

For Example:

Cylinder #1
Dimensions: radius = 2; height = 8
V ⇒ $\pi r^2 h$
   ⇒ $\pi(2)^2(8)$
   ⇒ 32π
SA ⇒ $2\pi r^2 + 2\pi rh$
   ⇒ $2\pi(2)^2 + 2\pi(2)(8)$
   ⇒ $8\pi + 32\pi$
   ⇒ 40π

Cylinder #2
Dimensions: radius = 4; height = 1
V ⇒ $\pi r^2 h$
   ⇒ $\pi(4)^2(1)$
   ⇒ 16π
SA ⇒ $2\pi r^2 + 2\pi rh$
   ⇒ $2\pi(4)^2 + 2\pi(4)(1)$
   ⇒ $32\pi + 8\pi$
   ⇒ 40π

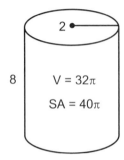

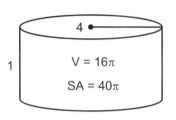

FACT #2: ⇒ Two or more cylinders with the same volume can have different shapes or dimensions (L, W, H).
⇒ Two or more cylinders with the same volume can have different areas.

For Example:

Cylinder #1
Dimensions: radius = 1; height = 20
V ⇒ $\pi r^2 h$
   ⇒ $\pi(1)^2(20)$
   ⇒ 20π
SA ⇒ $2\pi r^2 + 2\pi rh$
   ⇒ $2\pi(1)^2 + 2\pi(1)(20)$
   ⇒ $2\pi + 40\pi$
   ⇒ 42π

Cylinder #2
Dimensions: radius = 2; height = 5
V ⇒ $\pi r^2 h$
   ⇒ $\pi(2)^2(5)$
   ⇒ 20π
SA ⇒ $2\pi r^2 + 2\pi rh$
   ⇒ $2\pi(2)^2 + 2\pi(2)(5)$
   ⇒ $8\pi + 20\pi$
   ⇒ 28π

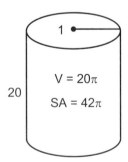

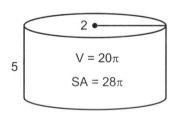

6.5: CONE:

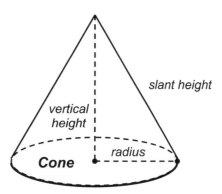

6.5.1: ABOUT CONES:

A circular cone is a solid in which a circular base is connected by a curved surface to its vertex. A Cone is a solid that has exactly one vertex and one circular base.

Examples of Cone: ice-cream cones, icing cones, etc.

Right Circular Cone: If the line from the vertex of the circular cone to the center of its base is perpendicular to the base, then the cone is called a right circular cone. For the purpose of your test and the scope of this book, you are only going to deal with right circular cones.

Cone is not a Uniform Solid: A cone is not a uniform or consistent solid; i.e., the cross sections are all circles, but are of different radii or sizes. In other words, a slice of a cone from the middle is bigger than a slice from the top and smaller than a slice from the bottom.

6.5.2: SURFACE AREA OF CONE:

SURFACE AREA OF CONE $\Rightarrow$ Lateral Surface Area + Area of the Circular Base
$$\Rightarrow \pi r l + \pi r^2$$

6.5.3: VOLUME OF CONE:

VOLUME OF CONE $\qquad \Rightarrow$ 1/3 (Volume of Cylinder)
$$\Rightarrow \frac{1}{3}\pi r^2 h$$

Example #1: If a right circular cone has a radius of 5 units and slant height of 6 units, then what is its surface area?
Solution: SA of Cone $\quad \Rightarrow \pi r l + \pi r^2$ [Write the appropriate formula]
$\qquad\qquad\qquad\quad \Rightarrow \pi(5)(6) + \pi(5)^2$ [Substitute the known values]
$\qquad\qquad\qquad\quad \Rightarrow 30\pi + 25\pi$ [Solve the exponent]
$\qquad\qquad\qquad\quad \Rightarrow 55\pi$ unit^2 [Do the multiplication]

Example #2: If a right circular cone has a radius of 5 units and vertical height of 6 units, then what is its volume?
Solution: Volume of Cone $\Rightarrow$ 1/3 $\pi r^2 h$ [Write the appropriate formula]
$\qquad\qquad\qquad\quad \Rightarrow 1/3\pi(5)^2(6)$ [Substitute the known values]
$\qquad\qquad\qquad\quad \Rightarrow 1/3\pi(25)(6)$ [Solve the exponent]
$\qquad\qquad\qquad\quad \Rightarrow 50\pi$ unit^3 [Do the multiplication]

6.6: SPHERE:

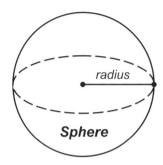

radius

Sphere

6.6.1: ABOUT SPHERES:

A sphere is a closed three-dimensional figure that is made up of a set or series of all the points in space (different planes) that are at the same distance (equidistant) from one fixed point, called the center point of the sphere.
- A sphere is a solid analogue of a circle, i.e., a sphere is like a three-dimensional circle.
- A sphere is a solid, which is round from all sides and has no edges or vertices.
- All the dimensions in a regular sphere are equal, i.e., all radii of a sphere are equal.

Radius of Sphere: The distance from the center to any point on the sphere is the radius of the sphere. In other words, the length of a line segment from any given point on the sphere to the center is called the radius of the sphere.

Examples of Spheres: basketball, inflated balloons, etc.

Sphere is not a Uniform Solid: A sphere is not a uniform or consistent solid; i.e., the cross sections are all circles, but are of different radii or sizes. In other words, a slice of a sphere from the middle is bigger than a slice from the top or the bottom.

Naming a Sphere: A sphere is denoted or labeled by a single letter, which is usually its center point. For example: sphere O means the sphere with center point *O*.

6.6.2: SURFACE AREA OF SPHERE:
SURFACE AREA OF SPHERE $\Rightarrow 4\pi r^2$

6.6.3: VOLUME OF SPHERE:
VOLUME OF SPHERE $\Rightarrow \dfrac{4}{3}\pi r^3$

Example #1:   If a sphere has a radius of 5 units, what is its surface area?

Solution: SA of Sphere

$\Rightarrow 4\pi r^2$ [Write the appropriate formula]

$\Rightarrow 4\pi(5)^2$ [Substitute the known values]

$\Rightarrow 4\pi(25)$ [Solve the exponent]

$\Rightarrow 100\pi$ unit^2 [Do the multiplication]

Example #2:   If a sphere has a radius of 6 units, what is its volume?

Solution: Volume of Sphere

$\Rightarrow \dfrac{4}{3}\pi r^3$ [Write the appropriate formula]

$\Rightarrow \dfrac{4}{3}\pi(6)^3$ [Substitute the known values]

$\Rightarrow \dfrac{4}{3}\pi(216)$ [Solve the exponent]

$\Rightarrow 288\pi$ unit^3 [Do the multiplication]

PRACTICE EXERCISE – QUESTIONS AND ANSWERS WITH EXPLANATIONS: SOLID GEOMETRY:

Question #1: If a rectangular solid has length = 7 units, width = 11 units, height = 12 units, what is its surface area?

Solution: SA of Rectangular Solid $\Rightarrow 2\,(LW + LH + WH)$ [Write the appropriate formula]
                                        $\Rightarrow 2[(7 \times 11) + (7 \times 12) + (11 \times 12)]$ [Substitute the known values]
                                          $\Rightarrow 2[77 + 84 + 132]$ [Solve within the parentheses]
                                          $\Rightarrow 2(293)$ [Solve within the brackets]
                                          $\Rightarrow 586 \text{ unit}^2$ [Do the multiplication]

Question #2: If a rectangular solid has length = 5 units, width = 6 units, height = 7 units, what is its volume?

Solution: Volume of Rectangular Box $\Rightarrow LWH$ [Write the appropriate formula]
                                          $\Rightarrow 5 \times 6 \times 7 = 210 \text{ unit}^3$ [Substitute the known values and simplify]

Question #3: If a rectangular box has, length = 6 units, width = 8 units, and height = 10 units, what is the length of its diagonal?

Solution: EZ Problem Set-Up $\Rightarrow D^2 = L^2 + W^2 + H^2$ (According to Diagonal Phenomenon of Rectangular Solids)
                                  $\Rightarrow D^2 = 6^2 + 8^2 + 10^2$ [Set up the equation]
                                  $\Rightarrow D^2 = 36 + 64 + 100$ [Solve the exponents]
                                  $\Rightarrow D^2 = 200$ [Combine like-terms]
                                  $\Rightarrow D = 10\sqrt{2}$ units   [Square root both sides]

Question #4: If a cube has an edge of 11 units, what is its surface area?

Solution: SA of Cube $\Rightarrow 6s^2$ [Write the appropriate formula]
                       $\Rightarrow 6(11)^2 = 6(121) = 726 \text{ unit}^2$ [Substitute the known values and simplify]

Question #5: If the surface area of a cube is 864 unit^2, what is the length of an edge of the cube?

Solution: SA of Cube $\Rightarrow 6s^2 = 864 \text{ unit}^2$ [Equate the SA formula with the given SA]
                       $\Rightarrow s^2 = 144 \text{ unit}^2$ [Divide both sides by 6]
                       $\Rightarrow s = 12$ units   [Square root both sides]

Question #6: If the area of a side of a cube is 576 unit^2, what is the length of an edge of the cube?

Solution: Area of side of Cube $\Rightarrow s^2 = 576 \text{ unit}^2$ [Equate the area formula with the given area]
                               $\Rightarrow s = 24$ units   [Square root both sides]

Question #7: If a cube has an edge of 9 units, what is its volume?

Solution: Volume of Cube $\Rightarrow s^3$ [Write the appropriate formula]
                         $\Rightarrow (9)^3 = 729 \text{ unit}^3$ [Substitute the known values and simplify]

Question #8: If a cube has a volume of 216 unit^3, what is the length of an edge of the cube?

Solution: Volume of Cube $\Rightarrow s^3 = 216 \text{ unit}^3$ [Equate the volume formula with the given volume]
                       $\Rightarrow s = 6$ units   [Cube root both sides]

Question #9: What is the surface area of a cube whose volume is 27 unit^3?

Solution: Volume of Cube $\Rightarrow s^3 = 27 \text{ unit}^3$ [Equate the volume formula with the given volume]
                       $\Rightarrow s = 3$ units   [Cube root both sides]
         SA of Cube $\Rightarrow 6s^2 =$ [Write the appropriate formula]
                       $\Rightarrow 6(3)^2 = 6(9) = 54 \text{ unit}^2$ [Substitute the known values and simplify]

Question #10: What is the volume of a cube whose surface area is 96 unit^2?

Solution: SA of Cube $\Rightarrow 6s^2 = 96 \text{ unit}^2$ [Equate the SA formula with the given SA]
                       $\Rightarrow s^2 = 16 \text{ unit}^2$ [Divide both sides by 6]
                       $\Rightarrow s = 4$ units   [Square root both sides]
         Volume of Cube $\Rightarrow s^3$ [Write the appropriate formula]

$$\Rightarrow (4)^3 \text{ unit}^3 = 64 \text{ unit}^3 \qquad \text{[Substitute the known values and simplify]}$$

Question #11: If the length of an edge of a cube is 5 units, what is the length of its diagonal?

Solution: Diagonal/Side Phenomenon of Cube $\Rightarrow$ Diagonal $= s\sqrt{3}$ [Write the appropriate formula]

$\Rightarrow$ Diagonal $= 5\sqrt{3}$ units   [Substitute the known values]

Question #12: If the length of a diagonal of a cube is $5\sqrt{3}$ units, what is the length of its edge?

Solution: Diagonal/Side Phenomenon of Cube $\Rightarrow$ Side $= \dfrac{d}{\sqrt{3}}$ [Write the appropriate formula]

$\Rightarrow$ Side $= \dfrac{5\sqrt{3}}{\sqrt{3}}$ [Substitute the known values]

$\Rightarrow$ Side = 5 units   [Simplify the fraction]

Question #13: If a right circular cylinder has a radius of 9 units and height of 2 units, what is its surface area?

Solution: SA of Cylinder $\Rightarrow 2\pi r^2 + 2\pi rh$ [Write the appropriate formula]

$\Rightarrow 2\pi(9)^2 + 2\pi(9)(2) = 162\pi + 36\pi = 198\pi \text{ unit}^2$ [Substitute values/simplify]

Question #14: If a right circular cylinder has a radius of 9 units and height of 2 units, what is its volume?

Solution: Volume of Cylinder $\Rightarrow \pi r^2 h$ [Write the appropriate formula]

$\Rightarrow \pi(9)^2(2) = \pi(81)(2) = 162\pi \text{ unit}^3$ [Substitute the known values and simplify]

Question #15: If a right cylinder with radius of 2 units has a volume of $100\pi \text{ unit}^3$, what is the height of the cylinder?

Solution: Volume of Cylinder $\Rightarrow \pi r^2 h = 100\pi$ [Equate the volume formula with the given volume]

$\Rightarrow \pi(2)^2 h = 100\pi$ [Substitute the known values]

$\Rightarrow 4h = 100$ [Solve the exponent]

$\Rightarrow h = 25$ units   [Divide both sides by 4]

Question #16: If a right cylinder with height of 25 units has a volume of $100\pi \text{ unit}^3$, what is the radius of the cylinder?

Solution: Volume of Cylinder $\Rightarrow \pi r^2 h = 100\pi$ [Equate the volume formula with the given volume]

$\Rightarrow \pi r^2(25) = 100\pi$ [Substitute the known values]

$\Rightarrow r^2 = 4$ [Divide both sides by 25π]

$\Rightarrow r = 2$ units   [Square root both sides]

Question #17: If a right circular cone has a radius of 9 units and slant height of 2 units, then what is its surface area?

Solution: SA of Cone $\Rightarrow \pi rl + \pi r^2$ [Write the appropriate formula]

$\Rightarrow \pi(9)(2) + \pi(9)^2 = 18\pi + 81\pi = 99 \text{ unit}^2$ [Substitute the known values and simplify]

Question #18: If a right circular cone has a radius of 9 units and height of 2 units, what is its volume?

Solution: Volume of Cone $\Rightarrow 1/3\pi r^2 h$ [Write the appropriate formula]

$\Rightarrow 1/3\pi(9)^2(2) = 54\pi \text{ unit}^3$ [Substitute the known values and simplify]

Question #19: If a sphere has a radius of 8 units, what is its surface area?

Solution: SA of Sphere $\Rightarrow 4\pi r^2$ [Write the appropriate formula]

$\Rightarrow 4\pi(8)^2 = 256\pi \text{ unit}^2$ [Substitute the known values and simplify]

Question #20: If a sphere has a radius of 9 units, what is its volume?

Solution: Volume of Sphere $\Rightarrow 4/3\pi r^3$ [Write the appropriate formula]

$\Rightarrow 4/3\pi(9)^3 = 972\pi \text{ unit}^3$ [Substitute the known values and simplify]

PART 7.0: COORDINATE GEOMETRY:

TABLE OF CONTENTS:

EZ REFERENCE: -To practice easy-to-medium level questions, please refer to our EZ Practice Basic Workbook.
-To practice medium-to-difficult level questions, please refer to our EZ Practice Advanced Workbook.

7.1: BASICS ABOUT COORDINATE GEOMETRY:

The *"coordinate geometry"* refers to the study of geometric figures and properties on the coordinate plane using algebraic principles – it involves both algebra and geometry. Coordinate geometry questions involve points, lines, and figures that lie in the coordinate plane. Coordinate geometry is commonly used to graph points and lines, to identify or locate points and lines, to find distance between any two given points, to find the mid-point between any two given points, and to find the slope of a line on a plane.

7.1.1: COORDINATE PLANE:

The *"coordinate plane"* is also known as *"Cartesian coordinate plane"* or *"rectangular coordinate plane"* or *"xy-coordinate system"* or *"xy-plane"*.

7.1.1.1: COORDINATE AXES:

The coordinate system is made up of two perpendicular real number lines or *"coordinate axes"* that intersect each other at right angles at the zero point of each number line.

X-Axis (abscissa): The horizontal number line is the x-axis, and it is perpendicular to the y-axis – it goes left and right.
Y-Axis (ordinate): The vertical number line is the y-axis, and it is perpendicular to the x-axis – it goes up and down.
Origin: The two number lines or axes intersect each other at their respective zeros. The point-of-intersection of these two axes is called the origin, and it is the zero point of both the number lines and axes.

PROPERTIES OF COORDINATE AXES:
- Both axes (x-axis & y-axis) function and act as a real number line, with the origin corresponding to zero.
- Both axes (x-axis & y-axis) are perpendicular to each other, i.e., angles created by intersection are 90° each.
- Both axes (x-axis & y-axis) intersect each other at their respective zeros at the origin.

7.1.1.2: COORDINATE POINTS:

Each point in the coordinate plane is identified by using an ordered pair of numbers that describes it, and is assigned a set of two numbers called *"coordinates"* or *"coordinate points,"* the x-coordinate and the y-coordinate. The coordinates of any point indicate how far it is from the origin. The coordinates of a point indicate its location relative to the number lines.
Coordinate points are always written as an *"ordered pair"* in parentheses: (x, y), in which the x-coordinate is written first, and the y-coordinate is written second, where:
(A) The 1st member of the ordered pair is x-coordinate $\Rightarrow$ corresponds to the point's location on the horizontal axis.
    $\Rightarrow$ It's the distance from the origin along the x-axis. It's the distance to the left (if negative) or to the right (if positive) of the y-axis.
(B) The 2nd member of the ordered pair is y-coordinate $\Rightarrow$ corresponds to the point's location on the vertical axis.
    $\Rightarrow$ It's the distance from the origin along the y-axis. It's the distance below (if negative) or above (if positive) the x-axis.
Note: Unless otherwise noted, the units used on the x-axis and the y-axis are the same.

COORDINATE POINTS ON EITHER SIDE OF THE AXES:
(A) Coordinates Points to the Right or Left of Y-axis:
    $\Rightarrow$ All points to the right of the y-axis have positive x-coordinates.
    $\Rightarrow$ All points to the left of the y-axis have negative x-coordinates.
(B) Coordinates Points Above or Below the X-axis:
    $\Rightarrow$ All points above the x-axis have positive y-coordinates.
    $\Rightarrow$ All points below the x-axis have negative y-coordinates.

Therefore, the coordinates of any given point P on the coordinate plane are defined by (x, y) if P is located by moving x-units left or right along the x-axis from the origin and then moving y-units up or down along the y-axis from the origin.

7.1.2: PARTS OF COORDINATE PLANE:

The coordinate axes divide or cut the coordinate plane into four quartered planes or quadrants. The axes and the area around the axes form a four-quartered plane. Each quarter plane is called a *"quadrant"*. The resulting four quadrants are labeled in counterclockwise direction starting from top right corner.

FIRST QUADRANT: The top right (North-East) quadrant is the First Quadrant. (Right & Above the Origin)
Quadrant I contains only those points whose value of x-coordinate is always positive and the value of y-coordinate is also always positive $\Rightarrow (+x, +y)$
For Example: $(+x, +y)$; $(+2, +5)$

SECOND QUADRANT: The top left (North-West) quadrant is the Second Quadrant. (Left & Above the Origin)
Quadrant II contains only those points whose value of x-coordinate is always negative and the value of the y-coordinate is always positive $(-x, +y)$
For Example: $(-x, +y)$; $(-2, +5)$

THIRD QUADRANT: The bottom left (South-West) quadrant is the Third Quadrant. (Left & Below the Origin)
Quadrant III contains only those points whose value of x-coordinate is always negative and the value of y-coordinate is also always negative $\Rightarrow (-x, -y)$
For Example: $(-x, -y)$; $(-2, -5)$

FOURTH QUADRANT: The bottom right (South-East) quadrant is the Fourth Quadrant. (Right & Below the Origin)
Quadrant IV contains only those points whose value of x-coordinate is always positive and the value of y-coordinate is always negative $(+x, -y)$
For Example: $(+x, -y)$; $(+2, -5)$

ORIGIN: The point at which the two axes intersect is the Origin.
$\Rightarrow$ It is the Center of all the four quadrants.
$\Rightarrow$ The coordinates of the origin are $(0, 0)$

WHICH COORDINATE LIES IN WHICH QUADRANT:
(A) If x-coordinate is positive & y-coordinate is positive $\Rightarrow$ then the point lies in the 1st Quadrant.
(B) If x-coordinate is negative & y-coordinate is positive $\Rightarrow$ then the point lies in the 2nd Quadrant.
(C) If x-coordinate is negative & y-coordinate is negative $\Rightarrow$ then the point lies in the 3rd Quadrant.
(D) If x-coordinate is positive & y-coordinate is negative $\Rightarrow$ then the point lies in the 4th Quadrant.
(E) If both of the coordinates are ZERO $\Rightarrow$ then the point lies on both of the axes,
i.e., on the origin $(0, 0)$
(F) If either of the coordinates is ZERO $\Rightarrow$ then the point lies on one of the axes.
(i) If x-coordinate is zero $\Rightarrow$ then the point lies on the y-axis.
(ii) If y-coordinate is zero $\Rightarrow$ then the point lies on the x-axis.

VALUE OF COORDINATE THAT LIES ON THE AXIS:
If a point lies on either one of the axes, then at least one of its coordinates has to be zero.
(A) The value of y-coordinate anywhere on the x-axis is zero $\Rightarrow$ i.e., if a point is on x-axis, its y-coordinate is 0.
(B) The value of x-coordinate anywhere on the y-axis is zero $\Rightarrow$ i.e., if a point is on y-axis, its x-coordinate is 0.

VALUE OF COORDINATE THAT LIES ON THE LINES PARALLEL TO THE AXES:
All the points that lie on a line parallel to one of the axes has the same x-coordinate or y-coordinate.
All the points on a horizontal line have the same y-coordinate $\Rightarrow$ i.e., all the points that are on any line parallel to x-axis have the same y-coordinate.

All the points on a vertical line have the same x-coordinate $\Rightarrow$ i.e., all the points that are on any line parallel to y-axis have the same x-coordinate.

COORDINATE GRID: A coordinate grid is a way of locating points that lie in a coordinate plane or flat surface.

7.2: PLOTTING COORDINATES:

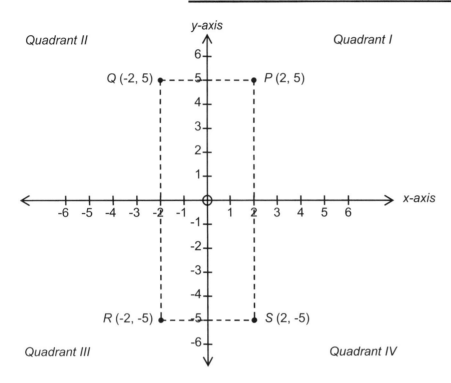

7.2.1: DIFFERENT WAYS OF PLOTTING COORDINATES:

7.2.1.1: BY DRAWING PERPENDICULAR LINE:

EZ STEP-BY-STEP METHOD: Apply the following step(s) to plot any point (x, y) when the coordinates are given:

STEP 1: First, locate the exact location of x-coordinate on the x-axis and draw a perpendicular line, which is parallel to the y-axis.

STEP 2: Similarly, locate the exact location of y-coordinate on the y-axis and draw a perpendicular line, which is parallel to the x-axis.

STEP 3: The point-of-intersection of these two perpendicular lines represents that specific coordinate.

EZ TIP: Use the number lines located on both the axis to find the exact location of coordinates.

7.2.1.2: BY MOVING ON THE AXIS:

EZ STEP-BY-STEP METHOD: Apply the following step(s) to plot any point (x, y) when the coordinates are given:

(A) To start from x-coordinate:

STEP 1: First, locate the x-coordinate on the x-axis. Starting from the origin $(0, 0)$, apply one of the following:
  (A) If the x-coordinate is positive, then from the origin, move horizontally right, the number of spaces indicated by the x-coordinate.
  (B) If the x-coordinate is negative, then from the origin, move horizontally left, the number of spaces indicated by the x-coordinate.

STEP 2: Once you locate the x-coordinate on the x-axis, starting from that x-coordinate, apply one of the following:
  (A) If the y-coordinate is positive, then from that position, move vertically up, the number of spaces indicated by the y-coordinate.
  (B) If the y-coordinate is negative, then from that position, move vertically down, the number of spaces indicated by the y-coordinate.
  $\Rightarrow$ The point at which you end up represents your ordered pair.

Method 2B: To start from *y*-coordinate:

STEP 1: First, locate the *y*-coordinate on the *y*-axis. Starting from the origin (0, 0), apply one of the following:
- **(A)** If the *y*-coordinate is positive, then from that position, move vertically up, the number of spaces indicated by the *y*-coordinate.
- **(B)** If the *y*-coordinate is negative, then from that position, move vertically down, the number of spaces indicated by the *y*-coordinate.

STEP 2: Once you locate the *y*-coordinate on the *y*-axis, starting from that y-coordinate, apply one of the following:
- **(A)** If the *x*-coordinate is positive, then from that position, move horizontally right, the number of spaces indicated by the *x*-coordinate.
- **(B)** If the *x*-coordinate is negative, then from that position, move horizontally left, the number of spaces indicated by the *x*-coordinate.
  ⇒ The point at which you end up represents your ordered pair.

For instance, in the figure given above:

Q1: If we have to plot the ordered pair *P* (2, 5), we would start from the origin, count 2 over to the right along the *x*-axis, and from that point count 5 up on the *y*-axis.
⇒ Conversely, the coordinates of *P* are (2, 5) since it's 2 units to the right of the *y*-axis (i.e., *x* = 2) and 5 units above the *x*-axis (i.e., *y* = 5).

Q2: If we have to plot the ordered pair *Q* (–2, 5), we would start from the origin, count 2 over to the left along the *x*-axis, and from that point count 5 up on the *y*-axis.
⇒ Conversely, the coordinates of *Q* are (–2, 5) since it's 2 units to the left of the *y*-axis (i.e., *x* = –2) and 5 units above the *x*-axis (i.e., *y* = 5).

Q3: If we have to plot the ordered pair *R* (–2, –5), we would start from the origin, count 2 over to the left along the *x*-axis, and from that point count 5 down on the *y*-axis.
⇒ Conversely, the coordinates of *R* are (–2, –5) since it's 2 units to the left of the *y*-axis (i.e., *x* = –2) and 5 units below the *x*-axis (i.e., *y* = –5).

Q4: If we have to plot the ordered pair *S* (2, –5), we would start from the origin, count 2 over to the right along the *x*-axis, and from that point count 5 down on the *y*-axis.
⇒ Conversely, the coordinates of *S* are (2, –5) since it's 2 units to the right of the *y*-axis (i.e., *x* = 2) and 5 units below the *x*-axis (i.e., *y* = –5).

MOVEMENT FROM ZERO ON THE AXIS:
(A) Movement From Zero on the *X*-Axis:
- **(i)** Positive *x*-coordinate value means a movement to the right from the origin.
- **(ii)** Negative *x*-coordinate value means a movement to the left from the origin.

(B) Movement From Zero on the *Y*-Axis:
- **(i)** Positive *y*-coordinate value means a movement up from the origin.
- **(ii)** Negative *y*-coordinate value means a movement down from the origin.

DIRECTIONS FOR POSITIVE AND NEGATIVE COORDINATES:
Right and Up ⇒ are the directions for positive numbers.   **Left and Down** ⇒ are the directions for negative numbers.
For Instance: Plotting (2, 5): Move 2 units to the right of the *x*-axis, and draw a perpendicular line; move 5 units along the *y*-axis, draw a perpendicular line. The point-of-intersection of these two lines represents the coordinate (2, 5).

FINDING COORDINATES OF A GIVEN PLOTTED POINT:
To find the coordinates of any given plotted point, apply the reverse of the process given above.

EZ STEP-BY-STEP METHOD: Apply the following step(s) to find the coordinates (*x*, *y*) when the coordinates are already plotted:

STEP 1: First, locate the exact location of the given coordinate and draw a perpendicular line from that point to the *x*-axis that is parallel to the *y*-axis ⇒ this is your *x*-coordinate.

STEP 2: Similarly, locate the exact location of the given coordinate and draw a perpendicular line from that point to the *y*-axis that is parallel to the *x*-axis ⇒ this is your *y*-coordinate.

STEP 3: The above two coordinates represent the specific coordinate ⇒ Write the above two coordinates as an ordered pair ⇒ the *x*-coordinate is written before the *y*-coordinate and a comma is used to separate the two.

EZ TIP: Use the number lines located on both the axis to find the exact location of coordinates.

7.3: DISTANCE BETWEEN TWO POINTS:

7.3.1: DISTANCE BETWEEN TWO POINTS WITH SAME "X" OR "Y" COORDINATES:

To find the distance between two points with the same x-coordinates or y-coordinates, that is, if they make a line segment that is parallel to either one of the axis ⇒ all you have to do is subtract the numbers that are different.

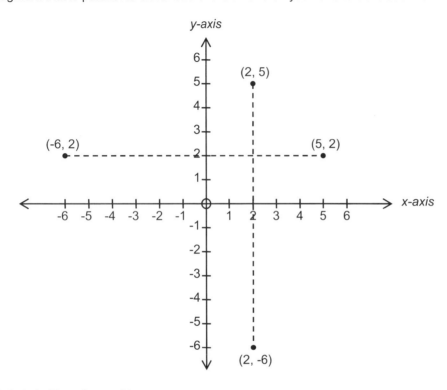

7.3.1.1: FOR SAME Y-COORDINATES:

EZ RULE: All the points on a horizontal line have the same y-coordinate.
i.e., all the points that are on any line parallel to x-axis have the same y-coordinate.
⇒ To find the distance between coordinate with same y-coordinates ⇒ subtract their x-coordinates.

For Example: What is the distance between (-6, 2) and (5, 2)?
Solution: Since the "y's" are the same in both the coordinates, simply subtract the "x's"
Distance ⇒ 5 – (-6) = 5 + 6 = 11

7.3.1.2: FOR SAME X-COORDINATES:

EZ RULE: All the points on a vertical line have the same x-coordinate.
i.e., all the points that are on any line parallel to y-axis have the same x-coordinate.
⇒ To find the distance between coordinates with same x-coordinates ⇒ subtract their y-coordinates.

For Example: What is the distance between (2, -6) and (2, 5)?
Solution: Since the "x's" are the same in both the coordinates, simply subtract the "y's"
Distance ⇒ 5 – (-6) = 5 + 6 = 11

7.3.2: DISTANCE BETWEEN TWO POINTS WITH DIFFERENT "X" & "Y" COORDINATES:

EZ RULE: To find the distance between two points with same or different x-coordinates and y-coordinates, that is, if they don't make a line segment that is parallel to either one of the axis – apply one of the following two methods:

7.3.2.1: FINDING DISTANCE BY USING DISTANCE FORMULA:

In a coordinate plane, the distance "d", between any two given points, A (x_1, y_1) and B (x_2, y_2) is represented by applying the following distance formula:

DISTANCE FORMULA = d = $AB \Rightarrow \sqrt{(x_1 - x_2)^2 + (y_1 - y_2)^2}$

EZ STEP-BY-STEP METHOD: Apply the following step(s) to find the distance between two points by using the distance formula:

STEP 1: Find the difference between the x-coordinates and square it

STEP 2: Find the difference between the y-coordinates and square it

STEP 3: Add the above two results

STEP 4: Finally square root it

For Example: What is the distance between (2, 2) and (5, 6)?

Solution: $d = \sqrt{(x_1 - x_2)^2 + (y_1 - y_2)^2} \Rightarrow \sqrt{(2-5)^2 + (2-6)^2} \Rightarrow \sqrt{(-3)^2 + (-4)^2} \Rightarrow \sqrt{(9) + (16)} \Rightarrow \sqrt{25} \Rightarrow 5$

Note: While using the distance formula, it doesn't matter which coordinate point you choose as (x_1, y_1) and which one you choose as (x_2, y_2) as long as you are consistent with what you pick.

7.3.2.2: FINDING DISTANCE BY USING PYTHAGOREAN THEOREM:

The distance formula is nothing more than a short form of the Pythagorean Theorem. In fact distance formula is derived from the Pythagorean Theorem. If you ever forget the formula, and you need the distance between any two given points that do not lie on the same horizontal or vertical line, just apply the following steps:

EZ STEP-BY-STEP METHOD: Apply the following step(s) to find the distance between two points by using Pythagorean Theorem:

STEP 1: If the coordinate grid is not given, first construct an arbitrary coordinate grid, and plot the two given points.

STEP 2: Connect the two given points with a line segment.

STEP 3: Create a right triangle by drawing a horizontal line through one of the points and a vertical line through the other, such that the line segment joining the two given points becomes the hypotenuse of the right triangle.

STEP 4: Finally, use Pythagorean Theorem, the value of the hypotenuse is the distance between the two given points.

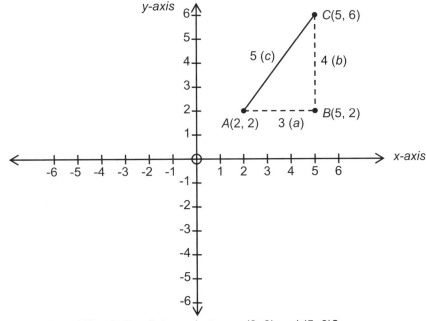

For Example: What is the distance between (2, 2) and (5, 6)?

Solution: Make a right triangle and use the Pythagorean Theorem: $a^2 + b^2 = c^2$

$\Rightarrow 3^2 + 4^2 = c^2 \quad \Rightarrow 9 + 16 = c^2 \quad \Rightarrow c = \sqrt{25} = 5$

7.4: MID-POINT BETWEEN TWO POINTS:

The mid-point, between any two given points $\Rightarrow$ A (x_1, y_1) and B (x_2, y_2) is represented by the following formula:

$$\text{MID-POINT FORMULA} = \text{MP} \Rightarrow \left(\frac{x_1 + x_2}{2}, \frac{y_1 + y_2}{2} \right)$$

EZ STEP-BY-STEP METHOD: Apply the following step(s) to find the midpoint between two points by using the mid-point formula:

STEP 1: First, find the average of x-coordinates $\Rightarrow$ add the x-coordinates together and divide by 2.

STEP 2: Next, find the average of y-coordinates $\Rightarrow$ add the y-coordinates together and divide by 2

STEP 3: Finally, write the above two averages as an ordered pair.

Note: While using the mid-point formula, it doesn't matter which coordinate point you choose as (x_1, y_1) and which one you choose as (x_2, y_2) as long as you are consistent with what you pick.

Example #1:   What is the mid-point between (2, 5) and (8, 7)?

Solution: $MP = (x_{midpoint}, y_{midpoint})$ $\Rightarrow \left(\dfrac{x_1 + x_2}{2}, \dfrac{y_1 + y_2}{2} \right)$ [Write the appropriate formula]

                                $\Rightarrow [(2 + 8) \div 2 \quad, \quad (5 + 7) \div 2]$ [Substitute the known values]
                                $\Rightarrow (10 \div 2 \quad, \quad 12 \div 2)$ [Solve within parentheses]
                                $\Rightarrow (5 \qquad\quad, \qquad 6)$ [Do the divisions]

Example #2:   If the midpoint of a line segment is (5, 7) and one of the endpoint is (2, 5), what are coordinates of the other endpoint?

Solution: $\Rightarrow MP \Rightarrow \left(\dfrac{x_1 + x_2}{2}, \dfrac{y_1 + y_2}{2} \right) = (5, 7)$ [Write the appropriate formula]

            $\Rightarrow \dfrac{x_1 + x_2}{2} = 5$ $\Rightarrow \dfrac{y_1 + y_2}{2} = 7$ [Set up the two equations]

            $\Rightarrow \dfrac{2 + x_2}{2} = 5$ $\Rightarrow \dfrac{5 + y_2}{2} = 7$ [Substitute the given values]

            $\Rightarrow 2 + x_2 = 10$ $\Rightarrow 5 + y_2 = 14$ [Cross-multiply each equation]
            $\Rightarrow x_2 = 8$ $\Rightarrow y_2 = 9$ [Isolate the variable in each equation]
            Coordinates of the other endpoint $\Rightarrow$ (8, 9)

7.5: INTERCEPTS OF LINE:

The point at which a line intersects the coordinate axes is called its *"intercepts"*. There are two types of intercepts, the *x-intercept* and the *y-intercept*. The following is the method to find the x- and y- Intercepts of a line:

X-INTERCEPT: The x-intercept of a line is the value of x-coordinate of the point at which the line intersects the x-axis, i.e., it's the value of x when y = 0 in the general equation.
⇒ The x-intercept is expressed using the ordered pair (x, 0), where x is the point at which the line intersects the x-axis. For instance: In the diagram given below, the x-intercept is 5, and is expressed by the ordered pair (5, 0).

Y-INTERCEPT: The y-intercept of a line is the value of y-coordinate of the point at which the line intersects the y-axis, i.e., it's the value of y when x = 0 in the general equation.
⇒ The y-intercept is expressed using the ordered pair (0, y), where y is the point at which the line intersects the y-axis. For instance: In the diagram given below, the y-intercept is 2, and is expressed by the ordered pair (0, 2).

Note: The y-intercept is also the value b when the equation is in the form: y = mx + b.

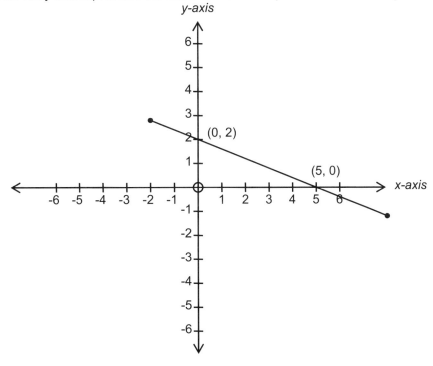

FINDING X & Y INTERCEPTS OF LINE FROM ITS EQUATION:

Y-Intercept: The y-intercept of a line is the y-coordinate of the point where the line intersects the y-axis.
To find the y-intercept of a line – set the equation by putting x = 0 and solve for y.
Alternately, the y-intercept of a line can also be defined by the given equation by setting it in the standard form y = mx + b, and then identifying the b-term.

For Example: In the xy-plane, what is the y-intercept of a line described by the equation 2 = 5x – y?
Solution: Set the equation by putting x = 0   ⇒ 2 = 5x – y
                                                 ⇒ 2 = 5(0) – y
                                                 ⇒ y = –2
         Alternatively: rewrite the equation in the standard form y = mx + b   ⇒ 2 = 5x – y
                                                                         ⇒ y = 5x – 2

         ⇒ y-intercept = –2

***X*-Intercept:** The *x*-intercept of a line is the *x*-coordinate of the point where the line intersects the *x*-axis.
To find the *x*-intercept of a line – set the equation by putting $y = 0$ and solve for *x*.
For Example: In the *xy*-plane, what is the *x*-intercept of a line described by the equation $2 = 5x - y$?
Solution: Set the equation by putting $y = 0$ $\Rightarrow 2 = 5x - y$
$\Rightarrow 2 = 5x - 0$
$\Rightarrow x = 2/5$

$\Rightarrow$ *x*-intercept = 2/5

FINDING WHICH QUADRANTS A GIVEN LINE PASSES THROUGH:

Sometimes you may be asked to determine which quadrants a given line passes through. It's simple, just find any two points and then plot them on the *xy*-coordinate plane and connect them. You'll clearly be able to see the position of the line in the *xy*-coordinate plane, and hence the quadrants it passes through.

For Example: In the *xy*-coordinate plane, which quadrants does the line $2x - y = -5$ passes through?
Solution: Rewrite the equation in general form $\Rightarrow y = mx + b$
$\Rightarrow 2x - y = -5$
$\Rightarrow y = 2x + 5$
Find the *x*-intercept by putting $y = 0$ $\Rightarrow y = 2x + 5$
$\Rightarrow 0 = 2x + 5$
$\Rightarrow 2x = -5$
$\Rightarrow x = -2.5$
One of the points on the line is (–2.5, 0) $\Rightarrow$ Point *A*
Find the *y*-intercept by putting $x = 0$ $\Rightarrow y = 2x + 5$
$\Rightarrow y = 2(0) + 5$
$\Rightarrow y = 5$
One of the other points on the line is (0, 5) $\Rightarrow$ Point *B*
Now, we have two points that are on the line $\Rightarrow$ (–2.5, 0) and (0, 5)
Finally, plot these two points on the *xy*-coordinate plane and connect them to form the line of the equation as shown below.

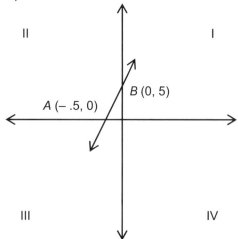

As can be clearly seen in the figure above, the line passes through Quadrants I, II, and III.

7.6: SLOPE OF LINE:

7.6.1: FINDING SLOPES:

The **"slope"** of a line is a measurement that indicates how steeply a line climbs or falls as it moves from left to right. The slope of a line is defined as the **rise** over the **run**, that is, the amount that the line rises vertically over the amount that the line runs horizontally.

EZ STEP-BY-STEP METHOD: Apply the following step(s) to find the slope of any given line:

STEP 1: Pick any two points on the line A (x_1, y_1) and B (x_2, y_2) that lie on the line.

STEP 2: Next, find the Rise and Run:

  Rise: The amount that the line rises vertically can be found by taking the difference between the y-coordinates, i.e., $y_1 - y_2$;

  Run: The amount that the line runs horizontally can be found by taking the difference between the x-coordinates, i.e., $x_1 - x_2$.

STEP 3: Finally, divide the Rise (difference of y-coordinate) by the Run (difference of x-coordinates).

Therefore, for any two given points on the line, the slope is defined to be the ratio of the difference in the y-coordinates to the difference in the x-coordinates.

The slope of a line can be determined from any two pairs of (x, y) coordinates. The slope of any given line with any two coordinates $\Rightarrow$ A (x_1, y_1) and B (x_2, y_2) that lie on the same line is calculated by the following formula:

$$\text{SLOPE} \Rightarrow \frac{rise}{run} = \frac{change\ in\ y}{change\ in\ x} = \frac{difference\ in\ y - coordinates}{difference\ in\ x - coordinates} = \frac{y_1 - y_2}{x_1 - x_2} \text{ or } \frac{y_2 - y_1}{x_2 - x_1}$$

EZ NOTE: You can subtract either pair from the other. While using the distance formula, it doesn't matter which coordinate point you choose as (x_1, y_1) and which one you choose as (x_2, y_2) as long as you are consistent with what you pick.

EZ CAUTION: Be careful to subtract corresponding values. For instance, do not subtract y_1 from y_2 and then subtract x_2 from x_1, or do not subtract y_2 from y_1 and then subtract x_1 from x_2.

For Example: What is the slope of the line that contains the points (7, 2) and (9, 7)?
Solution: Rise $\Rightarrow$ the line rises vertically from 2 to 7. This distance can be found by subtracting the y-coordinates: $7 - 2 = 5$. Thus, the line rises 5 units.
  Run $\Rightarrow$ the line runs horizontally from 7 to 9. This distance can be found by subtracting the x-coordinates: $9 - 7 = 2$. Thus, the line runs 2 units.

  $$\text{Slope} \Rightarrow \frac{rise}{run} = \frac{y_1 - y_2}{x_1 - x_2} = \frac{7 - 2}{9 - 7} = \frac{5}{2}$$

7.6.2: TYPES OF SLOPES:

The slope or **"steepness"** of a line is the change in y-values in relation to the change in corresponding x-values. Therefore, slope can define many things, such as, whether a line is diagonal, horizontal, or vertical and to what degree. Following are the four types of slopes that a line can have:

(A) POSITIVE UPWARD SLOPE: A positive slope (slants) **"rises upwards"** from left to right.
   $\Rightarrow$ The slope of any line that goes up as you move from left to right is positive.
   $\Rightarrow$ A line sloping upward from left to right has a positive slope (m).
   Positive Slopes and 45° angle:
      $\Rightarrow$ A line with a slope of 1, slopes upward from left to right at a 45° angle in relation to the x-axis.
      $(y_2 - y_1) = (x_2 - x_1)$
      $\Rightarrow$ A line with a fractional slope between 0 and 1 (such as, 0.2), slopes upward from left to right but at less than a 45° angle in relation to the x-axis.
      $\Rightarrow$ A line with a slope greater than 1 (such as, 2), slopes upward from left to right but at more than a 45° angle in relation to the x-axis.

(B) NEGATIVE DOWNWARD SLOPE: A negative slope (slants) *"falls downwards"* from left to right.
⇒ The slope of any line that goes down as you move from left to right is negative.
⇒ A line sloping downward from left to right has a negative slope (m).
Negative Slopes and 45° angle:
    ⇒ A line with a slope of –1, slopes downward from left to right at a 45° angle in relation to the x-axis.
    $(y_2 - y_1) = -(x_2 - x_1)$
    ⇒ A line with a fractional slope between 0 and –1 (such as, –0.2), slopes downward from left to right but at less then a 45° angle in relation to the x-axis.
    ⇒ A line with a slope less than –1 (such as, –2), slopes downward from left to right but at more than a 45° angle in relation to the x-axis.

(C) ZERO SLOPE: A zero slope is a *"straight horizontal line"*.
⇒ The slope of any horizontal straight line is zero. ($m = 0$ and $mx = 0 \Rightarrow y = b$)

Since there is no "rise" $\Rightarrow m = \dfrac{y_1 - y_2}{x_1 - x_2} = \dfrac{0}{x_1 - x_2} = 0$ (by definition, any fraction with a zero in the numerator is 0)

(D) UNDEFINED SLOPE: An undefined slope is a *"straight vertical line,"* also called *"no slope"*.
⇒ The slope of any vertical straight line is either undefined or indeterminate (the fraction's denominator is 0, so the m-term in the equation is ignored).
⇒ $x = k$, where k is the x-intercept.

Since there is no "run" $\Rightarrow m = \dfrac{y_1 - y_2}{x_1 - x_2} = \dfrac{y_1 - y_2}{0} =$ undefined (by definition, any fraction with a zero in the denominator is undefined)

Note: Vertical lines do not have slopes and they do not represent a function.

EZ TIP: Think of a slope as a running track that goes from left to right. If you ran along a line with a positive slope, you would run up. If you ran along a line with a negative slope, you would run down. If you ran along a zero slope, you would run straight across horizontally. If you ran along an undefined slope, you would run straight down vertically.

SLOPE AND ITS STEEPNESS:

Line's steepness can be used to determine its magnitude:
    ⇒ The steeper the line, the greater the slope; the flatter the line, the smaller the slope
    ⇒ An extremely positive slope is larger than a moderately positive slope
    ⇒ An extremely negative slope is smaller than a moderately negative slope
In the figure given below:
    ⇒ Lines a & b have positive slopes; Lines c & d have negative slopes; Line e has a 0 slope; Line f has an undefined slope.
    ⇒ Also, since line a is steeper than line b, slope of line a > slope of line b
    ⇒ Similarly, since line c is steeper than line d, slope of line c > slope of line d
    ⇒ Line b has a slope of +1 because it slopes upward at 45° as you move from left to right
    ⇒ Line d has a slope of –1 because it slopes downward at 45° as you move from left to right

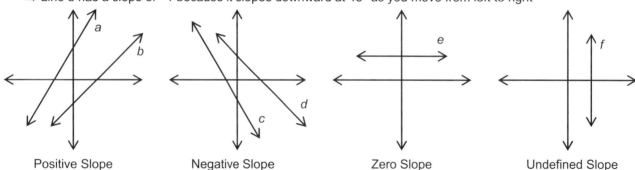

| Positive Slope | Negative Slope | Zero Slope | Undefined Slope |

7.6.3: SLOPE-INTERCEPT EQUATION:

Slope can also be explained by using the linear equation. Any straight line in the standard *xy*-coordinate plane can be defined/described by the equation of a straight line in the form: **y = mx + b**

Where: *y* and *x* = are the infinite number of coordinated (*x, y*) pairs that fall on that line.

(*x* and *y* are the coordinates of any point on the line)

Any (*x, y*) pair defining a point on the line can substitute for the variables *x* and *y*.

b   = the constant term *b* is the *y*-intercept of the line, or the value of *y* when *x* = 0 (the point at which the line intersects the *y*-axis)

m   = the *m*, the coefficient of *x* is the slope of the line = rise/run

For instance, a slope of 5 means that the line rises 5 steps for every 1 step it makes to the right.

Note that not all line equations are written in the slope-intercept form $y = mx + b$. In such cases, rewrite the equation so that it is expressed in the correct slope-intercept form by manipulation.

For Example: What is the slope-intercept form for a line with the equation: $10x + 5y = 25$?

Solution: General Equation $\Rightarrow y = mx + b$ [Write the general slope-intercept equation]

$\Rightarrow 10x + 5y = 25$ [Write the given equation]

$\Rightarrow 5y = 25 - 10x$ [Subtract 10x from both sides]

$\Rightarrow y = 5 - 2x$ [Divide the whole equation by 5]

$\Rightarrow y = -2x + 5$ [Rearrange the terms]

EQUATION OF HORIZONTAL AND VERTICAL LINES:

Horizontal and vertical lines are not expressed in the usual slope-intercept form: $y = mx + b$. Instead, they are expressed as simple, one-variable linear equations.

HORIZONTAL LINES: Horizontal lines are expressed in the form: y = some real number; such as, $y = 2$ or $y = -5$

All points on a horizontal line have the same y-coordinate $\Rightarrow$ i.e., all the points that are on any line parallel to *x*-axis have the same *y*-coordinate; this is why its equation is defined only by *y*.

For instance: In the diagram given below, the horizontal line $y = 2$ is expressed by a line parallel to the *x*-axis.

VERTICAL LINES: Vertical lines are expressed in the form: x = some number; such as, $x = 2$ or $x = -5$

All points on a vertical line have the same x-coordinate $\Rightarrow$ i.e., all the points that are on any line parallel to *y*-axis have the same *x*-coordinate; that is why its equation is defined only by *x*.

For instance: In the diagram given below, the vertical line $x = 5$ is expressed by a line parallel to the *y*-axis.

EZ NOTE: All the points that lie on a line parallel to one of the axes has the same *x*-coordinate or *y*-coordinate.

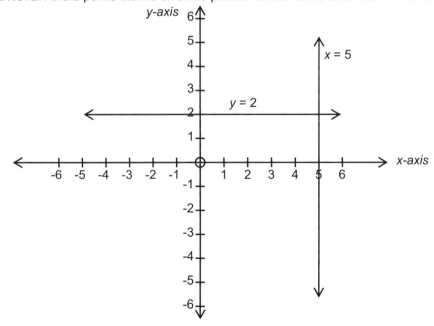

7.6.4: SLOPES OF PARALLEL LINES & PERPENDICULAR LINES:

Following are the important facts about parallel and perpendicular lines, and the relationship between their slopes:

FACT #1:   Two or more lines in the xy-coordinate plane are exactly parallel when their slopes are equal.
⇒ Slopes of parallel lines are always the same, i.e., the same m-term in the general equation.
If one line has a slope of m, any line parallel to it will also have the same slope of m.
For instance, if a line has a slope of 2/5, then any line parallel to it will also have the same slope of 2/5.

For Example: In the xy-plane, what is the slope of a line L, that is parallel to the line that contains (2, 8) and (7, 6)?

Solution: Slope of Line $L \Rightarrow \dfrac{y_1 - y_2}{x_1 - x_2} = \dfrac{6 - 8}{7 - 2} = -\dfrac{2}{5}$

Slope of the line parallel to line L is the same slope $\Rightarrow -\dfrac{2}{5}$

FACT #2:   If two lines are perpendicular and neither line is vertical (or horizontal), then the slope of one line is the negative reciprocal of the slope of the other line. The slopes of perpendicular lines are always the opposite reciprocal of each other.
Two lines in the xy-coordinate plane are exactly perpendicular when the product of their slopes is −1.
⇒ Since perpendicular lines have negative inverse slopes – flip the fraction and change the sign.
If one line has a slope of m, then any line perpendicular to it will have the slope of $-1/m$.
For instance, if a line has a slope of 2/5, then any line perpendicular to it will have a slope of −5/2.

For Example: In the xy-plane, what is the slope of a line L, which is perpendicular to the line that contains (2, 8) and (7, 6)?

Solution: Slope of Line $L \Rightarrow \dfrac{y_1 - y_2}{x_1 - x_2} = \dfrac{6 - 8}{7 - 2} = -\dfrac{2}{5}$

Slope of the line perpendicular to line L is the negative reciprocal of its slope $\Rightarrow$ Negative Reciprocal of $-\dfrac{2}{5} = \dfrac{5}{2}$

In the figure given below: Since Line p ‖ Line q ⇒ Slope of p = Slope of q
Since Line p & $q \perp$ Line $r \Rightarrow$ Slope of p & q = Negative Reciprocal of Slope of r
⇒ Slope of Line p × Slope of Line r = −1

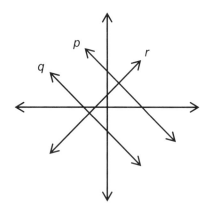

7.7: APPLICATIONS OF COORDINATE GEOMETRY:

7.7.1: FINDING SLOPE & Y-INTERCEPT OF LINE FROM ITS EQUATION:

To determine the slope and y-intercept of a line, given the equation of the line:
First: Put the equation in the standard form $y = mx + b$.
Next: Identify the m-term and b-term.

For Example:	In the xy-plane, what is the slope and y-intercept of a line described by the equation $2 = 5x - y$?
Solution:	General Equation	$\Rightarrow y = mx + b$	[Write the general slope-intercept equation]
		$\Rightarrow 2 = 5x - y$	[Write the given equation]
		$\Rightarrow y = 5x - 2$	[Rewrite the given equation in the general form]
	Value of Slope	$\Rightarrow m = 5$	
	Value of y-intercept	$\Rightarrow b = -2$	

7.7.2: FINDING EQUATION OF LINE FROM ITS SLOPE & ONE POINT:

To determine the equation of a line in general form, given the slope (m) and coordinates of at least one point (x_1, y_1) on the line:

METHOD #1: First: Find the y-intercept (b) by substituting the slope and the coordinates in the general equation.
            Next: Find the equation of the line by substituting the slope and y-intercept in the general equation.

METHOD #2: Apply the formula $\Rightarrow y - y_1 = m(x - x_1)$ [Where m is the given slope & (x_1, y_1) is the given coordinate]

For Example:	In the xy-pane, what is the equation of the line with slope 2, if the line contains the point (-1, 5)?
Solution:	Slope of Line	$\Rightarrow m = 2$	[Given]
	One coordinate	$\Rightarrow (x, y) = (-1, 5)$	[Given]
	General Equation	$\Rightarrow y = mx + b$	[Write the general slope-intercept equation]
		$\Rightarrow 5 = 2(-1) + b$	[Substitute the given coordinate and slope]
		$\Rightarrow 5 = -2 + b$	[Simplify the equation]
		$\Rightarrow b = 7$ (y-intercept)	[Add 2 to both sides]
	Equation of Line	$\Rightarrow y = mx + b$	[Write the general slope-intercept equation]
		$\Rightarrow y = 2x + 7$	[Substitute the slope and y-intercept]
	Alternate Solution:	$\Rightarrow y - y_1 = m(x - x_1)$	[Write the appropriate formula]
		$\Rightarrow y - 5 = 2[x - (-1)]$	[Substitute the known values]
		$\Rightarrow y - 5 = 2(x + 1)$	[Simplify within brackets]
		$\Rightarrow y - 5 = 2x + 2$	[Apply distributive property]
		$\Rightarrow y = 2x + 7$	[Add 5 to both sides]

7.7.3: FINDING Y-INTERCEPT OF LINE PASSING THROUGH TWO POINTS:

To determine the y-intercept of a line, given two points on the line:
First: Find the slope (m) of the line by using the slope formula from the two given coordinates.
Next: Find the y-intercept by substituting the slope and one of the given coordinates in the general equation.

For Example:	In the xy-plane, at what point along the y-axis does the line passing through points (5, 2) and (6, 7) intersects the y-axis?
Solution:	Two coordinates	$\Rightarrow (5, 2)$ and $(6, 7)$	[Given]
	Slope of Line	$\Rightarrow m = \dfrac{y_1 - y_2}{x_1 - x_2}$	[Write the appropriate formula]
		$\Rightarrow m = \dfrac{7 - 2}{6 - 5} = 5$	[Substitute the known values and simplify]
	General Equation	$\Rightarrow y = mx + b$	[Write the general slope-intercept equation]
		$\Rightarrow 7 = 5(6) + b$	[Substitute one of the given coordinate and slope]
		$\Rightarrow 7 = 30 + b$	[Simplify the equation]
		$\Rightarrow b = -23$ (y-intercept)	[Subtract 30 from both sides]
	The line intersect the y-axis at -23		

7.7.4: FINDING THE EQUATION OF LINE PASSING THROUGH TWO POINTS:

To determine the equation of a line in the general form:
First: Find the slope (m) of the line by using the slope formula.
Next: Find the y-intercept (b) of the line by substituting either (x, y) given coordinate pair in the general equation.
Finally: Find the equation of the line by plugging-in the value of m & b in general equation.

For Example: In the xy-plane, find the equation of the line containing the points (5, 2) and (6, 7).

Solution: Slope of the Line $\Rightarrow m = \dfrac{y_1 - y_2}{x_1 - x_2}$ [Write the appropriate formula]

$\Rightarrow \dfrac{7-2}{6-5} = 5$ [Substitute the known values and simplify]

General Equation $\Rightarrow y = mx + b$ [Write the general slope-intercept equation]
$\Rightarrow 2 = 5(5) + b$ [Substitute the given coordinate and slope]
$\Rightarrow 2 = 25 + b$ [Simplify the equation]
$\Rightarrow b = -23$ [Subtract 25 from both sides]

Equation of Line $\Rightarrow y = mx + b$ [Write the general slope-intercept equation]
$\Rightarrow y = 5x - 23$ [Substitute $m = 5$ and $b = -23$]

ALTERNATE METHOD: Alternately, you can also find the equation of a line from any two given points by applying the following process:

Given any two points (x_1, y_1) and (x_2, y_2) where $x_1 \neq x_2$, the equation of the line passing through these two points can also be found by applying the definition of slope $\Rightarrow$ Slope = $m = \dfrac{y_1 - y_2}{x_1 - x_2}$

Use a point that is known to be on the line, let's say (x_2, y_2), then any point (x, y) on the line must satisfy:

$\Rightarrow \dfrac{y - y_2}{x - x_2} = m$

$\Rightarrow y - y_2 = m(x - x_2)$

Note: Using (x_1, y_1) as the known point would result in an equivalent equation.

Now, let's solve the same example solved above:

For Example: In the xy-plane, find the equation of the line containing the points (5, 2) and (6, 7).

Solution: Slope of Line $\Rightarrow \dfrac{y_1 - y_2}{x_1 - x_2}$ [Write the appropriate formula]

$\Rightarrow \dfrac{7-2}{6-5} = 5$ [Substitute the known values and simplify]

Use either one of the given points, which must satisfy the following:

(5, 2)	(6, 7)	
$\Rightarrow y - y_2 = m(x - x_2)$	$\Rightarrow y - y_2 = m(x - x_2)$	[Write the appropriate formula]
$\Rightarrow y - 2 = 5(x - 5)$	$\Rightarrow y - 7 = 5(x - 6)$	[Substitute the known values]
$\Rightarrow y - 2 = 5x - 25$	$\Rightarrow y - 7 = 5x - 30$	[Apply distributive property]
$\Rightarrow y = 5x - 23$	$\Rightarrow y = 5x - 23$	[solve for y]

Note: both points yield the same equation.

7.7.5: FINDING THE EQUATION OF LINE FROM ONE POINT AND Y-INTERCEPT:

To determine the equation of a line from one given coordinate pair and y-intercept:
First: Find the value of another coordinate point from the y-intercept.
Next: Find the slope of the line by using the two coordinate points in the slope formula.
Finally: Find the equation of the line by plugging-in the value of m & b in general equation
Note: Sometimes you may be given only one point on the line, and also the y-intercept. Now, this is really the same thing as giving you two points on the line, because the y-intercept is also a point or an ordered pair with zero as the x-coordinate. For instance, a y-intercept of 5 is the same as the ordered pair (0, 5).

For Example: In the xy-plane, find the equation of the line containing the point (5, 2) and with a y-intercept of –23.

Solution:

One Coordinate Pair	$\Rightarrow$ (5, 2)	[Given]
Value of y-intercept	$\Rightarrow$ –23	[Given]
Other Coordinate Pair	$\Rightarrow$ (0, –23)	[The other coordinate pair is (0, b)]
Slope of Line	$\Rightarrow m = \dfrac{y_1 - y_2}{x_1 - x_2}$	[Write the appropriate formula]
	$\Rightarrow \dfrac{-23 - 2}{0 - 5} = 5$	[Substitute the known values and simplify]
Equation of Line	$\Rightarrow y = mx + b$	[Write the general slope-intercept equation]
	$\Rightarrow y = 5x - 23$	[Substitute $m = 5$ and $b = -23$]

7.7.6: FINDING POINT-OF-INTERSECTION OF TWO LINES:

To determine the point at which two non-parallel lines intersect on the coordinate plane:

First: Find the slope of each line by using the coordinate pairs in the slope formula.

Next: Find the equation of each line by substituting one of the coordinates and slope in the general equation

Finally: Find the point-of-intersection of the lines by equating the equation of both lines and solve for x and y by substitution method.

For Example: In the xy-plane, the (x, y) pairs (2, 5) and (6, 9) define line A, and the (x, y) pairs (6, 1) and (8, 5) define another line B. At which (x, y) points do the two lines intersect?

Solution:

Slope of Line A	$\Rightarrow \dfrac{y_1 - y_2}{x_1 - x_2}$	[Write the appropriate formula]
	$\Rightarrow \dfrac{9 - 5}{6 - 2} = 1$	[Substitute the known values and simplify]
General Equation	$\Rightarrow y = mx + b$	[Write the general slope-intercept equation]
	$\Rightarrow 5 = 1(2) + b$	[Substitute the (x, y) pair (2, 5) and $m = 1$]
	$\Rightarrow 5 = 2 + b$	[Simplify the equation]
	$\Rightarrow b = 3$ (y-intercept)	[Subtract 2 from both sides]
Equation for Line A	$\Rightarrow y = mx + b$	[Write the general slope-intercept equation]
	$\Rightarrow y = x + 3$	[Substitute the $m = 1$ and $b = 3$]
Slope of Line B	$\Rightarrow \dfrac{y_1 - y_2}{x_1 - x_2}$	[Write the appropriate formula]
	$\Rightarrow \dfrac{5 - 1}{8 - 6} = 2$	[Substitute the known values and simplify]
General Equation	$\Rightarrow y = mx + b$	[Write the general slope-intercept equation]
	$\Rightarrow 1 = 2(6) + b$	[Substitute the (x, y) pair (6, 1) and $m = 2$]
	$\Rightarrow 1 = 12 + b$	[Simplify the equation]
	$\Rightarrow b = -11$ (y-intercept)	[Subtract 12 from both sides]
Equation for Line B	$\Rightarrow y = mx + b$	[Write the general slope-intercept equation]
	$\Rightarrow y = 2x - 11$	[Substitute the $m = 2$ and $b = -11$]
Equate equations of Line A & B	$\Rightarrow$ Equation for Line A = Equation for Line B	
	$\Rightarrow x + 3 = 2x - 11$	[Write the equation of each line]
	$\Rightarrow x = 14$	[Isolate x on left side]
Substitute x value in 1st equation	$\Rightarrow y = x + 3$	[Rewrite the equation of Line A]
	$\Rightarrow y = 14 + 3$	[Substitute $x = 14$]
	$\Rightarrow y = 17$	[Do the addition]
Point of intersection	$\Rightarrow$ (14, 17)	

7.7.7: FINDING EQUATION OF PERPENDICULAR BISECTORS:

The perpendicular bisector of a line segment forms a right (90°) angle with the given segment and divides the segment exactly in half. The key to solving perpendicular bisector problems is to keep in mind that the perpendicular bisector has the negative inverse slope of the line segment it bisects.

To find the equation a perpendicular bisector:
First: Find the slope of the line by using the slope formula.
Second: Find the slope of the perpendicular bisector.
Third: Find the midpoint of the given line, which is also a point on the perpendicular bisector.
Fourth: Find the y-intercept of the perpendicular bisector by substituting the midpoint and slope in the general equation.
Fifth: Find the equation of the perpendicular bisector by substituting the slope and y-intercept in the general equation.

For Example: What is the equation of the line that is the perpendicular bisector of the line segment connecting points (5, 8) and (9, 6) in the xy-plane?

Solution: Slope of Line $\Rightarrow \dfrac{y_1 - y_2}{x_1 - x_2}$ [Write the appropriate formula]

$\Rightarrow \dfrac{6 - 8}{9 - 5} = -\frac{1}{2}$ [Substitute the known values and simplify]

Slope of Perpendicular Bisector = Negative Reciprocal of $-\frac{1}{2} \Rightarrow 2$
The perpendicular bisector passes through the midpoint of the given line. Therefore, if we find the midpoint of the given line, we will also have found a point on the perpendicular bisector.

$MP \Rightarrow \left(\dfrac{x_1 + x_2}{2}, \dfrac{y_1 + y_2}{2} \right)$ [Write the appropriate formula]

$\Rightarrow [(5 + 9) \div 2$, $(8 + 6) \div 2]$ [Substitute the known values]
$\Rightarrow [14 \div 2$, $14 \div 2]$ [Solve within parentheses]
$\Rightarrow (7$, $7)$ [Do the division]
General Equation $\Rightarrow y = mx + b$ [Write the general slope-intercept equation]
$\Rightarrow 7 = 2(7) + b$ [Substitute (7, 7) and m = 2 into the general equation]
$\Rightarrow 7 = 14 + b$ [Simplify the equation]
$\Rightarrow b = -7$ (y-intercept)   [Subtract 14 from both sides]
Equation for Line $\Rightarrow y = mx + b$ [Write the general slope-intercept equation]
$\Rightarrow y = 2x - 7$ [Substitute the slope and y-intercept]
Equation of the perpendicular bisector $\Rightarrow y = 2x - 7$

7.8: AREA & PERIMETER IN COORDINATE PLANE:

Coordinate geometry can often be used to solve for area and perimeter of some geometric figures that may not appear to involve coordinate geometry.

Example #1:   If $A(1, 1)$ and $B(7, 9)$ are the endpoints of one side of square $ABCD$, what is the area and perimeter of the square?

Solution: The area of square $ABCD = s^2$ where $s = AB = BC = CD = AD$

$$d \Rightarrow \sqrt{(x_1 - x_2)^2 + (y_1 - y_2)^2} = \sqrt{(1-7)^2 + (1-9)^2} = \sqrt{(-6)^2 + (-8)^2} = \sqrt{(36)+(64)} = \sqrt{100} = 10$$

Area of Square $ABCD$	$\Rightarrow s^2$	[Write the appropriate formula]
	$\Rightarrow 10^2$	[Substitute the known values]
	$\Rightarrow 100$	[Solve the exponent]
Perimeter of Square $ABCD$	$\Rightarrow 4s$	[Write the appropriate formula]
	$\Rightarrow 4 \times 10$	[Substitute the known values]
	$\Rightarrow 40$	[Do the multiplication]

Example #2:   If the coordinate of the rectangle $ABCD$ are $A(-2, 7)$, $B(-2, 1)$, $C(8, 1)$, and $D(8, 7)$, what is the area and perimeter of the rectangle?

Solution: Since the diagram is not provided in the question, let's get oriented by drawing the following diagram:

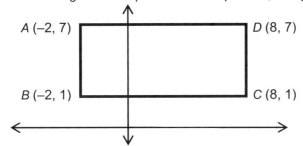

Length of $ABCD$	$\Rightarrow BC = 8 - (-2) = 10$	[B & C lie on the same horizontal line
Width of $ABCD$	$\Rightarrow AB = 7 - 1 = 6$	[A & B lie on the same vertical line
Area of Rectangle $ABCD$	$\Rightarrow$ Length × Width	[Write the appropriate formula]
	$\Rightarrow 10 \times 6$	[Substitute the known values]
	$\Rightarrow 60$	[Do the multiplication]
Perimeter of Rectangle $ABCD$	$\Rightarrow 2(L + W)$	[Write the appropriate formula]
	$\Rightarrow 2(10 + 6)$	[Substitute the known values]
	$\Rightarrow 2(16)$	[Solve within parentheses]
	$\Rightarrow 32$	[Do the multiplication]

PRACTICE EXERCISE – QUESTIONS AND ANSWERS WITH EXPLANATIONS: COORDINATE GEOMETRY:

Question #1: Find the distance between point (2, 1) and (8, 9)

Solution:
$$d \Rightarrow \sqrt{(x_1 - x_2)^2 + (y_1 - y_2)^2}$$
$$\Rightarrow \sqrt{(2-8)^2 + (1-9)^2} = \sqrt{(-6)^2 + (-8)^2} = \sqrt{36 + 64} = \sqrt{100} = 10$$

Question #2: If point A has coordinates (2, 1) and point B has coordinates (x, 9), and the distance between points A and B is 10 units, what is the value of x?

Solution:

$d \Rightarrow AB \Rightarrow \sqrt{(x_1 - x_2)^2 + (y_1 - y_2)^2} = 10$ [Equate the distance formula with the given distance]

$\Rightarrow \sqrt{(2-x)^2 + (1-9)^2} = 10$ [Substitute the known values]

$\Rightarrow \sqrt{(2-x)^2 + (-8)^2} = 10$ [Simplify within parentheses]

$\Rightarrow \sqrt{4 + x^2 - 4x + 64} = 10$ [Solve the exponents]

$\Rightarrow x^2 - 4x + 68 = 100$ [Square both sides]

$\Rightarrow x^2 - 4x - 32 = 0$ [Subtract 100 from both sides]

$\Rightarrow (x - 8)(x + 4) = 0$ [Factor the trinomial into two binomials]

$\Rightarrow x - 8 = 0$ or $x + 4 = 0$ [Equate each factor equal to zero]

$\Rightarrow x = 8 \qquad x = -4$ [Solve for both value of x]

Question #3: Find the midpoint between point (2, 1) and (8, 9)

Solution:
$$MP \Rightarrow \left(\frac{x_1 + x_2}{2}, \frac{y_1 + y_2}{2} \right)$$
$$\Rightarrow \left(\frac{2+8}{2}, \frac{1+9}{2} \right) = \left(\frac{10}{2}, \frac{10}{2} \right) = (5, 5)$$

Question #4: If the midpoint of a line segment is (7, 9) and one of the endpoint is (1, 2), what are coordinates of the other endpoint?

Solution:

$\Rightarrow MP \Rightarrow \left(\dfrac{x_1 + x_2}{2}, \dfrac{y_1 + y_2}{2} \right) = (7, 9)$ [Write the appropriate formula]

$\Rightarrow \dfrac{x_1 + x_2}{2} = 7 \qquad \Rightarrow \dfrac{y_1 + y_2}{2} = 9$ [Set up the two equations]

$\Rightarrow \dfrac{1 + x_2}{2} = 7 \qquad \Rightarrow \dfrac{2 + y_2}{2} = 9$ [Substitute the given values]

$\Rightarrow 1 + x_2 = 14 \qquad \Rightarrow 2 + y_2 = 18$ [Cross-multiply each equation]

$\Rightarrow x_2 = 13 \qquad \Rightarrow y_2 = 16$ [Isolate the variable in each equation]

Coordinates of the other endpoint $\Rightarrow$ (13, 16)

Question #5: What is the slope of the line that contains the points (11, 12) and (6, 5)?

Solution:
Slope $\Rightarrow \dfrac{y_1 - y_2}{x_1 - x_2}$
$$\Rightarrow \frac{12 - 5}{11 - 6} = \frac{7}{5}$$

Question #6: What is the slope of the line that contains the points (16, 8) and (9, 17)?

Solution:
Slope $\Rightarrow \dfrac{y_1 - y_2}{x_1 - x_2}$

$$\Rightarrow \frac{8-17}{16-9} = -\frac{9}{7}$$

Question #7: What is the slope of the line that contains the points (19, 7) and (12, 7)?

Solution: Slope $\Rightarrow \dfrac{y_1 - y_2}{x_1 - x_2}$

$$\Rightarrow \frac{7-7}{19-12} = \frac{0}{7} = 0$$

Question #8: What is the slope of the line that contains the points (7, 19) and (7, 12)?

Solution: Slope $\Rightarrow \dfrac{y_1 - y_2}{x_1 - x_2}$

$$\Rightarrow \frac{19-12}{7-7} = \frac{7}{0} = \text{undefined}$$

Question #9: In the xy-plane, what is the slope of a line L, that is parallel to the line that contains (9, 6) and (2, 8)?

Solution: Slope of Line $L \Rightarrow \dfrac{y_1 - y_2}{x_1 - x_2} \Rightarrow \dfrac{6-8}{9-2} = -\dfrac{2}{7}$

Slope of the line parallel to line L is the same slope $\Rightarrow -\dfrac{2}{7}$

Question #10: In the xy-plane, what is the slope of a line L, that is perpendicular to the line that contains (9, 2) and (2, 7)?

Solution: Slope of Line $L \Rightarrow \dfrac{y_1 - y_2}{x_1 - x_2} \Rightarrow \dfrac{2-7}{9-2} = -\dfrac{5}{7}$

Slope of line perpendicular to line L is the negative reciprocal of its slope $\Rightarrow$ –ve reciprocal of $-\dfrac{5}{7} = \dfrac{7}{5}$

Question #11: In the xy-plane, if lines P and Q intersect at point (5, 2) and lines Q and R intersect at point (12, 11), what is the slope of line Q?

Solution: If line P and Q intersect at point (5, 2), and line Q and R intersect at point (12, 11), this means that both of the given points lie on line Q.

Slope of Line $Q \Rightarrow \dfrac{y_1 - y_2}{x_1 - x_2} = \dfrac{11-2}{12-5} = \dfrac{9}{7}$

Question #12: In the xy-plane, what is the slope of a line described by the equation $9 = 7x - y$?

Solution:
General Equation	$\Rightarrow y = mx + b$	[Write the general slope-intercept equation]
	$\Rightarrow 9 = 7x - y$	[Write the given equation]
	$\Rightarrow y = 7x - 9$	[Rewrite the given equation in the general form]
Value of Slope	$\Rightarrow m = 7$	
Value of y-intercept	$\Rightarrow b = -9$	

Question #13: In the xy-pane, what is the equation of the line with slope 5, if the line contains the point (–2, 7)?

Solution:
Slope of Line	$\Rightarrow m = 5$	[Given]
One coordinate	$\Rightarrow (x, y) = (-2, 7)$	[Given]
General Equation	$\Rightarrow y = mx + b$	[Write the general slope-intercept equation]
	$\Rightarrow 7 = 5(-2) + b$	[Substitute the given coordinate and slope]
	$\Rightarrow 7 = -10 + b$	[Simplify the equation]
	$\Rightarrow b = 17$ (y-intercept)	[Add 10 to both sides]
Equation for Line	$\Rightarrow y = mx + b$	[Write the general slope-intercept equation]
	$\Rightarrow y = 5x + 17$	[Substitute the slope and y-intercept]
Alternate Solution:	$\Rightarrow y - y_1 = m(x - x_1)$	[Write the appropriate formula]
	$\Rightarrow y - 7 = 5[x - (-2)]$	[Substitute the known values]

$\Rightarrow y - 7 = 5(x + 2)$ [Simplify within brackets]
$\Rightarrow y - 7 = 5x + 10$ [Apply distributive property]
$\Rightarrow y = 5x + 17$ [Add 7 to both sides]

Question #14: In the *xy*-plane, at what point along the *y*-axis does the line passing through points (6, 8) and (5, 7) intersect the *y*-axis?

Solution:
Two coordinates	$\Rightarrow (6, 8)$ and $(5, 7)$	[Given]
Slope of Line	$\Rightarrow m = \dfrac{y_1 - y_2}{x_1 - x_2}$	[Write the appropriate formula]
	$\Rightarrow \dfrac{8-7}{6-5} = 1$	[Substitute the known values and simplify]
General Equation	$\Rightarrow y = mx + b$	[Write the general slope-intercept equation]
	$\Rightarrow 8 = 1(6) + b$	[Substitute one of the given coordinate and slope]
	$\Rightarrow 8 = 6 + b$	[Simplify the equation]
	$\Rightarrow b = 2$ (*y*-intercept)	[Subtract 6 from both sides]

Line intersects the *y*-axis at 2.

Question #15: In the *xy*-plane, at what point along the *y*-axis does the line passing through points (6, 8) and (5, 7) intersect the *y*-axis?

Solution:
Slope of the Line	$\Rightarrow m = \dfrac{y_1 - y_2}{x_1 - x_2}$	[Write the appropriate formula]
	$\Rightarrow \dfrac{8-7}{6-5} = 1$	[Substitute the known values and simplify]
General Equation	$\Rightarrow y = mx + b$	[Write the general slope-intercept equation]
	$\Rightarrow 8 = 1(6) + b$	[Substitute the given coordinate and slope]
	$\Rightarrow 8 = 6 + b$	[Simplify the equation]
	$\Rightarrow b = 2$	[Subtract 6 from both sides]
Equation of Line	$\Rightarrow y = mx + b$	[Write the general slope-intercept equation]
	$\Rightarrow y = x + 2$	[Substitute $m = 1$ and $b = 2$]

Question #16: In the *xy*-plane, find the equation of the line containing the point (5, 7) and with a *y*-intercept of 2.

Solution:
One Coordinate Pair	$\Rightarrow (5, 7)$	[Given]
Value of *y*-intercept	$\Rightarrow 2$	[Given]
Other Coordinate Pair	$\Rightarrow (0, 2)$	[The other coordinate pair is (0, *b*)]
Slope of the Line	$\Rightarrow m = \dfrac{y_1 - y_2}{x_1 - x_2}$	[Write the appropriate formula]
	$\Rightarrow \dfrac{2-7}{0-5} = 1$	[Substitute the known values and simplify]
Equation of Line	$\Rightarrow y = mx + b$	[Write the general slope-intercept equation]
	$\Rightarrow y = x + 2$	[Substitute $m = 1$ and $b = 2$]

Question #17: In the *xy*-plane, the (*x*, *y*) pairs (6, 1) and (2, 5) define line *A*, and the (*x*, *y*) pairs (8, 5) and (6, 9) define another line *B*. At which point do the two lines intersect?

Solution:
Slope of Line *A*	$\Rightarrow \dfrac{y_1 - y_2}{x_1 - x_2}$	[Write the appropriate formula]
	$\Rightarrow \dfrac{1-5}{6-2} = -1$	[Substitute the known values and simplify]
General Equation	$\Rightarrow y = mx + b$	[Write the general slope-intercept equation]
	$\Rightarrow 5 = -1(2) + b$	[Substitute the (*x*, *y*) pair (2, 5) and $m = -1$]
	$\Rightarrow 5 = -2 + b$	[Simplify the equation]
	$\Rightarrow b = 7$ (*y*-intercept)	[Add 2 to both sides]
Equation for Line *A*	$\Rightarrow y = mx + b$	[Write the general slope-intercept equation]
	$\Rightarrow y = -x + 7$	[Substitute the $m = -1$ and $b = 7$]

Slope of Line B	$\Rightarrow \dfrac{y_1 - y_2}{x_1 - x_2}$	[Write the appropriate formula]
	$\Rightarrow \dfrac{5 - 9}{8 - 6} = -2$	[Substitute the known values and simplify]
General Equation	$\Rightarrow y = mx + b$	[Write the general slope-intercept equation]
	$\Rightarrow 9 = -2(6) + b$	[Substitute the (x, y) pair (6, 9) and $m = -2$]
	$\Rightarrow 9 = -12 + b$	[Simplify the equation]
	$\Rightarrow b = 21$ (y-intercept)	[Add 12 to both sides]
Equation for Line B	$\Rightarrow y = mx + b$	[Write the general slope-intercept equation]
	$\Rightarrow y = -2x + 21$	[Substitute the $m = -2$ and $b = 21$]
Equate equations of A & B	$\Rightarrow$ Equation for Line A = Equation for Line B	
	$\Rightarrow -x + 7 = -2x + 11$	[Write the equation of each line]
	$\Rightarrow x = 4$	[Isolate x on left side]
Substitute x value in 1st equation	$\Rightarrow y = -x + 7$	[Rewrite the equation of Line A]
	$\Rightarrow y = -4 + 7$	[Substitute $x = 4$]
	$\Rightarrow y = 3$	[Combine like-terms]

Point of intersection $\Rightarrow$ (4, 3)

Question #18: What is the equation of the line that is the perpendicular bisector of the line segment connecting points (12, 9) and (2, 11) in the xy-plane?

Solution:

Slope of Line	$\Rightarrow \dfrac{y_1 - y_2}{x_1 - x_2}$	[Write the appropriate formula]
	$\Rightarrow \dfrac{9 - 11}{12 - 2} = -\dfrac{1}{5}$	[Substitute the known values and simplify]

Slope of the perpendicular bisector = negative reciprocal of $-1/5 \Rightarrow 5$
The perpendicular bisector passes through the midpoint of the given line. Therefore, if we find the midpoint of the given line, we will also have found a point on the perpendicular bisector.

$MP \Rightarrow \left(\dfrac{x_1 + x_2}{2}, \dfrac{y_1 + y_2}{2} \right)$		[Write the appropriate formula]
$\Rightarrow [(2 + 12) \div 2 \quad , \quad (11 + 9) \div 2]$		[Substitute the known values]
$\Rightarrow (14 \div 2 \quad , \quad 20 \div 2)$		[Solve within parentheses]
$\Rightarrow (7 \quad , \quad 10)$		[Do the division]
General Equation	$\Rightarrow y = mx + b$	[Write the general slope-intercept equation]
	$\Rightarrow 10 = 5(7) + b$	[Substitute (7, 10) and $m = 5$]
	$\Rightarrow 10 = 35 + b$	[Simplify the equation]
	$\Rightarrow b = -25$ (y-intercept)	[Subtract 35 from both sides]
Equation for Line	$\Rightarrow y = mx + b$	[Write the general slope-intercept equation]
	$\Rightarrow y = 5x - 25$	[Substitute the slope and y-intercept]

Equation of the perpendicular bisector $\Rightarrow y = 5x - 25$

Question #19: If A(6, 6) and B(15, 18) are the endpoints of one side of square $ABCD$, what is the area and perimeter of the square?

Solution:

Length of Side	$\Rightarrow \sqrt{(x_1 - x_2)^2 + (y_1 - y_2)^2}$	[Use distance formula to find length]

$\Rightarrow \sqrt{(6 - 15)^2 + (6 - 18)^2} = \sqrt{(-9)^2 + (-12)^2} = \sqrt{(81) + (144)} = \sqrt{225} \Rightarrow 25$

Area of Square $ABCD$	$\Rightarrow s^2 = 15^2 = 225$	[Use area formula to find area]
Perimeter of Square $ABCD$	$\Rightarrow 4s = 4 \times 15 = 60$	[Use perimeter formula to find perimeter]

Question #20: If the coordinate of the rectangle $ABCD$ are A(–5, 7), B(–5, 1), C(15, 1), and D(15, 7), what is the area and perimeter of the rectangle?

Solution: Since the diagram is not provided in the question, let's get oriented by drawing the following diagram:

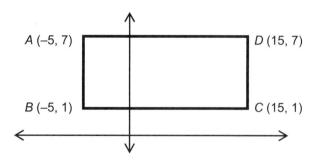

Length of Rectangle $\Rightarrow BC = 15 - (-5) = 20$ [B & C lie on the same horizontal line]
Width of Rectangle $\Rightarrow AB = 7 - 1 = 6$ [A & B lie on the same vertical line]
Area of Rectangle $\Rightarrow L \times W = 20 \times 6 = 120$ [Use area formula to find area]
Perimeter of Rectangle $\Rightarrow 2(L + W) = 2(20+6) = 2(26) = 52$[Use perimeter formula to find perimeter]

PART 8.0: MULTIPLE FIGURES:

TABLE OF CONTENTS:

EZ REFERENCE: -To practice easy-to-medium level questions, please refer to our EZ Practice Basic Workbook.
                        -To practice medium-to-difficult level questions, please refer to our EZ Practice Advanced Workbook.

8.1: BASICS ABOUT MULTIPLE FIGURES:

There will be some problems on your math test that combine and involve several different types of geometric figures. As the name suggests, these types of questions require the use of multiple formulas and multiple concepts in one single question.

These problems essentially test your understanding of various geometric concepts and relationships collectively, not just your ability to memorize a few formulas applicable to specific geometric figures. For instance, the hypotenuse of a right triangle may be the side of a neighboring square or rectangle, or the diameter of a circumscribed circle. You have to keep looking for the relationships between different figures until you find one that leads you to the correct path or answer.

In other words, in a problem that combines figures, you have to look for the relationship between the figures. Look for pieces the figures have in common. For instance, if two figures share a side or an angle, information about that side or angle will probably be the key.

Moreover, as long as you have a clear understanding of lines, angles, triangles, polygons, circles, etc., you shouldn't have much problem dealing with such questions. Like in any geometry question, just remember not to be overwhelmed or bogged down by extraneous and irrelevant information. Break these problems down into their separate parts. Think about what information you need, and then, one by one, apply the concepts you already know to solve the problem.

8.2: IRREGULAR FIGURES:

An *"irregular figure"* is a combination of two or more geometric figures to form a new irregular or complex shape. The most common type of irregular figure questions involve finding the perimeter or area of irregularly shaped regions formed by two or more overlapping figures, often with two or more known regions.

8.2.1: PERIMETER OF IRREGULAR OR COMPLEX FIGURES:

EZ STEP-BY-STEP METHOD: Apply the following step(s) to find the perimeter of an irregular or complex figure:

STEP 1: If the measures of some of its sides are not given, first figure out (deduce) the measures of its missing sides using measures given for the other sides.

STEP 2: Next, add the measures of all the sides.

PERIMETER OF REQUIRED REGION $\Rightarrow$ **Sum of the Measures of All Sides**

For Example: A room has the dimensions shown in the figure given below, find its perimeter.

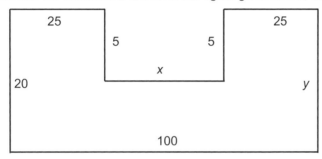

Solution: Length of x $\Rightarrow 100 - 25 - 25 = 50$ [Lengths of opposite sides are equal]
                Length of y $\Rightarrow 20$ [Lengths of opposite sides are equal]
                Perimeter $\Rightarrow$ Add all Sides $= 100 + 20 + 20 + 50 + 25 + 25 + 5 + 5 = 250$ units

8.2.2: AREA OF IRREGULAR OR COMPLEX FIGURES:

EZ STEP-BY-STEP METHOD: Apply the following step(s) to find the area of an irregular or complex figure:

STEP 1: Try dropping lines to break or divide the figure into familiar shapes that you can easily work with, such as – rectangles, squares, and triangles.

STEP 2: If the measures of some of its sides are not given, first figure out (deduce) the measures of its missing sides using measures given for the other sides.

STEP 3: Next, apply the correct area formula of each shape to find their areas separately.

STEP 4: Finally, add them together to find the area of the whole figure.

AREA OF REQUIRED REGION $\Rightarrow$ **Sum of the Area of Each Individual Piece**

For Example: A room has the dimensions shown in the figure given above, find its area. (Use the figure given above)
Solution: Length of x $\Rightarrow 100 - 25 - 25 = 50$ [Lengths of opposite sides are equal]
                Length of y $\Rightarrow 20$ [Lengths of opposite sides are equal]
                Area of Left Rectangle $= 25 \times 5$ $\Rightarrow + \quad 125$
                Area of Right Rectangle $= 25 \times 5$ $\Rightarrow + \quad 125$
                Area of Middle Rectangle $= 100 \times 15$ $\Rightarrow +1,500$
                Total Area of the Figure $\Rightarrow \underline{\ 1,750}$
Alternately: Find the area of the whole rectangle and subtract the small missing rectangle:
                Area of Irregular Figure = Area of Regular Figure – Missing Piece
                Area of Whole Rectangle $= 100 \times 20$ $\Rightarrow 2,000$
                Area of Missing Rectangle $= 50 \times 5$ $\Rightarrow -\ 250$
                Area of the Enclosed Figure $\Rightarrow \underline{1,750}$

8.3: INSCRIBED OR CIRCUMSCRIBED FIGURES:

(I) POLYGON INSCRIBED IN A CIRCLE OR CIRCLE CIRCUMSCRIBED ABOUT A POLYGON:

A polygon is said to be **"inscribed"** in a circle or a circle is **"circumscribed"** about a polygon if each vertex of the polygon is a point that lies on the circle. In other words, the circle passes through all the vertices of the polygon.

For Example: In the figure given below, *PQR* is an inscribed triangle and *ABCD* is an inscribed rectangle in the circle. Or the circle is circumscribed about triangle *PQR* and rectangle *ABCD*.

Vertices *A*, *B*, *C*, *D* of the rectangle, and *P*, *Q*, *R* of the triangle, are all points on the circle.

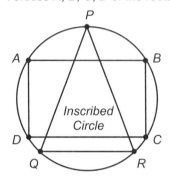

AREA OF INSCRIBED FIGURES:

Case #1: If the Area of Square is given:
For Example: Area of Square $\Rightarrow 100$
$\Rightarrow side^2 = 100$
$\Rightarrow side = 10$

Diagonal of Square $\Rightarrow 10\sqrt{2}$

Diameter of Circle = Diagonal of Square = $10\sqrt{2}$

Radius of Circle $\Rightarrow \frac{1}{2}(10\sqrt{2}) = 5\sqrt{2}$

Area of Circle $\Rightarrow \pi r^2 = \pi(5\sqrt{2})^2 = 50\pi$

Case #2: If the Area of Circle is given:
For Example: Area of Circle $\Rightarrow 50\pi$
$\Rightarrow \pi r^2 = 50\pi$
$\Rightarrow r = 5\sqrt{2}$

Diameter of Circle = $2r = 2(5\sqrt{2}) = 10\sqrt{2}$

Diagonal of Square = Diameter Circle = $10\sqrt{2}$

Side of Square = 10

Area of Square $\Rightarrow s^2 = 10^2 = 100$

(II) CIRCLE INSCRIBED IN A POLYGON OR POLYGON CIRCUMSCRIBED ABOUT A CIRCLE:

A circle is said to be **"inscribed"** in a polygon or a polygon is **"circumscribed"** about a circle if each side of the polygon is tangent to the circle, that is, the circle touches all the sides of the polygon at only one point. This is the same as saying that a polygon is circumscribed about a circle if all the sides of the polygon are tangent to the circle.

For Example: In the figure given below, the circle is inscribed in the square *ABCD*. Or the square *ABCD* is circumscribed about the circle.

Sides *AB*, *BC*, *CD*, *DA* of the square are all tangent to the circle at points *E*, *F*, *G*, *H*.

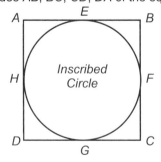

AREA OF CIRCUMSCRIBED FIGURES:

Case #1: If the Area of Square is given:
For Example: Area of Square $\Rightarrow side^2 = 100$
                               $\Rightarrow side = 10$
Diameter of Circle = Side of Square = 10
Radius of Circle = ½d = ½(10) = 5
Area of Circle $\Rightarrow \pi r^2 = \pi(5)^2 = 25\pi$

Case #2: If the Area of Circle is given:
For Example: Area of Circle $\Rightarrow \pi r^2 = 25\pi$
                               $\Rightarrow r = 5$
Diameter of Circle $\Rightarrow 2r = 2(5) = 10$
Side of Square = Diameter of Circle = 10
Area of Square $\Rightarrow s^2 = 10^2 = 100$

IN POLYGONS CIRCUMSCRIBED ABOUT CIRCLES, POINT OF TANGENCY BISECTS LINE SEGMENTS:

In any regular polygon (in which all sides are congruent) that circumscribes a circle, the point of tangency between each line segment and the circle bisects the line segment.

For instance: In the figures given below, each circle is circumscribed by a regular polygon (equilateral triangle, square, regular pentagon, and regular hexagon); all line segments are bisected by the points of tangency highlighted along the circles' circumferences:

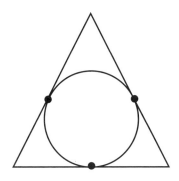 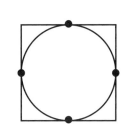  

Example #1:   In the figure given below, a regular hexagon is tangent to the circle at six points. If the perimeter of the hexagon is 144, what is the length of *PX*?

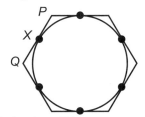

Solution: Perimeter of Hexagon $\Rightarrow 6s = 144$ [Equate the hexagon perimeter formula with given perimeter]
             Length of *PQ* $\Rightarrow s = 24$ [Divide both sides by 6]
             Length of *PX* $\Rightarrow$ ½PQ = ½(24) = 12   [Point *X* is the midpoint of *PQ*]]

Example #2:   In the figure given below, a regular pentagon is tangent to the circle at five points. If the perimeter of the pentagon is 70, what is the length of *PX*?

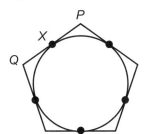

Solution: Perimeter of Pentagon $\Rightarrow 5s = 70$ [Equate the pentagon perimeter formula with given perimeter]
             Length of *PQ* $\Rightarrow s = 14$ [Divide both sides by 5]
             Length of *PX* $\Rightarrow$ ½PQ = ½(14) = 7   [Point *X* is the midpoint of *PQ*]]

8.4: NON-OVERLAPPING FIGURES:

8.4.1: NON-OVERLAPPING 2-DIMENSIONAL SURFACES:

EZ RULE: Remember, when fitting 2-dimensional surfaces onto other 2-dimensional surfaces, knowing the respective areas is not enough; it is important to know the specific dimensions (length and width) of each surface to determine if it can fit and how many can fit.

For Instance: How many non-overlapping identical rectangular post cards, each with an area of 24 inch^2, can be pasted on a rectangular bulletin board with an area of 1200 inch^2?

Wrong Solution $\Rightarrow$ Area of Board $\div$ Area of Cards = 1200 $\div$ 24 = 50

The easiest solution is to answer 50 cards; however, this is incorrect, because we don't know the exact dimensions of each rectangular card or the bulletin board. Each rectangular card or bulletin board could have one of the possible dimension:

Possible Dimensions of a 1200 inch^2 board $\Rightarrow$ 600 × 2; 200 × 6; 60 × 20; 40 × 30; etc.

Possible Dimensions of a 24 inch^2 cards $\Rightarrow$ 24 × 1; 12 × 2; 8 × 3; 6 × 4; 16 × 1.5; etc.

Although, all these card dimensions have an area of 24 inch^2, they have different rectangular shapes. Without knowing the exact dimensions (or shapes) of all the boards and the cards, it's impossible to say how many cards can be pasted on the board.

For Example: A rectangular garden measures 62 feet by 28 feet. What is the greatest number of non-overlapping 5-foot square plots that be ruled off in this garden?

Solution: Length of Rectangular Garden   = 62 feet $\Rightarrow$ 62 $\div$ 5 = 12 and remainder = 2

$\Rightarrow$ A maximum of 12 square plots that can fit horizontally along the length of the rectangular plot.

Width of Rectangular Garden = 28 feet $\Rightarrow$ 28 $\div$ 5 = 5 and remainder = 3

$\Rightarrow$ A maximum of 5 square plots that can fit vertically along the width of the rectangular plot.

Total Number of 5-foot Square plots that can fit into the rectangular garden $\Rightarrow$ 12 × 5 = 60

The 2-feet strip along length and 3-feet strip along width will go waste, the 5-foot squares can't fit in it.

8.4.2: NON-OVERLAPPING 3-DIMENSIONAL OBJECTS:

EZ RULE: Remember, when fitting 3-dimensional objects into other 3-dimensional objects, knowing the respective volumes is not enough; it is important to know the specific dimensions (length, width, and height) of each object to determine if it can fit and how many can fit.

For Instance: How many books, each with a volume of 100 inch^3, can be packed into a container with a volume of 50,000 inch^3?

Wrong Solution $\Rightarrow$ Volume of Container $\div$ Volume of Book = 50,000 $\div$ 100 = 500

The easiest solution is to answer 500 books; however, this is incorrect, because we don't know the exact dimensions of each book or the container. Each book/container can have one of the possible dimension:

Possible Dimensions of a 50,000 inch^3 container $\Rightarrow$ 50 × 1000 × 1; 5 × 100 × 100; 500 × 10 × 10; etc.

Possible Dimensions of a 100 inch^3 book $\Rightarrow$ 10 × 10 × 1; 10 × 5 × 2; 5 × 5 × 4; 25 × 2 × 2; 50 × 2 × 1; 20 × 5 × 1; 25 × 4 × 1; 100 × 1 × 1; 200 × 0.5 × 1; 20 × 2 × 2.5; etc.

Although, all these books' dimensions have a volume of 100 inch^3, they have different rectangular shapes. Without knowing the exact dimensions (or shapes) of the container and the books, it's impossible to say if they would all fit into the container or how many books would fit into one container.

For Example: What is the maximum number of rectangular blocks, each measuring 2 feet by 12 feet by 9 feet, which can fit inside a rectangular box with dimensions of 19 feet by 61 feet by 109 feet?

Solution: Length of Blocks = 2 feet $\Rightarrow$ (19 $\div$ 2) = 9 and remainder = 1

$\Rightarrow$ The maximum number of blocks that can be lined up across the 19-foot dimension is 9

Width of Blocks   = 12 feet $\Rightarrow$ (61 $\div$ 12) = 5 and remainder = 1

$\Rightarrow$ The maximum number of blocks that can be lined up across the 61-foot dimension is 5

Height of Blocks = 9 feet $\Rightarrow$ (109 $\div$ 9) = 12 and remainder = 1

$\Rightarrow$ The maximum number of blocks that can be lined up across the 109-foot dimension is 12

The total number of blocks $\Rightarrow$ 9 × 5 × 12 = 540

The 1-foot strip along length and 1-foot strip along width and 1-foot strip along height will go to waste as the blocks can't fit in it.

8.5: AREA OF SHADED/WHITE REGION:

The other most common type of multiple figure questions involve irregularly shaped regions formed by two or more overlapping figures, often with one or more shaded region. In fact, it's common to find geometry problems asking to find area of shaded or white regions.

TIPS FOR MULTIPLE FIGURE PROBLEMS:

While answering multiple figure questions, make sure to use one or more of the following tips:

TIP #1: To find the area of the shaded region – The easiest way is to find the area of the white region and subtract it from the total area of the figure.
⇒ **Area of Shaded Region = Total Area – Area of White Region**

TIP #2: To find the area of the white region – The easiest way is to find the area of the shaded region and subtract it from the total area of the figure.
⇒ **Area of White Region = Total Area – Area of Shaded Region**

TIP #3: To find the total area of the figure, and if it cannot be found directly – The easiest way is to find the area of the shaded region and find the area of the white region and then add them together.
⇒ **Total Area = Area of Shaded Region + Area of White Region**

Example #1: In the figure below, the small rectangle with sides 10 and 5 placed right in the center of the big rectangle with sides 20 and 10, what is the area of the shaded region?

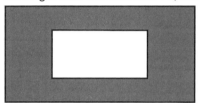

Solution: Area of Big Rectangle   ⇒ *Length* × *Width* = 20 × 10 = 200
Area of Small Rectangle ⇒ *Length* × *Width* = 10 × 5 = 50
Area of Shaded Region   ⇒ Area of Big Rectangle – Area of Small Rectangle
⇒ 200 – 50 = 150

Example #2: In the figure below, if in two concentric circles, the smaller circle has a radius of 5 units and the bigger circle has a radius of 11 units, what is the area of the shaded area?

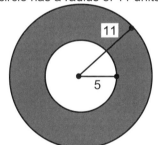

Solution: Radius of Small Circle   ⇒ 5 units
Area of Small Circle   ⇒ $\pi r^2 = \pi \times 5^2 = 25\pi$ unit^2
Radius of Big Circle   ⇒ 11 units
Area of Big Circle   ⇒ $\pi r^2 = \pi \times 11^2 = 121\pi$ unit^2
Area of Shaded Region   ⇒ Area of Big Circle – Area of Small Circle
⇒ $121\pi – 25\pi = 96\pi$ unit^2

8.6: GEOMETRIC TRANSFORMATIONS:

Understanding the concepts of basic geometric transformations will be helpful while working through some of the geometry problems. Geometric transformation can be of three different types: **translations**, **rotations**, and **reflections**.

8.6.1: GEOMETRIC TRANSLATIONS:

A *"geometric translation"* means **translating**, **shifting**, or **moving** all points of a figure or object either horizontally and/or vertically, without involving any rotation or reflection. In other words, a figure is moved from its current location to a different location without turning it. After translation, every point of the translated image is the same distance from the corresponding point of the original image.

For instance: In the diagram below, square A on the left has been translated a few units up, that is, in the positive *y*-direction to get the square A' on the right.

 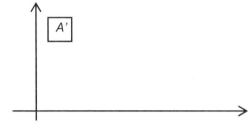

8.6.2: GEOMETRIC ROTATION:

A *"geometric rotation"* means **rotating** or **turning** a figure or an object about a point, which is called the center of rotation, without involving any movement or reflection. After rotation, every point of the rotated image is the same distance from the point of rotation as the corresponding point of the original image.

For instance: In the diagram below, the clock A on the left is rotated by 90° clockwise to get the clock B on the right.

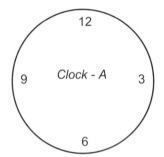 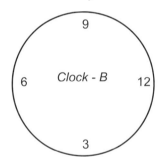

8.6.3: GEOMETRIC REFLECTION:

A *"geometric reflection"* means to **reflect** or produce a figure's or an object's **mirror image** with respect to a line, which is called the *"line of reflection,"* without involving any movement or rotation. A mirror image is produced on the other side of the line. In other words, to reflect an object means to produce its mirror image without moving or rotating it. After reflection, every point of the reflected image is the same distance from the line of reflection as the corresponding point of the original image.

For instance: In the diagram below, the triangle on the left is reflected across the line on the other side on the right.

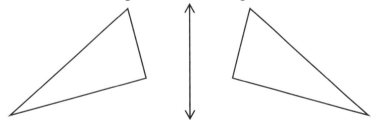

Reflecting a Figure Twice: If a figure has been reflected twice across the same line, it results back in the original figure. This brings us to the concept of symmetry, which is reviewed next.

8.6.4: SYMMETRY:
There are two types of symmetries: ***reflectional symmetry*** or symmetry about a line and ***rotational symmetry*** or symmetry about a point.

(A) REFLECTIONAL SYMMETRY OR SYMMETRY ABOUT A LINE:
A figure has ***"reflectional symmetry"*** or symmetry about a line if reflection across a fixed line produces an identical figure. The line is called the ***"line of symmetry"***.

For instance, in the diagram below, the dashed line divides the hexagon into two equal parts or halves. If the left half of the hexagon is reflected across the dashed line, the result is the right half, and vice versa. In other words, if the hexagon is reflected across the dashed line, it will result in the same hexagon. The hexagon is said to be symmetrical about the dashed line, and that dashed line is called a line of symmetry for the hexagon.

Figures with more than one Line of Symmetry: A geometric figure may have one line of symmetry (such as the hexagon above), more than one line of symmetry (such as a rectangle), or it may have no lines of symmetry.

(B) ROTATIONAL SYMMETRY OR SYMMETRIC ABOUT A POINT:
A figure has ***"rotational symmetry"*** or symmetry about a point if a rotation of n degrees, where $0° < n < 360°$, either clockwise, or counterclockwise, about a fixed point produces an identical figure. The point is called the ***"point of symmetry"***.

For instance, in the diagram below, there is a hexagon with a point P at its center. If the hexagon is rotated by $60°$, $120°$, $180°$, or $240°$ (either clockwise or counterclockwise) around point P, then it will result in the same hexagon. The hexagon is said to be symmetrical around the point P, and P is called a point of symmetry for the hexagon.

EZ NOTE: Symmetry about a line and symmetry about a point are two different properties. A given figure may have one type of symmetry and not the other, or it may have both types of symmetry, or neither type of symmetry.

GEOMETRIC PERCEPTION: You may also be asked questions that require you to visualize a plane figure or a solid from different views or orientations. These are the questions using geometric perception.

For Example: A triangle ABC is reflected across the y-axis to have the image $\triangle A'B'C'$ in the standard (x, y) coordinate plane; in such a way that A reflects to A', B reflects to B', and C reflects to C'. If the coordinates of A are (p, q), what are the coordinates of A'?

Solution: The coordinates of A are (p, q). Since both coordinates of point A are positive, point A lies in the first quadrant. When $\triangle ABC$ is reflected across the y-axis, the reflection of point A, which is A', will be in the second quadrant. Hence the coordinates of point A' would be $(-p, q)$. Note that the reflection across the y-axis does not change the sign or value of y-coordinate, but it does change the sign of the x-coordinate to the opposite sign. It may be helpful to draw a rough sketch to visualize the problem.

PRACTICE EXERCISE – QUESTIONS AND ANSWERS WITH EXPLANATIONS: MULTIPLE FIGURES:

Question #1: If a room has the dimensions shown in the figure given below, what is its area and perimeter?

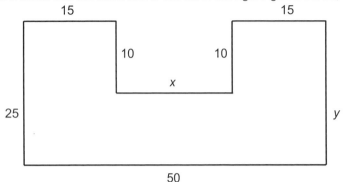

Solution: First, find the missing measurements

Length of x $\Rightarrow 50 - 15 - 15 = 20$ [Lengths of opposite sides are equal]
Length of y $\Rightarrow 25$ [Lengths of opposite sides are equal]
Perimeter $\Rightarrow 50 + 25 + 25 + 20 + 15 + 15 + 10 + 10 = 170$
Area of Left Rectangle $= 15 \times 10$ $\Rightarrow +150$
Area of Right Rectangle $= 15 \times 10$ $\Rightarrow +150$
Area of Middle Rectangle $= 50 \times 15$ $\Rightarrow \underline{+750}$
Total Area of the Figure $\Rightarrow \underline{1050}$

Question #2: If a circle is inscribed in a square of area 256, what is the area and circumference of that circle?
Solution:
Area of Square $\Rightarrow side^2 = 256$ [Equate the area formula with the given area]
$\Rightarrow side = 16$ [Square root both sides]
Diameter of Circle $\Rightarrow 16$ [Diameter of circle is same as side of square]
Radius of Circle $\Rightarrow \frac{1}{2}d = \frac{1}{2}(16) = 8$ [Radius is half of diameter]
Area of Circle $\Rightarrow \pi r^2 = \pi(8)^2 = 64\pi$ [Apply appropriate formula and simplify]
Circumference of Circle $\Rightarrow 2\pi r = 2\pi(8) = 16\pi$ [Apply appropriate formula and simplify]

Question #3: If a circle of area 64π is inscribed in a square, what is the area and perimeter of that square?
Solution:
Area of Circle $\Rightarrow \pi r^2 = 64\pi$ [Equate the area formula with the given area]
$\Rightarrow r^2 = 64$ [Divide both sides by π]
$\Rightarrow r = 8$ [Square root both sides]
Diameter of Circle $\Rightarrow 2r = 2(8) = 16$ [Diameter is twice the radius]
Side of Square $\Rightarrow 16$ [Diameter of circle is same as side of square]
Area of Square $\Rightarrow s^2 = 16^2 = 256$ [Apply appropriate formula and simplify]
Perimeter of Square $\Rightarrow 4s = 4(16) = 64$ [Apply appropriate formula and simplify]

Question #4: If a square of area 256 is inscribed in a circle, what is the area and circumference of the circle?
Solution:
Area of Square $\Rightarrow side^2 = 256$ [Equate the area formula with the given area]
$\Rightarrow side = 16$ [Square root both sides]
Diagonal of Square $\Rightarrow 16\sqrt{2}$ [Diagonal of square is side times $\sqrt{2}$]
Diameter of Circle $\Rightarrow 16\sqrt{2}$ [Diameter of circle is same as diagonal of square]
Radius $\Rightarrow \frac{1}{2}d = \frac{1}{2}(16\sqrt{2}) = 8\sqrt{2}$ [Radius is half of diameter]
Area of Circle $\Rightarrow \pi r^2 = \pi \times (8\sqrt{2})^2 = 128\pi$ [Apply appropriate formula and simplify]
Circumference $\Rightarrow 2\pi r = 2\pi(8\sqrt{2}) = 16\sqrt{2}\pi$ [Apply appropriate formula and simplify]

Question #5: If a square is inscribed in a circle or area 128π, what is the area and perimeter of the square?

Solution:

Area of Circle	$\Rightarrow \pi r^2 = 128\pi$	[Equate the area formula with the given area]
	$\Rightarrow r^2 = 128$	[Divide both sides by π]
	$\Rightarrow r = 8\sqrt{2}$	[Square root both sides]
Diameter of Circle	$\Rightarrow 2(8\sqrt{2}) = 16\sqrt{2}$	[Diameter is twice of radius]
Diagonal of Square	$\Rightarrow 16\sqrt{2}$	[Diagonal of square is same as diameter of circle]
Side of Square	$\Rightarrow 16$	[Side of square is side divided by $\sqrt{2}$]
Area of Square	$\Rightarrow s^2 = 16^2 = 256$	[Apply appropriate formula and simplify]
Perimeter of Square	$\Rightarrow 4s = 4(16) = 64$	[Apply appropriate formula and simplify]

Question #6: A rectangular garden measures 77 feet by 26 feet. What is the greatest number of non-overlapping 5-foot square plots that be ruled off in this garden?

Solution: Length of Rectangular Garden = 77 feet $\Rightarrow 77 \div 5 = 15$ and remainder = 2
$\Rightarrow$ A maximum of 15 square plots that can fit horizontally along the length of the rectangular plot.
Width of Rectangular Garden = 26 feet $\Rightarrow 26 \div 5 = 5$ and remainder = 1
$\Rightarrow$ A maximum of 5 square plots that can fit vertically along the width of the rectangular plot.
Total Number of 5-foot Square plots that can fit into the rectangular garden $\Rightarrow 15 \times 5 = 75$
Note: the 2 feet strip along the length and 1 foot strip along the width will go waste, as the 5-foot squares can't fit into it.

Question #7: The area of a square is equal to the area of a rectangle whose length is 25 and width is 9. What is the perimeter of the square?

Solution:

Area of Rectangle	$\Rightarrow LW = 25 \times 9 = 225$	[Apply appropriate formula and simplify]
Area of Square	$\Rightarrow s^2 = 225$	[Equate the are formula with the actual area]
	$\Rightarrow s = 15$	[Square root both sides]
Perimeter of Square	$\Rightarrow 4s = 4 \times 15 = 60$	[Apply appropriate formula and simplify]

Question #8: The perimeter of a square is equal to the perimeter of a rectangle whose length is 25 and width is 9. What is the area of the square?

Solution: Perimeter of Rectangle $\Rightarrow 2(L + W) = 2(25 + 9) = 2(34) = 68$

EZ Problem Set-Up	$\Rightarrow$ Perimeter of Square = Perimeter of Rectangle	
	$\Rightarrow 4s = 68$	[Set up the equation]
	$\Rightarrow s = 17$	[Divide both sides by 4]
Area of Square	$\Rightarrow s^2 = 17^2 = 289$	[Apply appropriate formula and simplify]

Question #9: If the area of a circle is equal to twice its circumference, then what is the area of the circle?

Solution:

EZ Problem Set-Up	$\Rightarrow$ Area of Circle = 2(Circumference of Circle)	
	$\Rightarrow \pi r^2 = 2(2\pi r)$	[Set up the equation]
	$\Rightarrow r = 4$	[Divide both sides by πr]
Area of Circle	$\Rightarrow \pi r^2 = \pi(4)^2 = 16\pi$	[Apply appropriate formula and simplify]

Question #10: If the circumference of a circle is equal to twice its area, then what is the circumference of the circle?

Solution:

EZ Problem Set-Up	$\Rightarrow$ Circumference of Circle = 2(Area of Circle)	
	$\Rightarrow 2\pi r = 2(\pi r^2)$	[Set up the equation]
	$\Rightarrow r = 1$	[Divide both sides by $2\pi r$]
Circumference of Circle	$\Rightarrow 2\pi r = 2\pi(1) = 2\pi$	[Apply appropriate formula and simplify]

Question #11: What is the maximum number of rectangular blocks, each measuring 2 inches by 12 inches by 9 inches, which can fit inside a rectangular box with dimensions 17 inches by 73 inches by 163 inches?

Solution: Length of Blocks = 2 inches $\Rightarrow (17 \div 2) = 8$ and remainder = 1
$\Rightarrow$ The maximum number of blocks that can be lined up across the 17-inch dimension is 9
Width of Blocks = 12 inches = $(73 \div 12) = 6$ and remainder = 1
$\Rightarrow$ The maximum number of blocks that can be lined up across the 73-inch dimension is 5
Height of Blocks = 9 inches = $(163 \div 9) = 18$ and remainder = 1
$\Rightarrow$ The maximum number of blocks that can be lined up across the 163-inch dimension is 12
Total number of blocks = $8 \times 6 \times 18 = 864$

Note: the 1 foot strip along the length and 1 foot strip along the width and 1 foot strip along the height will go waste as the blocks can't fit into it.

Question #12: A rectangular box measures 26 units by 5 units by 7 units. What is the greatest number of 2- unit radius iron balls that can fit inside the box such that none of the balls obtrudes from the box?

Solution: Let's draw the following diagram to help visualize the problem:

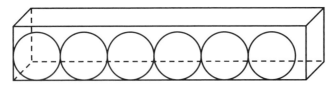

Radius of Iron Ball = 2 units & Diameter of Iron Ball = 4 units
Length of the Rectangular Box = 26 units
Start filling in the balls one by one, along the length of the box.
Divide the length of the box by the diameter of the ball $\Rightarrow$ 26 ÷ 4 = 6 and reminder = 2 (left over space)
Note that the width or height of the box is not big enough to accommodate more than 1 adjacent ball.
Therefore, at most 6 balls can fit into the box.

Question #13: A cube and a rectangular solid have the same volume. If the lengths of the edges of the rectangular solid are 2, 9, and 12 units, what is the length of the edge of the cube?

Solution: EZ Problem Set-Up $\Rightarrow$ Volume of Cube = Volume of Rectangular Solid
$\Rightarrow s^3 = LWH$ [Equate the volume formula with the given volume]
$\Rightarrow s^3 = 2 \times 9 \times 12$ [Substitute the values]
$\Rightarrow s^3 = 216$ [Do the multiplication]
$\Rightarrow s = \sqrt[3]{216} = 6$ units   [Cube root both sides]

Question #14: A rectangular tank 10 units by 8 units by 2 units is filled with oil. If all of the oil without loosing a drop is to be transferred to smaller tanks in the form of cubes all of which are 2 units wide on a side, how many of these cubical tanks are needed?

Solution: V of Rectangular Tank $\Rightarrow LWH = 10 \times 8 \times 2 = 160$ unit^3 [Apply appropriate formula and simplify]
V of Cubical Tank $\Rightarrow s^3 = 2^3 = 8$ unit^3 [Apply appropriate formula and simplify]
No. of Cubical Tanks needed $\Rightarrow \dfrac{160}{8} = 20$ [Divide volume of rectangular tank by cubical tank]

Question #15: What is the maximum number of rectangular blocks with dimensions 2 units by 3 units by 4 units that could fit in a cube-shaped box with a side of 12 units?

Solution: V of Cube $\Rightarrow s^3 = 12^3 = 1,728$ unit^3 [Apply appropriate formula and simplify]
V of each Rectangular Block $\Rightarrow LWH = 2 \times 3 \times 4 = 24$ unit^3 [Apply appropriate formula and simplify]
No. of Rectangular Block that would fit in the Cube $\Rightarrow 1728 \div 24 = 72$
Note: Since 2, 3, and 4 are all divisible by 12, we can divide the two volumes.

Example #16: In the figure below, A is the center of the larger circle, and B is the center of the smaller shaded circle. If the radius of the smaller circle is 5, what is the area of the non-shaded region?

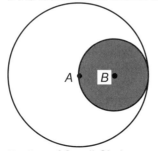

Solution: Radius of Small Circle $\Rightarrow 5$
Area of Small Circle $\Rightarrow \pi r^2 = \pi(5)^2 = 25\pi$
Radius of Big Circle $\Rightarrow$ Diameter of Smaller Circle = 5 × 2 = 10

Area of Big Circle $\quad\Rightarrow \pi r^2 = \pi(10)^2 = 100\pi$
Area of White Region $\quad\Rightarrow$ Area of Larger Circle – Area of Smaller Circle
$\quad\Rightarrow 100\pi - 25\pi = 75\pi$

Question #17: In the figure given below, if the circle with center A has a radius of 16, what is the area of the shaded region?

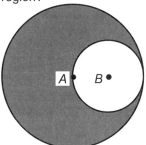

Solution:

Radius of Circle A	$\Rightarrow 16$
Area of Circle A	$\Rightarrow \pi r^2 = \pi(16)^2 = 256\pi$
Diameter of Circle B	$\Rightarrow$ Radius of Circle $A = 16$
Radius of Circle B	$\Rightarrow \frac{1}{2}(16) = 8$
Area of Circle B	$\Rightarrow \pi r^2 = \pi(8)^2 = 64\pi$
Area of Shaded Region	$\Rightarrow$ Area of Circle A – Area of Circle B
	$\Rightarrow 256\pi - 64\pi = 192\pi$

Question #18: In the figure given below, M and N are midpoints of two of the sides of the square $ABCD$. What is the area of the shaded region?

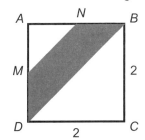

Solution:

Area of $\triangle ABD \quad\Rightarrow \frac{1}{2}(b)(h) = \frac{1}{2}(2)(2) = 2$ unit^2
Area of $\triangle AMN \quad\Rightarrow \frac{1}{2}bh = \frac{1}{2}(1)(1) = \frac{1}{2}$ unit^2
Area of the shaded region $\quad\Rightarrow$ Area of $\triangle ABD$ – Area of $\triangle AMN$
$\quad\Rightarrow 2 - \frac{1}{2} = 1.5$ unit^2

Question #19: In the figure given below, the circle is inscribed in the square $ABCD$, touching it at E, F, G, and H. If the radius of the circle is 5, what is the area of the shaded region?

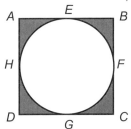

Solution:

Radius of Circle	$\Rightarrow 5$
Diameter of Circle	$\Rightarrow 2r = 2(5) = 10$
Area of Circle	$\Rightarrow \pi r^2 = \pi(5)^2 = 25\pi$
Side of Square	$\Rightarrow 10$
Area of Square	$\Rightarrow s^2 = 10^2 = 100$
Area of Shaded Region	$\Rightarrow$ Area of Square – Area of Circle

$$\Rightarrow 100 - 25\pi$$

Question #20: In the figure given below, the square $ABCD$, with side $AB = 8$, is overlaid with a circle, with a diameter BC. What is the area of the shaded region?

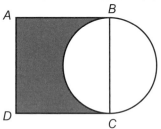

Solution:

Area of Square $ABCD$	$\Rightarrow s^2 = 8^2 = 64$
Side of Square	$\Rightarrow s = 8$
Diameter of Circle	$\Rightarrow 8$
Radius of Circle	$\Rightarrow \frac{1}{2}(8) = 4$
Area of Circle	$\Rightarrow \pi r^2 = \pi(4)^2 = 16\pi$
Area of Half Circle	$\Rightarrow \frac{1}{2}(16\pi) = 8\pi$
Area of Shaded Region	$\Rightarrow$ Area of Square – Area of Half Circle
	$\Rightarrow 64 - 8\pi$

EZ SOLUTIONS ORDERS & SALES:

ORDERS & SALES INFORMATION: EZ Solutions products and services can be ordered via one of the following methods:

🖥 ON-LINE ORDERS:
On-line Orders can be placed 24/7 via internet by going to: www.EZmethods.com

✉ E-MAIL ORDERS:
E-Mail Orders can be placed 24/7 via internet by emailing: orders@EZmethods.com

☎ PHONE ORDERS:
Phone Orders can be placed via telephone by calling: (Please check our website for most updated information)

📠 FAX ORDERS:
Fax Orders can be placed via fax by faxing: (Please check our website for most updated information)

📧 MAIL ORDERS:
Mail Orders can be placed via regular mail by mailing to the address given below:
EZ Solutions
Orders Department
P.O. Box 10755
Silver Spring, MD 20914
USA

OTHER OPTIONS: EZ Solutions books are also available at most major bookstores.

Institutional Sales: For volume/bulk sales to bookstores, libraries, schools, colleges, universities, organization, and institutions, please contact us. Quantity discount and special pricing is available.

EZ SOLUTIONS PRODUCTS & SERVICES:

LIST OF EZ TEST PREP SERIES OF BOOKS:

EZ Solutions Test Prep Series Books are available for the following sections:
- EZ Solutions – Test Prep Series – General – Test Taker's Manual
- EZ Solutions – Test Prep Series – Math Review – Arithmetic
- EZ Solutions – Test Prep Series – Math Review – Algebra
- EZ Solutions – Test Prep Series – Math Review – Applications
- EZ Solutions – Test Prep Series – Math Review – Geometry
- EZ Solutions – Test Prep Series – Math Review – Word Problems
- EZ Solutions – Test Prep Series – Math Review – Logic & Stats
- EZ Solutions – Test Prep Series – Math Practice – Basic Workbook
- EZ Solutions – Test Prep Series – Math Practice – Advanced Workbook
- EZ Solutions – Test Prep Series – Math Strategies – Math Test Taking Strategies
- EZ Solutions – Test Prep Series – Math – Data Sufficiency
- EZ Solutions – Test Prep Series – Verbal Section – Reading Comprehension
- EZ Solutions – Test Prep Series – Verbal Section – Sentence Correction/Completion
- EZ Solutions – Test Prep Series – Verbal Section – Vocabulary
- EZ Solutions – Test Prep Series – Verbal Section – Grammar
- EZ Solutions – Test Prep Series – Verbal Section – Critical Reasoning
- EZ Solutions – Test Prep Series – Verbal Section – Writing Skills

Note: Most of these books have already been published and others will be released shortly.

EZ Solutions Test Prep Series Books are available for the following standardized tests:
- EZ Solutions GMAT Test Prep Series of Books
- EZ Solutions GRE Test Prep Series of Books
- EZ Solutions SAT Test Prep Series of Books
- EZ Solutions ACT Test Prep Series of Books
- EZ Solutions LSAT Test Prep Series of Books
- EZ Solutions PRAXIS Test Prep Series of Books
- EZ Solutions POWER MATH/ENGLISH Test Prep Series of Books